Education and the Politics of Becoming

This collection examines education in the light of a politics of becoming. It takes a non-hierarchical transdisciplinary approach, challenging the macropolitics of pre-established governmental and economic agendas for education. Drawing on the philosophy of Gilles Deleuze and Felix Guattari, the contributors consider questions such as how education might engage a politics of becoming, and how education and becoming function in a society of control. Since Deleuze and Guattari contend that a society is defined by its becomings, its transformations, this collection asks how education, itself a process in becoming, may contribute 'collective creations' to a society in continual flux.

The chapters bring theory and praxis together, deploying power, affect, cartography, space, relationality, assemblage and multiple literacies in order to experiment with music, art, language, teacher education, curriculum and policy studies. This collection is an innovative resource, creating an encounter with the macropolitics of education, and altering teaching, learning, evaluation and curriculum.

This book was originally published as a special issue of *Discourse: Studies in the Cultural Politics of Education*.

Diana Masny is Professor Emerita and founding member of the Multiple Literacies Research Unit at the Faculty of Education, University of Ottawa, Canada. She is also Adjunct Professor at Queensland University of Technology, Australia. She developed MLT (Multiple Literacies Theory) a transdisciplinary lens to study mainly, but not exclusively, early childhood education, education and Deleuze, immigration, citizenship and minority language education. She has co-authored *Mapping Multiple Literacies: An introduction to Deleuzian Literacy Studies* (2012), has edited *Cartographies of becoming in Education: A Deleuze-Guattari perspective* (2013) and co-edited *Deleuze and Education* (2013).

David R. Cole is an Associate Professor at the University of Western Sydney, Australia. He is a trained philosopher and educational thinker, concerned with opening up new modes of thought. David researches and writes in a multidisciplinary manner, harnessing, impacting and motivating ideas to move away from subjugation to any one modality or form of containment. So far, this approach has yielded eight books (including a novel called *A Mushroom of Glass*) and numerous articles, book chapters, research grants and presentations. David's latest monograph is called *Educational Lifeforms: Deleuzian Teaching and Learning Practice*.

Education and the Politics of Becoming

Edited by
Diana Masny and David R. Cole

LONDON AND NEW YORK

First published 2014
by Routledge
2 Park Square, Milton Park, Abingdon, Oxon, OX14 4RN, UK

and by Routledge
711 Third Avenue, New York, NY 10017, USA

Routledge is an imprint of the Taylor & Francis Group, an informa business

© 2014 Taylor & Francis

All rights reserved. No part of this book may be reprinted or reproduced or utilised in any form or by any electronic, mechanical, or other means, now known or hereafter invented, including photocopying and recording, or in any information storage or retrieval system, without permission in writing from the publishers.

Trademark notice: Product or corporate names may be trademarks or registered trademarks, and are used only for identification and explanation without intent to infringe.

British Library Cataloguing in Publication Data
A catalogue record for this book is available from the British Library

ISBN 13: 978-0-415-74119-4

Typeset in Times New Roman
by Taylor & Francis Books

Publisher's Note
The publisher accepts responsibility for any inconsistencies that may have arisen during the conversion of this book from journal articles to book chapters, namely the possible inclusion of journal terminology.

Disclaimer
Every effort has been made to contact copyright holders for their permission to reprint material in this book. The publishers would be grateful to hear from any copyright holder who is not here acknowledged and will undertake to rectify any errors or omissions in future editions of this book.

Contents

Citation Information	vii
Notes on Contributors	ix

1. Introduction: Education and the politics of becoming
   David R. Cole and Diana Masny — 1

2. Travelling and sticky affects: Exploring teens and sexualized cyberbullying through a Butlerian-Deleuzian-Guattarian lens
   Jette Kofoed and Jessica Ringrose — 5

3. Becoming-teacher: Encounters with the Other in teacher education
   Stephen Marble — 21

4. Latino families becoming-literate in Australia: Deleuze, literacy and the politics of immigration
   David R. Cole — 33

5. Living, learning, loving: Constructing a new ethics of integration in education
   Inna Semetsky — 47

6. 'It's all about relationships': Hesitation, friendship and pedagogical assemblage
   Sam Sellar — 61

7. Uprooting music education pedagogies and curricula: Becoming-musician and the Deleuzian refrain
   Elizabeth Gould — 75

8. Policy prolepsis in education: Encounters, becomings, and phantasms
   P. Taylor Webb and Kalervo N. Gulson — 87

9. Grotesque gestures or sensuous signs? Rethinking notions of apprenticeship in early childhood education
   Linda Knight — 101

10. Multiple Literacies Theory: Discourse, sensation, resonance and becoming
    Diana Masny — 113

CONTENTS

11. 'We don't believe media anymore': Mapping critical literacies in an adult immigrant language classroom
    Monica Waterhouse   129

12. Bon mots for bad thoughts
    Jason J. Wallin   147

    Index   163

Citation Information

The chapters in this book were originally published in *Discourse: Studies in the Cultural Politics of Education*, volume 33, issue 1 (February 2012). When citing this material, please use the original page numbering for each article, as follows:

Chapter 1
Introduction to Special Issue: Education and the politics of becoming
David R. Cole and Diana Masny
Discourse: Studies in the Cultural Politics of Education, volume 33, issue 1
(February 2012) pp. 1–4

Chapter 2
Travelling and sticky affects: Exploring teens and sexualized cyberbullying through a Butlerian-Deleuzian-Guattarian lens
Jette Kofoed and Jessica Ringrose
Discourse: Studies in the Cultural Politics of Education, volume 33, issue 1
(February 2012) pp. 5–20

Chapter 3
Becoming-teacher: Encounters with the Other in teacher education
Stephen Marble
Discourse: Studies in the Cultural Politics of Education, volume 33, issue 1
(February 2012) pp. 21–32

Chapter 4
Latino families becoming-literate in Australia: Deleuze, literacy and the politics of immigration
David R. Cole
Discourse: Studies in the Cultural Politics of Education, volume 33, issue 1
(February 2012) pp. 33–46

Chapter 5
Living, learning, loving: Constructing a new ethics of integration in education
Inna Semetsky
Discourse: Studies in the Cultural Politics of Education, volume 33, issue 1
(February 2012) pp. 47–60

CITATION INFORMATION

Chapter 6

'It's all about relationships': Hesitation, friendship and pedagogical assemblage
Sam Sellar
Discourse: Studies in the Cultural Politics of Education, volume 33, issue 1 (February 2012) pp. 61–74

Chapter 7

Uprooting music education pedagogies and curricula: Becoming-musician and the Deleuzian refrain
Elizabeth Gould
Discourse: Studies in the Cultural Politics of Education, volume 33, issue 1 (February 2012) pp. 75–86

Chapter 8

Policy prolepsis in education: Encounters, becomings, and phantasms
P. Taylor Webb and Kalervo N. Gulson
Discourse: Studies in the Cultural Politics of Education, volume 33, issue 1 (February 2012) pp. 87–100

Chapter 9

Grotesque gestures or sensuous signs? Rethinking notions of apprenticeship in early childhood education
Linda Knight
Discourse: Studies in the Cultural Politics of Education, volume 33, issue 1 (February 2012) pp. 101–112

Chapter 10

Multiple Literacies Theory: Discourse, sensation, resonance and becoming
Diana Masny
Discourse: Studies in the Cultural Politics of Education, volume 33, issue 1 (February 2012) pp. 113–128

Chapter 11

'We don't believe media anymore': Mapping critical literacies in an adult immigrant language classroom
Monica Waterhouse
Discourse: Studies in the Cultural Politics of Education, volume 33, issue 1 (February 2012) pp. 129–146

Chapter 12

Bon mots for bad thoughts
Jason J. Wallin
Discourse: Studies in the Cultural Politics of Education, volume 33, issue 1 (February 2012) pp. 147–162

Please direct any queries you may have about the citations to
clsuk.permissions@cengage.com

Notes on Contributors

David R. Cole, University of Western Sydney, Australia

Elizabeth Gould, University of Toronto, Canada

Kalervo N. Gulson, University of New South Wales, Australia

Linda Knight, Queensland University of Technology, Australia

Jette Kofoed, University of Aarhus, Denmark

Stephen Marble, Southwestern University, USA

Diana Masny, University of Ottawa, Canada and Queensland University of Technology, Australia

Jessica Ringrose, Institute of Education, University of London, UK

Sam Sellar, The University of Queensland, Australia

Inna Semetsky, University of Waikato, New Zealand

Jason J. Wallin, University of Alberta, Canada

Monica Waterhouse, Université Laval, Canada

P. Taylor Webb, University of British Columbia, Canada

INTRODUCTION

Education and the politics of becoming

David R. Cole and Diana Masny

> One can envisage education becoming less and less a closed site differentiated from the workspace as another closed site, but both disappearing and giving way to frightful continual training – to continual monitoring of worker-schoolkids or bureaucrat-students. They try to present this as a reform of the school system, but it's really its dismantling (Deleuze, 1990).

The future that Gilles Deleuze envisaged in conversation with Antonio Negri in 1990 is already upon us. Advances in digital technology have aided the universal culture of management systems being set into place throughout education, often in the name of reform and even under the title of revolution. Yet why has education become so riddled with the presence of control? What factors have lead to Deleuze's diagnosis about education becoming true?

This special issue of *Discourse: Studies in the Cultural Politics of Education* looks to answer these questions through a collection of international essays that take questions about power, agency, identity and politics seriously, and have turned to the philosophy of Gilles Deleuze for some possible escape routes from enclosure. The politics of becoming is a good way to understand this search for an exit door in education, as becoming is suitably 'light' in that it is not centred on a counter politics or sites of resistance to the tactics of control as they are now manifest in education. This tactic is useful because any such subjectivity in educational politics would likely become taken over by dominating paradigms that are intent on control and exploitation. For example, the use of the term 'radical' was taken over by the Right during the 1980s, and has come to signify economic reform, henceforth confusing the left-wing revolutionary intent of the term. The image of *Che Guevara* has been packaged and commodified and is now the epitome of capitalist cool.

Deleuzian philosophy demands that we analyse terms and images down to the affective level in order to understand their impact and intentionality. Affect is bound to becoming through the ways in which one may affect and be affected, which define a continuum of change that gets inside of what it means to exist in a situation. For example, classrooms have definite affects that can be analysed and articulated, teacher education colleges have discernible affects that are often different from the rest of the university, in that pre-service teachers and teacher trainers often bring with them the atmospheres of the classroom! The job of the Deleuzian analyst is to understand these affects and to try to get inside of them in terms of explaining how they work. This job also defines an aspect of the politics of becoming.

Contiguous with the microanalysis of situations and their requisite affects, is the macro political situation within which educational events occurs. Governmental intervention, which is often aligned with the requisites of big business and societal concern, has made the educational sphere riddled with power concerns and directives that alter the practice of teaching and learning. Once again, the politics of becoming does not define an outside to these pressure points and exposures, but looks at these influences in a new manner. This new manner has the aim of producing difference in education, not as a rhetorical slogan or political banner, but as a grounding in the ontological realities that beset education. This is why the use of data is important in the politics of becoming, and several papers in this collection take the conjunction between Deleuzian theory and empirical study seriously as a fresh means to building ontological matters in education that are supple, lithe and pertinent (see Cole, Kofoed & Ringrose, Waterhouse, and Masny in this special issue). Of course, using Deleuzian philosophy helps to build parallel educational theory, which is aptly demonstrated in this issue through Semetsky, Wallin, and Webb & Gulson's papers.

However, the educational theory that one might take from Deleuze also responds to the politics of becoming. This is not theory meant to cast otherness and aspersions on the realities of real life in and through the educational box. This theory takes the lives of those of us inside the educational machine and enhances this reality by pushing at points of non-equilibrium, by working through the interstices, by adding colour to educational thought. This series of essays simultaneously works on the level of praxis, whereby data can be theorised and theory can be broken down into data. Marble, Knight, Gould and Sellars' papers show how this can be achieved, and to what ends one might infuse educational practice with Deleuze.

So, how can attending to the politics of becoming help us in education? What are the objectives of the politics of becoming and how might one achieve them? Becoming is a process, and this process is an introduction and prelude to a future generation of educators and their education. The potential of the politics of becoming and its activation through education, hovers in a virtual cloud, it is locatable as distributed systems of affective relations and experimental bodily tendencies. Unlike traditional party politics, the politics of becoming does not come about through learning a pre-written script or memorising the party line on any particular topic. The politics of becoming is more creative, perhaps harder to fathom, and has access points via serious thought and the total commitment to unearthing assumptions in one's practice. We, the authors, would like to commend to you – the readers of this edition – the journey and the challenge of this politics of becoming. This special issue represents different stages in this journey, from grappling with the theory, to using the theory to analyse data, to enacting the theory through practice.

The politics of becoming is not connected to representative politics. Deleuze (1997) discussed this point in conversation with Michel Foucault, where he suggests that when people are empowered to speak for themselves, they do not transfer one form of representation for another. On the contrary, the politics of becoming in education is not about representing any particular teacher, student, or set of views, but relies on digging through the layers of political interference that currently overlay practice.

References

Deleuze, G. (1990). Control and becoming: Gilles Deleuze in conversation with Antonio Negri (M. Joughin, Trans.). *Futur Anterieur, 1* (Spring).

Deleuze, G. (1997). Intellectuals and power: A conversation between Michel Foucault and Gilles Deleuze (D.F. Bouchard, & S. Simon, Trans.). In D.F. Bouchard (Ed.), *Language, counter-memory, practice* (pp. 205–217). Ithaca, NY: Cornell University Press. (Original interview 1972.)

Travelling and sticky affects: Exploring teens and sexualized cyberbullying through a Butlerian-Deleuzian-Guattarian lens

Jette Kofoed and Jessica Ringrose

In this paper we combine the thinking of Deleuze and Guattari (1984, 1987) with Judith Butler's (1990, 1993, 2004, 2009) work to follow the rhizomatic becomings of young people's affective relations in a range of on- and off-line school spaces. In particular we explore how events that may be designated as sexual cyberbullying are constituted and how they are mediated by technology (such as texting or in/through social networking sites). Drawing on findings from two different studies looking at teens' uses of and experiences with social networking sites, Arto in Denmark, and Bebo in the UK, we use this approach to think about how affects flow, are distributed, and become fixed in assemblages. We map how affects are manoeuvred and potentially disrupted by young people, suggesting that in the incidences discussed affects travel as well as stick in points of fixation. We argue that we need to grasp both affective flow and fixity in order to gain knowledge of how subjectification of the gendered/classed/racialised/sexualised body emerges. A Butlerian-Deleuzian-Guattarian frame helps us to map some of these affective complexities that shape sexualized cyberbully events; and to recognize technologically mediated lines of flight when subjectifications are at least temporarily disrupted and new terms of recognition and intelligibility staked out.

Introduction

This paper aims to contribute to applying Deleuzian theory to practical problems in education by looking at problems of understanding and responding to cyberbullying in on-line communities and schools. We combine a Butlerian approach to exploring discursive subjectification with a Deleuzian and Guattarian approach to mapping affective flows. Moving beyond a discursive analytical approach (that is, Davies & Harre, 1990, Ellwood & Davies, 2010), we argue Deleuze and Guattari's thinking helps us understand affect as bound in, but not limited to, discursive signification. The open-ness of what we will call a Butlerian/Deleuzian/Guattarian approach helps us understand both fixity and becoming in how young people navigate conflict and extreme exclusions. In this paper we draw on these lines of thinking and focus the analytical lens to affective processes of becoming and to how an affective tenor of being (temporarily) included and excluded is maintained and shifting when technologies are mediating the processes of bullying.

EDUCATION AND THE POLITICS OF BECOMING

To illustrate our points we draw on two data sets focused on young people's experiences at social networking sites, *Arto* in Denmark and *Bebo* in the UK. We bring together two diverse projects engaging in a dual analysis. While aware of methodological limitations in bringing together data from diverse studies, we limit the purpose of this joint analysis to re-conceptualize cyber fights as 'events' across time/space/locations. For this purpose, analyses across the two datasets have proven fruitful in investigating cases which involve a number of different subjects and a number of different technologies. Here we focus on incidences where sexual subjectification happens via networked communications in school and cyber assemblages. Cross-data-analyses have helped us understand the singularities of our own research findings and the commonalities across contexts.

Researching cyberbullying

In this paper we draw on the field of cyberbullying studies and argue for ways to develop a theoretically refined approach to the particularity of bullying when it is technologically mediated. We will first highlight the basic assumption within bullying research (both socalled traditional bullying and cyberbullying); second, we highlight the particularities of cyberlife, and third, we move on to the arguments of why we introduce a theoretical framework to grasp the specificities of technologically mediated bullying. Within bullying research there is a general and widely acknowledged assumption that a number of relative stable positions are at work in cases recognized as bullying. Those would be that of the victim, the bully, and the bystanders (Olweus, 1993; Salmivalli & Niemenen, 2002; Smith, 2009; Smith et al., 2002; Smith et al., 2008). Much work is based on this assumption of stable, individualised positions.[1] Apart from this focus on a recognizable number of positions, it is in addition assumed that these positions are fixed in the sense that a position over time is taken up by the same individual. In the most quoted definitions of bullying this is referred to as exposure to negative action on the part of one or more persons, to patterns of repetition, and intentional harm (Olweus, 1993; Smith et al., 2008). Personalities of individuals play a significant and central role in these definitions of bullying. This classical work was coined by Dan Olweus during the 1970s and has been influential internationally over the past 30 years not only in research but also within the development of local and national intervention programmes (for critical analysis of this, see Schott, 2009; Eriksson et al., 2002).

Within cyberbullying studies there is widespread agreement that specific characteristics characterize cyberbullying. First is anonymity, that is, the possibility of hiding the identity of the sender and to blur the number of subjects involved. This is also referred to as 'disinhibition' (Shariff, 2008), where young people borrow each others' phones, use each others' profiles (whether with or without the acceptance of the owner of the profile), or the practice of sending messages collectively, for instance, four people agree upon a message that is sent in the name of one of them. Thus there is uncertainty of the correspondence between the name displayed on the screen and the actual sender (Kowalski & Limber, 2007; Shariff, 2008; Spears et al., 2009). In addition, there is general agreement that the impossibility of escaping derogatory messages is crucial in understanding cyberbullying. There is no sanctuary, as Kowalski and Limber put it (2007, p. 23). The fact that cyberbullying can occur at any time raises the experience of vulnerability. A third characteristic of cyberbullying

6

is the possible infinite audience that can witness the evaluations posted online (Shariff, 2008). It makes a difference whether a negative evaluation is witnessed by and commented on by close peers or by possibly 'the whole world'. A fourth trait of cyberbullying is how a distinction between in and out school activities is blurred (Hinduja & Patchin, 2009; Slonje & Smith, 2008) because messages are sent during classes and recess and late at night, by and to classmates. Boundaries are less clear. We would like to add a fifth trait: the non-simultaneity of emotional intensity in cases of cyberbullying. Technologies slow down and accelerate the pace of communication in such a way that communication is characterized by non-simultaneity in emotional intensity (Kofoed, 2009a).

In this paper we focus both on the individuals and on social and cultural aspects of the becoming of individuals, groups and the organisation of schools. In our view, bullying is a social rather than an individual phenomenon. In developing this perspective we build on the findings and assumptions of the first generation of bullying research, and embed this in a larger pool of possible interrelated complex constituents. The basic assumption is that the socio-emotional condition of a child is important in ways in which bullying is constituted, maintained and changed; but social-emotional conditions are not the only forces enacted in cases of bullying. Recent research illustrates that a number of interacting forces are producing the phenomenon of bullying. Such forces are social and cultural, material and technological, historical and affective (Kofoed & Søndergaard, 2009; Ringrose, 2010; Schott, 2009). These assumptions are based on theoretically informed empirical analysis and suggest that the explanatory power is not limited to the socio-emotional capacity of an individual. The point of departure is that these diverse kinds of forces must be taken into consideration in the specificities of every local context. We thus argue for generating a complexity-sensitive knowledge of bullying that does not reject simplicity, but takes into careful consideration the number of forces that possibly interact in cases of bullying (Kofoed & Søndergaard, 2009).

Cyberbullying therefore requires complex theoretical and methodological approaches. In addition, other researchers suggest the importance of studying the interface and relationship between on-line and off-line phenomena (Patchin & Hinduja, 2009) like bullying and cyberbullying, viewing each as informing one another so we can better understand how the internet is 'reconfiguring' young people's social experiences (Kofoed, 2008; Livingstone & Haddon, 2009).

Outline of theoretical approach

Bronwyn Davies (1990), a key poststructural theorist in educational research, has offered important theoretical tools in understanding discursive positionings of subjects in social contexts, drawing on Foucauldian analyses (see also Walkerdine, 1991; Ellwood & Davies, 2010). Davies and others (see Ringrose & Renold, 2010) have recently offered a discursive analysis of school violence and bullying, using Foucault and Butler to explore how 'the real world is produced through the mobilisation of statements (enonces) or things said about violence in schools' (Ellwood & Davies, 2010, p. 86). As Ellwood and Davies suggest, discourses are 'not merely spoken words' but involve –

... signification which concerns not merely how it is that certain signifiers come to mean what they mean, but how certain discursive forms articulate objects and subjects in their intelligibility (2010, p. 86).

They use this analysis to look at how discourses of bullying mark out some subjects as individually pathological with bad intentions, and other subjects as having a good 'consciousness' in educational contexts. Similar arguments were presented by Ringrose and Renold (2010) in their Butlerian analysis of how bullying was constituted as pathological for both boys and girls in school, whereas much everyday cruelty was noted as unremarkable 'normative' gender play for children.

We want to build on this discursive analysis of bullying with an affective approach to understanding cyberbullying. We will join up further concepts from Butler's theories of subjectification, with the thinking of Deleuze and Guattari, whose philosophy offers ways of analysing the movement of affect and bodies through their theories of immanent becoming.

It is crucial to begin with a nuanced analysis of subjectification derived from Butler's body of work on gender/sexuality. Butler develops a post-Lacanian framework to argue that sex/gender is constituted through a subjectifying 'heterosexual matrix' (1990, p. 151) where performing certain normalized and idealised gender norms render the subject as gender 'intelligible' or 'unintelligible.' Exploring cyberbullying through this line of thinking helps us to argue that cyberbullying is also a set of discursive processes where certain subject positions are annulled, and derived of intelligibility. In cases of cyberbullying, we argue, some lives become (temporarily) unliveable and threatened with unviability (Butler, 2004). Teen's lives become unliveable for shorter or longer periods of time due to, for instance, hate groups on Facebook, fake profiles, daily evaluations of body sizes and body forms, sexual preferences, or alleged wrongdoings during school life. We assume that the viability of the subjects involved in the analysis is dependent not only on themselves individually, but on each other, and on the social norms that reign in the settings and situations in which they find themselves. What seems to be shared by the subjects in the cases studied in this paper is the experience of being 'threatened with unviability' (Butler, 2004, p. 3). Butler reminds us that –

> Some lives are grievable, others are not. The differential allocation of grievability that decides what kind of subject is and must be grieved and which kind of subject must not, operates to produce and maintain certain exclusionary conceptions of who is normatively human: what counts as a livable life and a grievable death? (Butler, 2004)

Her approach helps us reframe essential bullying questions slightly differently by asking 'which life is viable, which conflicts grievable'? By grievable we mean the sense in which conflicts matter or can be recognised and therefore addressed and 'grieved' in the everyday, mundane world of school policy and practice. We need to think about how liveability or grievability becomes manifest in specific social time/space contexts like schools, and in relation to particular gendered and sexualised cultural norms, which regulate and discipline young people's bodies via the 'heterosexual matrix' (Renold & Ringrose, 2008; Ringrose & Renold, 2010).

Butler's emphasis on gender normativity is crucial for our analysis, but we are concerned about the teleological reduction in some poststructural accounts that subjects are simply captured and/or fixed within the structural/discursive order

(Blackman et al., 2007). We are drawn to conceptual moves that are foregrounding the messy complexity of affects, and attempting to break down binaries between 'body and mind' and 'reason and passions', offering 'a complex view of causality' (Hardt, 2007). A body of thought often referred to as the 'affective turn' (Clough & Halley, 2007) encompasses attempts to theorize 'both our power to affect the world around us and our power to be affected by it, along with the relationship between these two powers' (Hardt, 2007, p. 10). We hope to contribute to a move towards an 'affective turn' in trying to map out some of the affective complexities that shape what is recognized as sexualised cyberbullying events.

In thinking through an affective lens to understanding cyberbullying, we develop the terminology of 'travelling and sticky affects', drawing on Butler's theories of subjectification and Deleuze and Guattari's (1984) theories of affect. According to Colman (in Parr, 2005, p. 11) –

> Affects in a Deleuzian-Guattarian understanding 'is the change, or variation, that occurs when bodies collide, or come into contact. As a body, affect is the knowable product of an encounter [...], yet is is also as indefinite as the experience of a sunset, transformation, or ghost'.

This understanding of affect as change and 'becoming' through relational affective processes helps us to qualify but also trouble poststructuralist assumptions of processes of subjectification (Davies, 2006; Kofoed, 2007; Søndergaard, 2002)[2] and is useful in staging the type of nuanced empirical analysis of processes of inclusion and exclusion we are aiming to make. In particular, we include Brian Massumi's interpretation of Deleuze's concept of affect. Here affect is described in terms of the intrinsic connection between movement and sensation.

> Feelings have a way of folding into each other, resonating each other, interfering with each other, mutually intensifying, all in unquantifiable ways apt to unfold again in action, often unpredictably. (Massumi, 2002, p. 1)

We thus understand affect to be intensities and sensations that fold and change in both unforeseen ways, and predictable ways (Kofoed, 2010; Staunæs & Bjerg, 2011). We set out to investigate these (un)predictable foldings and becomings in empirical data.

The term 'sticky' emerged out of our analysis of cyberbullying events, and we use it to refer to force relations which (temporarily) glue certain affects to certain bodies; 'travelling' in contrast, refers to the relational lines between subjects and the promiscuity and flowing nature of affects.[3] By following (through analysis of data) when affects stick and travel, we can qualify situated processes of subjectification and complex manouverings of positionings in empirical research findings. There are points of overlap and resonance in Butler's and Deleuze and Guattari's approach so that fixation occurs through processes where subjects are regulated and disciplined through heterosexual norms in ways that relate to Deleuze and Guattari's notions of bodily capture through force relations.

Deleuze and Guattari also use the notion of 'assemblages' to think about the relationships between bodies and the flows of affect through space and time. Assemblages have been described as social entities or 'wholes whose properties emerge from the interactions between the parts' (De Landa, in Tamboukou, 2009, p. 9).

The specific relationships and connections between bodies form assemblages, but the body itself is also an assemblage which interacts with and has various capacities to affect other bodies and other scales of assemblages: 'A body's function or potential or "meaning" becomes entirely dependent on which other bodies or machines it forms an assemblage with' (Malins, 2004, p. 85). Bodies interact with and plug into technological machines creating whole new assemblages and new rhizomatic movements. Affect flows via these connections, and subjectification happens, shaping affective possibilities. But affect may also exceed the discursive power of subjectification. Because we are focusing on the cyber or virtual space, our analysis will centre on bodily-technologically-mediated affective flows and subjectification. To summarize, the notion of assemblage helps us to think about how bodies and parts of bodies interact with non-human technology forming 'affective assemblages' of various scales and intensities (De Landa, 2006) that interact with and mutually affect one another in complex ways (Deleuze & Guattari, 1987; Massumi, 1987; Kofoed, 2009a; Ringrose, 2010).[4]

Deleuze and Guattari are also interested in power and force relations in ways that resonate strongly with Butler (and Foucault). They outline the 'affective' capacities of bodies to 'affect' each other (Coleman, 2008) in either 'life affirming' or 'life destroying ways' (Bonta & Protevi, 2004). This resonates in important ways with Butler's notions of liveable and grievable lives. We are interested in when lives become at least temporarily un-liveable through the life-destroying affects circulating in networked peer assemblages in cyberbully events. This therefore constitutes the ethical axis, and we aim to map this in our data analysis (see also Ringrose, 2010; Kofoed, 2005). In theorizing power, Delueze and Guattari (1984, 1987) develop further language to understand the flows of affect in relation to whether affective effects either align with or disrupt what they call the 'molar' (i.e. normative) lines or power formations (Jackson, 2010). They suggest that rhizomatic, molecular 'lines of flight' can break off from molar (normative) identities and power formations and go in new directions (Deleuze & Guattari, 1984; Renold & Ringrose, 2008; Tamboukou, 2008). But lines of flight are also readily re-coupled back to the norm (Deleuze & Guattari, 1984; Renold & Ringrose, 2008). These concepts help us in mapping what is happening or 'becoming' in particular cyberbully events and relations. We show how the fixing of affects onto bodies happens in sexualised ways in our data, but also illustrate how affects do not flow or 'travel' or stick in only predictable ways. Indeed in the second part of our data analysis, we point to examples where the sexual subjectification of cyberbullying exceeds the discursive regulation through complex flows and molecular lines of flight where the affective assemblages end up 'queering' (that is mix-up, complicate and subvert) conventional meanings of gendered norms (see also Renold & Ringrose, 2008).

Methodology

As noted, we draw on two different studies, one in Denmark and the other in the UK, which are exploring teens' uses and experiences of social networking sites (SNSs). While one study focused on cyberbullying as an analytical focus, the other focused on friendship and conflict in digital peer groups more generally. The Denmark study focused on the uses of the SNS Arto, and the UK study looked at young people's uses of the SNS Bebo. In the studies, teenagers and technologies have been followed across a number of sites: in the classroom, in the schoolyard, into the streets, over into the park, following the technologies, into the chat rooms, through the cell phones and back into the classroom. Thus the local sites extend into the national and global and back again to the micro networks of the schools. In the Danish-study, the choices of field schools were based on specific cases of cyber bullying. Some incident had been reported to the police or the head of the school as cases of cyberbullying. In the UK study, more general dynamics of teen's digital engagement were mapped but when specific events and incidences of conflict were recounted, they were addressed in individual interviews and followed online. The Danish study is based on eXbus's research (a Copenhagen based research project on bullying: Exploring Bullying in Schools). The data consists of qualitative fieldwork including observations, virtual fieldwork, school based fieldwork, interview, drawings and written essays from five schools in the vicinity of Copenhagen. Grades 4–7 are addressed, though the excerpts analysed in this paper stem from Danish grade 7 (14 year olds). The UK research was a study of 'Young people's uses of social networking sites' was conducted in 2 UK schools in rural Suffolk and urban London, across UK grades 9 and 11 (14–16 year olds). The data consisted of in school and on-line observations, focus group and individual interviews. For this paper we draw on data from 14 and 15 year old girls.

Analysis

When exploring both datasets, there seemed to be overarching issues of heightened intensity and sexualised content of name-calling. This heightened intensity is expressed throughout the interviews in an ongoing negotiation of who is to blame and in sexualized name-calling such as: fat slag, whore, slut, bitch, khaba (whore in Arabic). Reflections throughout the interviews are characterized by high speed and high emotional pitch. The transcripts present a whirlpool of sexualised drama and affectivity, all of it rife with the contradictions of living sex and gender in the temporality of teenage life. We will address these issues by recounting three assemblages in which three cyberbully events are staged. The following will introduce these assemblages and the subjects involved.

Celia (girl aged 14) and Saad (boy aged 14) are 7th graders. On the Danish social networking site, Arto, Saad posted an evaluation which according to their peers point at Celia, though no names were mentioned. It said:

> Fuck u, and your bitch ass crew. U bitch, you can put your opinion up your hairy ass. The day we became friends was the worst day of my life now that I realize how fucked up people can be. It was fucking nice to get you out of my life you have been a waste of time. Someone like you shouldn't be anyone's friend. You are so ugly, you think that you are perfect and beautiful. Khaba! No way!! You are uglier than ugly!!!! Die slow!!!

The ways in which Celia reflected upon the event suggested that she – in this pronunciation – was rendered unintelligible and unviable in the fixation. Throughout the interviews, this evaluation on Arto stands out as particularly important and sticky – and the school positioned Saad and Celia as involved in cyberbullying as bully and victim, respectively. The chain of events started like this: Saad texted Celia admitting that he looked at her breasts. The breasts seemed to be the point from where things take speed. Cecilia replied that this was perfectly all right. Rania became aware of Saad's gaze at Celia's breasts. She altered between judgments of it being gross and wanting such attention herself. More girls got involved in the confession. Rania encouraged Celia to ask Saad whether he checked out Rania's breasts as well. Celia declined but left her phone on the table when going to the toilet. Rania and the others girls texted Saad and asked him if he fancied Rania's breasts also – in Celia's name. Saad got upset. And from then on the messages were exchanged at high speed. The desires, competition and gazing at breasts travelled and informed the heightened sexual force of the entire teen school assemblage. Breasts, the preference for them and the desire for desired breasts accelerated after Saad's first text message and culminated in the above evaluation.

These sexualized affects seemed to travel among the peers, with a range of affects upon more bodies than those immediately involved. Envy, fear, distrust, embarrassment seemed to travel among the subjects involved in ways that allowed envy to merge into fear, into embarrassment, into relief, into indefinite affects. It did so because technologies were both detached and attached to specific bodies which ruled out the possibility of definitively linking subjects to messages. Celia's cell (mobile) phone was associated with her when her name was displayed in the receiving phone, yet finger's belonging to other bodies quickly keyed messages in her name.[5] Such detachment created new possibilities for virtual subjectification and we need to map both the fixity and the travelling of affects.

The main reason for the unequivocal agreement that this evaluation addresses Celia is the pronunciation of 'Khaba', which means whore in several Arabic dialects. As we go on to argue, terms like whore, slag and slut are not innocent pronouncements, but are affective terms which hold the power to (hetero)sexually subjectify. Khaba 'stuck' to Celia because it left no doubt in the minds of her peers that she was the one, due to the local connotation of Khaba as 'Moroccan'. Celia's body was read as ethnic and racial Other, particularly Moroccan, in relation to the associated Danishness and whiteness of many of her peers. In this on-line evaluation, 'Khaba' is both gendered,sexualized, and ethnic-racialized and appears to be the final referent that rules out the possibility that the evaluation which refers to 'you' and not a named subject, could refer to any of Celia's white peers. It apparently left no situated doubt that 'khaba' pointed at Celia who sensed how other affects and pronunciations might travel, but how this particular pronouncement wouldn't travel, but stuck to her body, her position and how it produced affects of discomfort and unease that stayed with her and temporarily made life unviable.

Temporarily unliveable lives

Our second example stems from the UK study in which we will focus on a significant affective event – a cyber and physical fight ostensibly between two girls, Louise (15) and Marie (15). Louise, was socially rejected through the SNS Bebo – she was no one's top friend, her romantic 'interest', Jay, would not formalize their relationship on their Bebo sites, and she was apparently called a 'fat slag' online by one of her 'friends', Marie. Marie was described as saying Louise went 'round with everyone' and 'tried to get with everyone's exes' in an instant messaging exchange. The virtual conflict erupted into 'real' violence the morning after the online interactions around 'fat slag', when Louise attacked Marie at school and was thereafter positioned as a

EDUCATION AND THE POLITICS OF BECOMING

violent bully with anger management problems by the school. The following excerpt is from a group interview with Louise, Marie and 3 other girls in their grade.

> L: An MSN[6] argument ... It would just travel down the line and then it will get to my friend and it would be like 'Oh yeah, I know her' and then it would just like... be like me ... I would be stuck in the middle ...We've literally been in a fight before because things have been ... said that's like, one of my mates told me on MSN that she called me a fat slag and everything like that so then I ... waited for her outside before school one day and I said 'Why are you saying this for?' and ...
> M: She punched me in my back.
> L: I punched her in the back, she razzed in my face, she tried walking away, I grabbed her, punched her again, everything right, because all these things that people say to ... wind people up ... she sits there and cries their eyes out, right and I beg to differ that I will never, ever do it again and I promise ...
> M: Because you love me!
> L: I love you! But the things that people say they don't realise what, how much trouble it can actually cause.
> M: Like people were saying to me that, 'Well, she'd been saying that she don't like me, she hates me, she's never liked me' and then they were saying to her, I'd been calling her a fat slag, I'd been calling her this ...
> L: So either way everything's been getting twisted ... this MSN argument and it turned out to be a punch-up between me and her although you didn't hit me.
> M: No ...
> L: For some strange reason. If I hit you, why didn't you hit me back?
> M: Louise! Look at me ... Then look at you!
> L: What are you trying to say, that I'm fat and ugly?
> M: No, you're not fat ... you're taller than me ... I'm a midget ... I'll Die!!

The excerpt illustrates the affective flow underway – rumour flows through friend networks vis-a-vis SNSs and instant messaging. The fight is described through spatial dynamics like gossip 'travelling' and girls 'being stuck in the middle' and everything getting 'twisted'. Bodily responses of 'razzing', grabbing, punching and crying are described. And affective states such as blame, hate, love, envy, despair are moving around through the discussion. Marie's suggestion that she would likely 'die' in any further physical encounter with Louise, is at one level a turn of phrase, but at another a description of an affective state of dread and anxiety, which sits in relation to the excitement of heightened affective states like 'love and hate' propelling the fight.

As in the assemblage of Saad and Celia and peer group, it becomes exceedingly difficult to bifurcate the experiences into the classical two subject positions of bully/victim. Such an analysis would miss the affective fabric and the speed, and prevent us from further conceptual work on the complex daily affective processes of inclusion and exclusion.

As with Celia and Saad, sexualized affect forms the fabric of this assemblage, where desires for inclusion and mechanisms of exclusion circulate and produce insecurity that moves amongst the peer group with various effects. What we find crucial about this assemblage is again a point of fixation. Louise was accused of going 'round with everyone' and trying to 'get with everyone's exes'. In relation to the 'heterosexual matrix' of competitive power relations of the school space (Renold & Ringrose, 2008), the subjectification is meant to work to literally put her in her place. By calling up corporeal abjectness (fatness) (see Kristeva and Butler, in Ringrose &

EDUCATION AND THE POLITICS OF BECOMING

Walkerdine, 2008) and classed discourses of moral suspicion – sexual impurity (slagness) and being 'loose', Louise's self-assemblage in the school culture was at once fixed *and* rendered unviable, so the effect was at least temporarily life-destroying. Like Khaba, the Moroccan variation of 'whore' stuck to Celia, 'fat slag' stuck to Louise in particular, as the overweight and therefore unjustifiably desired and desiring teen in their peer group.

As has emerged throughout the paper, the pejoratives around whore and slag work as points of fixation in both a discursive sense, but also in aligning with molar power formations so that fat slag restricted Louise's movement leading to hardenings of segmentations fixing her, a form of affective and bodily capture. The effects of this were an affective intensity so extreme that Louise literally physically exploded in the school yard when she attacked Marie. This physical violence worked to further fixate her as abject feminine subject, since she became positioned as a 'bully' through the behavioural interventions set in motion in the school.

There is also a great deal of movement within the peer assemblage, however, the displacement of the affective rush and drama of the altercations are also described through the narrative as shifting among a wider group as Louise talked about what 'people were saying to me' and 'people were saying to her' (Marie), just as Celia talked about how the evaluations were witnessed and commented upon by her peers. We find the so-called 'infinite audience' that witnessed the evaluations in cyber space (Shariff, 2008). There was generalized uncertainty and instability about the knowledge circulating via the electronic circuits, so Louise repeatedly referred to a mass form of 'lying', where Celia referred to an 'unknowing' about the origin or end point of the words which circulated about her. We see a generalized sense of anxiety and unease at the insecurity of whom and how many witnesses the exchanges include.

Subversive potentials

So far we have shown how Celia and Louise were kept in place and how these assemblages involved 'pinning' to a ethnic-racialised, gendered and classed screen (Deleuze & Parnet, 2002) or grid of positions (Massumi, 2002) and how Celia, Saad and Louise were delicately balancing these pinnings and renegotiating the affective tenor. In the following we will show – even if not for long – how such pronouncements could also be subverted. The pejorative, molar identities like whore and slag were not completely closed, with some girls attempting to negotiate the sexual signification of these signs, queering (so a disruption of the affective capture of fixed gender regulations) through 'lines of flight' that became possible in the virtual SNS assemblage. In the next examples we explore the subversive potentialities that were afforded through the technological platform and assemblage of the social networking site. This illustrates more fully how social networking sites may create new affective conditions for manoeuvring sexual bullying in intriguing ways.

Daniella (14) from the UK study, had been called a 'slut' by 'loads of people' at her school the previous year. This resembles the interactions among Celia and Saad. Daniella's way of negotiating 'slut', however, differed in some ways from Celia's negotiations, perhaps representing a more radical line of flight. In part as a response to the sexual bullying, Daniella adopted 'slut' as her user name for her Bebo profile, while her friend Nicole used the user name 'whore'. Daniella discussed how her use

EDUCATION AND THE POLITICS OF BECOMING

of slut in the digital space of the SNS was a direct response to sexualized bullying from 'older girls' at school.

> D: I didn't know what you would think, because like my username is slut ... but I don't mean it as like I'm a slut. Because if you look down on my friends list ... One of her ... [Nicola] her username is Whore ... We have this little thing, like she's my slut, I'm her whore. Because loads of people used to call us it, so we just thought whatever, we'll just be them then. And like one day we just found a background like it, and we were like, oh, that's quite nice. And people are like, why have you got slut ... and it's like, I don't mean it like that. But 'cos I didn't know, like if you read it if you'd be thinking, o my god!"

> J: So you mean that people used to say that you were a slut ... what do you mean by that?

> D: Well, 'cos our group, like some people, like older girls that saw us, like with someone would be like, oh you slag or you slut because ... just because they didn't know us, but just because they wanted to insult us ... 'Cos we used to really care about it, and then we just got a bit like oh I don't care anymore ... we just got used to it, and then ... I don't really know what happened but it was just a random thing of where we were just like ... she's my whore and I'm her slut. Whatever! Get over it. And then she'd say the same.

In the previous examples we have been exploring how terms like slag or whore stuck with an affective force that made the girls' lives temporarily unliveable. What is striking about the example of Daniella was how something new was happening via the technological assemblage of the SNS. The SNS appeared to afford a virtual space, and affective movement and molecular lines of flight away from the pejorative bodily capture of 'slut'. Through taking up these positions on their SNSs, Daniella and Nicola were shifting the possibility of the injury through this signifier, they were partially re-signifying and queering the notions of slut and whore, as Daniella explicitly repeated: 'She's my whore and I'm her slut. Whatever! Get over it'. This 'queering' of the notions of 'slut' and 'whore' happened through the girls proclaiming they were each others' whore and slut, rather than the conventional meanings that tied these markers as prostitution, sexual promiscuity or sexual servicing.

Researchers (Atwood, 2007) have shown how the meanings of 'slut' are shifting, and may have new currency as 'cool' and 'sexed up' ways of performing a feminine sexuality in the larger popular 'sexualised' media contexts in the West. A Deleuzian-Guattarian analysis builds on this, to show the specific ways the affective meanings, directions and force of slut and whore are manouevered here, so using 'slut' is not simply reactive but puzzling, blurring boundaries and affirming new meanings. It is a rhizomatic, molecular *becoming* of a specific sort where the coercive, molar line of 'slut' is opened up (at least temporarily), allowing for play and joy, and strengthening of the affective bonds between Daniella and Nicola. This manoevering is not, however, without constraints

Indeed, Deleuze and Guattari's theories of becoming are not simply about an ontological move to pure positivity, as some commentators mistakenly suggest (Gilbert, 2004). Deleuze and Guattari's writings caution us to not build up an analysis to find a grand political re-significaiton or a conscious 'mockery [and] disrespect to the dominance of hetersexuality and the power of norms', suggesting instead shifting 'the focus to the micro, the molecular: singular acts and practices of a

15

EDUCATION AND THE POLITICS OF BECOMING

non-referential nature' (Nigianni, 2009, p. 4). Bearing this caution in mind, we find that there was a queering in the case of Daniella and Nicola, but that it was an unstable one. Later Daniella ended up erasing the experiment with digital slut changing her on-line identity in what seemed to correspond with the end of her heterosexual dating relationship with the popular and attractive Sam. Perhaps slut proved too difficult a subject position to occupy and stretched the meanings when Daniella was outside the protective space of a known heterosexual union with a popular guy at school?

A range of possible additional complex factors limit the possibilities of maneouverabilty around fixed, sticky sexualized signifiers, and constrain subjects via their affective meanings and force. Norms of beauty, or erotic capital (Hakim, 2010), which tie into issues of class and race need to be addressed and tie together our three analyses. Part of the possible reason that Daniella was able to move around with the notion of 'slut' was because her physical body aligned with many of the norms of whiteness and beauty in Western media contexts. Daniella's body carried markers that highlighted her desirability, and she was dating a popular boy during the first part of the research. Some of her freedom to harness the 'cool' 'sexy' factor of 'slut', lay in her positioning as a desirable girl in the school on-line and off-line assemblage. In contrast, the cyberbully event where Louise was called 'fat slag', worked to position her as undesirable (fat) and also low class (slag) chasing after other girls' property (boys). Louise's bodily qualities of largeness were marked out as abject in relation to ideal feminine norms of young, small petite-ness (Ringrose & Walkerdine, 2008; Søndergaard, 2009) and fixed her as undesireable, although she did try to speak back in general ways to these attacks via her Bebo page.

The cyberbully event of fixing Celia as 'khaba' has points of similarity and difference to the cases of Daniella and Louise. Celia's body, like Daniella's, carried signs that aligned her with idealized versions of femininity, though racialised differently, because Celia was not white. These signs were the basis of attack on her on Arto. Recall how Saad was accused of looking at Celia's breasts and that he protested saying even though Celia thought she was 'perfect and beautiful', she was 'uglier than ugly' and 'Khaba'. Yet where Daniella was able to use her body signs to play around with 'slut', the specific cultural and racial nature of the Danish school community formed an assemblage where 'khaba' was more difficult to manouver; and we speculate this may have been because 'khaba' carried affective racialised and sexualised force and intensity different to that of 'slut'. In this way 'Khaba' was racialized, like 'slag' was classed, and there was less scope for resisting these notions, or for re-claiming a 'sexy' and cool identity out of the identity of 'slut', as we saw with Daniella.

Conclusion

In this analysis we have attempted to show how, rather than the singularities of either bully, victim, or by-stander, we find conflict dispersing via 'travelling affects'. Desires, positions and subjects are displaced, dispersed and moved around. Technology mediates desires, blurring the ownership and accelerates the circulations of affects within assemblages that apparently have no 'outer border', as Conley (2009) puts it. Our analysis shows how cyberbulling happens as conflicts move through and are mobilized via a larger assemblage than the limited number of individuals involved in the eventual exchange, *and* affects are charged with meaning and content.

It is the sexualized charge that circulates through the teens, and it is sexualized 'order words' (Cole, 2010), 'Khaba' and 'fat slag', that are introduced into the flow and which work to re-fix and harden an injurious and regulatory sense of sexual abjectness. The effects of the sexualized order words are both fixity and further displacement, particularly an anxiety again for the girls in the peer groups about where these signifiers might land next time they are deployed in the assemblage. If the 'cartographic task … aims at mapping the composition of lines inherent to every assemblage' (Bergen, 2010, p. 36), it is our job as cartographers of youth affect and deconstructors of the phenomena of 'cyberbullying' to outline the intensities of 'khaba', 'fat slag', and 'slut'. As we have been exploring, whore and fat slag work as molar gender identities foisted onto various girls to capture and discipline them through heterosexually striated, coercive space, and the affective effects are moments that render the girls involved as unviable and make school life at least temporarily unliveable, drawing out the implications of Butler's theories of (hetero)sexual subjectification. What Deleuze and Guattari also allow us to explore is how subjects negotiate such fixity, with surprising effects. What is important and what needs to be noted in overviewing the analytical points we are making, is that by using the combined theoretical tools we have elaborated, we can make detailed mappings of the ways affects travel and stick and are maneouvered in *specific* school assemblages. These mappings differ from the insights that would be available to us in either understandings of 'bullies' and 'victims' or even in discourse analysis that illustrate discursive positionings.

In closing, our approach contributes to research on sexualised cyberbullying by allowing us to see how different sexualized signifiers do not all subjectify in the same ways, or hold the same affective force. Indeed, there is differential scope for moving, disrupting and queering injurious sexual identifiers, depending on the raced, classed and encultured specificities of the encounters within a particular school, on-line and off-line assemblages, and meanings in wider popular culture, as we have illustrated. The approach we've outlined continues to challenge us to map these rich complexities of how affects travel across temporalities, between bodies, through in/significant evaluations and technologies. We believe mapping this movement of affect helps us to understand desire, technologically mediated exclusions, and the multiple affective permutations of becoming in school life in more nuanced ways.

Notes

1. In psychological accounts analysing a bullying event in time, the positions of victim and bully tend to be positioned in a binary and this formulation tends to pathologize both positions (see Ringrose, 2008). Where movement is suggested is the risk that the victim could become the bully.
2. There is considerable debate around the possibilities of bringing Butler and Deleuzian approaches together. We, like others, do not see these approaches as inimical and seek to build up a dialogue between the theories through the interweaving of specific theoretical concepts that help us understand the relational processes of subjectification through an affective lens (see also Hickey-Moody & Rasmussen (2009) and Renold & Ringrose (2008)

for feminist and educational discussions of working at the interstices between Butler and Deleuze).
3. Sara Ahmed in her work elaborates how 'what sticks' operates (Ahmed, 2004). There are obvious similarities between Ahmed 2004 and our analysis, which is in part inspired by her creative work on affect. However, our theoretical framework is directly conceptually organised around describing how concepts from Butler, Deleuze and Guattari help us to understand the movement of affect in our empirical research accounts.
4. For a longer discussion of the concept of 'affective assemblages', see Ringrose, 2010.
5. Recent research has discussed the exchange of sexually explicit content (text and images) on mobile phones or online as a phenomenon of 'sexting' (see for instance, Lenhart, 2009; Livingstone et al., 2011). The notion of 'sexting' is certainly provocative if defined widely, as it can help us think about how specifically *sexualised* affects are circulating through mobile technologies.
6. MSN refers here to the instant messaging 'chat' feature.

References

Ahmed, S. (2004). *The cultural politics of emotions*. Edinburgh: Edinburgh University Press.
Attwood, F. (2007). Sluts and riot girls. Female identity and sexual agency. *Journal of Gender Studies, 16*(3), 231–245.
Blackman, L., Cromby, J., Hook, D., Papadopoulos, D., & Walkerdine, V. (2007). Creating subjectivities. *Subjectivity, 22*(1), 1–27.
Bergen, V. (2010). Politics as the orientation of every assemblage. *New formations: A Journal of Culture/Theory/Politics: Deleuzian Politics, 68*, 34–41.
Bonta, M., & Protevi, J. (2004). *Deleuze and geophilosophy: A guide and glossary*. Edinburgh: Edinburgh University Press.
Butler, J. (1990). *Gender trouble*. London: Routledge.
Butler, J. (1993). *Bodies that matter: On the discursive limits of 'sex'*. New York: Routledge.
Butler, J. (2004). *Precarious life: The powers of mourning and violence*. London: Verso.
Butler, J. (2009). *Frames of war: When is life grievable?* London: Verso.
Clough, P.T., & Halley, J. (2007). *The affective turn: Theorizing the social*. Durham: Duke University Press.
Cole, D. (2011). The actions of affect in Deleuze: Others using language and the language that we make. *Educational Philosophy and Theory, 43*(6), 549–561.
Colman, F.J. (2005). Affect. In A. Parr (Ed.), *The Deleuze Dictionary*. Edinburgh: Edinburgh University Press.
Coleman, B. (2008). The becoming of bodies. *Feminist Media Studies, 8*(2), 163–179.
Conley, E. (2009) Borders, motion, and excess in Dante's Commedia, ECLS Student Scholarship. Paper 21. http://scholar.oxy.edu/ecls_student/21, Accessed 20 May 2010.
Davies, B. (2006). Subjectification: The relevance of Butler's analysis for education. *British Journal of Sociology of Education, 27*(4), 425–438.
Davies, B., & Harre, R. (1990). Positioning: The discursive production of selves. *Journal for the Theory of Social Behaviour, 20*(1), 43–63.
DeLanda, M. (2006). *A new philosophy of society*. London: Continuum.
Deleuze, G., & Guattari, F. (1984/2004). *Anti-Oedipus: Capitalism and schizophrenia*. London: Continuum.
Deleuze, G., & Guattari, F. (1987/2004). *A thousand plateaus: Capitalism and schizophrenia*. (Trans. and foreword by Brian Massumi.) London: Continuum.
Deleuze, G., & Parnet, C. (1977/2002). *Dialogues II* (H. Tomlison, B. Habberjam, & E.R. Albert, Trans.) London: The Athlone Press.
Ellwood, C., & Davies, B. (2010). Violence and the moral order in contemporary schooling: A discursive analysis. *Qualitative Research in Psychology, 7*(2), 85–98.
Eriksson, B.O., Lindberg, E., Flygare, J., & Daneback, K. (2002). *Skolan – en arena för mobning (The school. An arena for bullying)*. Stockholm: Skolverket.

EDUCATION AND THE POLITICS OF BECOMING

Gilbert, J. (2004). Signifying nothing: 'Culture', 'discourse', and the sociality of affect, *Culture Machine*, 6 http://www.culturemachine.net/index.php/cm/article/viewArticle/8/7, Accessed 20 August 2009.

Hakim, C. (2010). Erotic capital. *European Sociological Review, 26*(5), 499–518.

Hardt, M. (2007). Foreward: What affects are good for. In P.T. Clough & J. Halley (Eds.), *The affective turn: Theorizing the social* (pp. ix–xiii). Durham: Duke University Press.

Hickey-Moody, A.C., & Rasmussen, M.L. (2009). In-between Deleuze & Butler. In C. Nigianni (Ed.), *Deleuze and queer theory* (pp. 37–53). Edinburgh: Edinburgh University Press.

Hinduja, S., & Patchin, J.W. (2009). *Bullying beyond the schoolyard: Preventing and responding to cyberbullying*. Thousand Oaks, CA: Sage Publications (Corwin Press).

Jackson, A.Y. (2010). Deleuze and the girl. *International Journal of Qualitative Studies in Education, 23*(5), 579–587.

Kofoed, J. (2005). Elevpli. Arbitrære punktummer i skoleliv og forskning (Arbitrary full stops in school life and research). Nordiske Udkast. Tidsskrift for kritisk samfundsforskning (Nordic Sketches). *Journal of Critical Social Science, 33*(2), 67–75.

Kofoed, J. (2007). Ansvar for egen elevhed. Suspensive komparationer på arbejde (Responsible for your own pupilhood). In J. Kofoed & D. Staunæs (Eds.), *Magtballader – 14 fortællinger om magt, modstand og menneskers tilblivelse (PowerTroubles. 14 accounts of power, resistance and human becoming)* (pp. 99–121). Copenhagen: Danmarks Pædagogiske Universitetsforlag.

Kofoed, J. (2009a). Genkendelser af digital mobning: Freja vs Ronja vs Arto vs Sara vs Emma (Recognitions of cyberbullying. Freja vs Ronja vs Arto vs Sara vs Emma). In J. Kofoed & D.M. Søndergaard (Eds.), *Mobning. Sociale processer på afveje (Bullying. Social processes astray)* (pp. 99–133). Copenhagen: Hans Reitzels Forlag.

Kofoed, J. (2009b). Emotional evaluations in cases recognized as cyberbullying. In *Proceedings of conference 'The Good, the Bad and the Challenging'*, Copenhagen, 13–15 May 2009.

Kofoed, J. (2010). Mobile affects: Envy in/through phones. Paper presented at the annual national gender conference, 24 April 2010. Odense: University of Southern Denmark.

Kofoed, J., & Søndergaard, D.M. (Eds.). (2009). *Mobning. Sociale processer på afveje (Bullying. Social processes astray.)*. Copenhagen: Hans Reitzels Forlag.

Kowalski, R.M., & Limber, S.P. (2007). Electronic bullying among middle school students. *Journal of Adolescent Health, 41*, S22–S30.

Lenhart, A. (2009). Teens and sexting: How and why minor teens are sending sexually suggestive nude or nearly nude images via text messaging. *Pew Research Centre Report*, accessed 25 January 2011, http://pewresearch.org/assets/pdf/teens-and-sexting.pdf

Livingstone, S., & L. Haddon (Eds.) (2009). *Kids online. Opportunities and risks for children*. Bristol: The Policy Press.

Livingstone, S., Haddon, L., Görzig, A., & Ólafsson, K. (2011). Risks and safety on the internet: The perspective of European children. Full Findings. LSE, London: EU Kids Online. http://www2.lse.ac.uk/media@lse/research/ERKidsOnline/ERKidsII%20(2009-11)/EUKidsOnlineIIReports/D4FullFindings.pdf, Accessed 20 March 2011.

Malins, P. (2004). Machinic assemblages: Deleuze, Guattari and an ethico-aesthetics of drug use. *Janus Head, 7*(1), 84–104.

Massumi, B. (1987). Notes on the translation and acknowledgements. In G. Deleuze & F. Guattari (Eds.), *A Thousand Plateaus*. Minneapolis, MN: University of Minnesota Press.

Massumi, B. (2002). *Parables for the virtual: Movement, affect, sensation*. Montreal: Post Contemporary Interventions.

Nigianni, C. (2009). Introduction. In C. Nigianni & M. Storr (Eds.), *Deleuze and queer studies* (pp. 1–13). Edinburgh: Edinburgh University Press.

Olweus, D. (1993). *Bullying at school: What we know and what we can do*. Oxford: Blackwell.

Renold, E., & Ringrose, J. (2008). Regulation and rupture: Mapping tween and teenage girls' 'resistance' to the heterosexual matrix. *Feminist Theory: An International Interdisciplinary Journal, 9*(3), 335–360.

Ringrose, J. (2008). 'Just be friends': Exposing the limits of educational bully discourses for understanding teen girls' heterosexualized friendships and conflicts. *British Journal of Sociology of Education, 29*(5), 509–522.

EDUCATION AND THE POLITICS OF BECOMING

Ringrose, J. (2011). Beyond discourse? Using Deleuze and Guattari's schizoanalysis to explore affective assemblages, heterosexually striated space, and lines of flight online and at school. *Educational Philosophy & Theory, 43*(6), 598–618.

Ringrose, J., & Renold, E. (2010). Normative cruelties and gender deviants: The performative effects of bully discourses for girls and boys in school. *British Educational Research Journal, 36*(4), 573–596.

Ringrose, J., & Walkerdine, V. (2008). Regulating the abject: The TV make-over as site of neo-liberal reinvention toward bourgeois femininity. *Feminist Media Studies, 8*(3), 227–246.

Schott, R.M. (2009). Mobning som socialt fænomen. Filosofiske refleksioner over definitioner (Bullying as a social phenomenon. Philosophical reflections on definitions). In J. Kofoed & D.M. Søndergaard (Eds.), *Mobning. Sociale processer på afveje* (*Bullying: Social processes astray*) (pp. 222–259). Copenhagen: Hans Reitzels Forlag.

Shariff, S. (2008). *Cyberbullying: Issues and solutions for the school, the classroom, and the home.* New York: Routledge.

Slonje, R., & Smith, P.K. (2008). Cyberbullying: Another main type of bullying? *Scandinavian Journal of Psychology, 49*, 147–154.

Smith, P.K. (2009). Cyberbullying: Abusive relationships in cyberspace. *Journal of Psychology, 217*(4), 180–181.

Smith, P.K., Cowie, H., Olafsson, R.F., & Liefooghe, A.P.D. (2002). Definitions of bullying: A comparison of terms used, and age and gender differences, in a fourteenth-country international comparison. *Child Development, 73*(4), 1119–1133.

Smith, P.K., Mahdavi, J., Carvalho, M., Fisher, S., Russell, S., & Tippett, N. (2008). Cyberbullying: Its nature and impact in secondary school pupils. *Journal of Child Psychology and Psychiatry, 49*(4), 376–385.

Søndergaard, D.M. (2002). Poststructuralist approaches to empirical analysis. *Qualitative Studies in Education, 15*(2), 187–204.

Søndergaard, D.M. (2009). Mobning og social eksklusionsangst (Bullying and Social Fear of Exclusion). In J. Kofoed & D.M. Søndergaard (Eds.), *Mobning. Sociale processer på afveje* (*Bullying. Social processes astray*) (pp. 21–59). Copenhagen: Hans Reitzels Forlag.

Spears, B.P., Slee, L., Owens, J., & Johnson, B. (2009). Behind the scenes and screens: Insights into the human dimension of covert and cyber bullying. *Zeitschrift für Psychologie / Journal of Psychology, 217*(4), 189–197.

Staunæs, D., & Bjerg, H. (2011). Anerkendende ledelse og blussende ører (Appreciative leaderhsip and flushed ears). In M. Juelskjær, H. Knudsen, J. Pors & D. Staunæs (Eds.), *Ledelse af uddannelse – at lede det potentielle* (*Leading of education-leading the potential*). Frederiksberg: Samfundslitteratur.

Tamboukou, M. (2008). Machinic assemblages: Women, art education and space. *Discourse: Studies in the Cultural Politics of Education, 29*(3), 359–375.

Walkerdine, V. (1991). *Schoolgirl fictions.* London: Verso.

Becoming-teacher: Encounters with the Other in teacher education

Stephen Marble

> Teacher education – as currently practised – is solidly based on a developmental model of growing expertise, where novices move from error to effective practice by replicating the strategies and classroom moves of model teachers. Short timelines and limited opportunities for experience create challenges for students wishing to become teachers. Deleuze's construct of Becoming opens new perspectives on what it means for prospective teachers to explore the notion of Becoming-teacher, where learning about teaching is an encounter with ever-new situations and relationships. This chapter concludes with an invitation to teacher educators to experiment in their own practice, to do with their students, to fully explore the potentialities of Becoming-Teachers.

Pre-service teachers frequently wonder about how life will be when they too finally become teachers. Without a doubt, their more experienced school colleagues are 'teachers' but this professional title rarely stretches to include 'student' teachers. Then one day, there is a shift in their discourse and they no longer describe themselves as *wanting to become* a teacher, but *as* teachers. This shift in identity raises questions important for teacher education. What does it mean to 'become' a teacher? Does every prospective teacher become one? How? When in time does this happen: at the moment of licensure, upon completing student teaching, with the first letter of hire, on the first day of work? And does *being* a teacher prevent one from continuing to *become* a teacher?

I have argued elsewhere (Marble, 1997) that pre-service students *become* teachers when novices self-identify with others who are teachers, when 'they' changes to 'we' in their discourse about practice. Students in a two-year graduate teacher education program self-identified as teachers during the first of four semesters, long before they ever actually taught and right around the moment when they presented the results of a 'school portrait' research project to the school faculty. Communicating 'insider' information and ideas about the school to teachers as peers, I proposed, promoted their membership in the school community, casting them within a role in the school narrative, a belonging. Seeing the actions and beliefs of experienced teachers reproduced in themselves prompted teacher candidates to recognize themselves as teachers, doing what teachers do, in the same environments, and with the same groups.

But is it enough to simply identify oneself as a teacher in order to become a teacher? If not, what *does* it mean for someone to 'become' a teacher? In this article

I examine this question through two very different lenses. One looks through the widely accepted developmental lens at the process by which beginning teachers learn the craft, a perspective relying heavily on representational language. In this process, novices move through a linear continuum of identifiable, measureable, and replicable practices while they acquire contextual experience, beginning with reproducing the skills and knowledge of more accomplished teachers. Eventually, given enough experience, they too might become experts. The article then explores what it means to become a teacher from a very different perspective, one rooted in the philosophy of Gilles Deleuze. When seen through a Deleuzean lens, *Becoming-teacher* no longer describes the acquisition of identities or replication of accepted sets of behaviours, but rather involves the creative responding to always-new situations and relationships that classrooms and schools make possible. A Becoming-teacher does not move from A to B (student-teacher to real teacher, for example) but 'makes a multiplicity' through 'changes in nature as it expands its connections' (Deleuze & Guattari, 1987, p. 8).

Becoming a teacher

Many if not all pre-service teacher education programs assume that becoming a teacher involves novice candidates acquiring the knowledge and skills of teachers, a process that requires both mentoring and practice. The metamorphosis from candidate to teacher can occur in several ways, depending on which side of the *born vs made* debate you root for. One involves teacher candidates discovering within themselves the characteristics they share with 'good' or expert teachers. Alternatively, candidates can acquire and grow these teaching skills through guided practice. In either case, the goal is for the candidate to identify and shape their practice to replicate the behaviours of others, in this case more experienced professionals. Student teaching serves as the culminating pre-service experience, a performance during which 'candidates' transform into 'teachers' through trials in real classrooms guided and monitored by experienced teachers and university supervisors.

David Berliner (1988) proposed a typology of teaching expertise to theorize the development of teaching practice, beginning with novice teachers and working through five stages to the ultimate expert teacher. The first three stages he defined as the domain of teacher education programs. In the first, novices are taught to follow rules without context as requisite for beginning teaching, since only marginal performance can be expected from these 'green horns'. With some experience, novices become advanced beginners, aware that rules sometimes can be ignored as situations and learners vary. With additional experience and guidance, the teacher candidate can become a competent performer, making conscious choices about classroom activities and knowing what is important to attend to and what is not. Teacher education programs, Berliner argues, should expect to accomplish little more than promoting competent teaching performance characterized by rational approaches to planning and contextual sensibilities in execution.

Two more experienced stages continue the development of teacher expertise beyond the purview of teacher pre-service education. Competent teachers can eventually become Proficient ones when they begin to work with the intuition and know-how arising from extensive experience. Teachers at this fourth stage can *feel* how well lessons are going, develop generalizations about similarities between disparate events, and predict events more precisely based on common understandings of what should be happening. And ultimately, some – but not all – teachers reach an even deeper understanding of practice Berliner identifies as 'expert':

> If novices, advanced beginners, and competent performers are rational, and proficient performers are intuitive, we might categorize experts as 'a-rational'. They have an intuitive grasp of a situation and seem to sense in non-analytic, non-deliberative ways the appropriate response to make. They show fluid performance, as we all do when we no longer have to choose our words when speaking or think about where to place our feet when walking ... They are acting effortlessly and fluidly, behaving in ways that are not easily described as deductive or analytic. (Berliner, 1988, p. 5)

Most importantly, however, Berliner found that experts act without calculation or deliberative thought. They don't need to, he argues because they can focus on fewer details, quickly honing in on those that differ from their expectations, developed over long practice. 'Experience seems to change people so they literally see differently ...' (Berliner, 1988, p. 18). This enables experts to more quickly process and react in situations with which they are familiar or have sufficient information. However, Berliner reports an interesting and unexpected finding: when asked to plan a lesson given simulated classroom information, the experts became 'quite angry about the task and quite disappointed in their performance' remembering their 'discomfort, stress and terror' (Berliner, 1988, p. 19) long after the experiment ended. Berliner argues this anger arises because the experiment minimized the contextual information that experts are so quick to process and understand, forcing them to work in unfamiliar situations.

Berliner proposes that this developmental typology of teaching has important implications for teacher education, implications that have widely influenced teacher education programs. Beginning teachers should focus on accumulating experience, he argues, learning to see what experts 'see' and how to understand classroom events in 'expert' terms, pushing the visions of experts onto novices as a way of developing these images of teaching. Beginning teachers should not be expected to create lessons or explore alternatives to standard lessons, but should be given scripts and forms to follow and learn from as they gain experience. Learning classroom decision-making skills should be postponed until after teachers become competent, and instead routines for handling the everyday work of teaching should hold the centre of their attention. And teacher educators working in real world classrooms should choose mentors who are good coaches rather than focus on teacher experts, who may not be able to articulate exactly what they do and why.

Not all of Berliner's suggestions have been widely implemented. He argues that, rather than preparing future teachers for some generic future placement, we should be preparing beginning teachers for very specific grade levels and content assignments. If pre-service teachers knew what grades they would be teaching in their first year on the job, he reasons, their chances for a successful experience would greatly improve. He claims not to be advocating for a narrow form of on-the-job training, however, since our expectations should be that it takes a long time to develop competent practitioners and longer to develop expertise in a profession as complicated as teaching (Berliner, 1988, p. 27).

Learning to teach for Berliner and many others, then, is an extended linear process where beginners copy more experienced practitioners as they gain contextual expertise, at which point some few transform into 'a-rational' experts whose practice is fluid and no longer easily analysed. Teacher education, confined to the lower ends of the taxonomy, focuses heavily on the replication of known practices. Most programs designed to teach new teachers how to practise in their field follow this outline. Lesson planning, instruction, and assessment are first modelled and evaluated by more experienced mentors who guide students away from novice error toward the faithful reproduction of expert practice.

Berliner's theoretical description of developmental stages in learning to teach was proposed in a time of increasing awareness of the variability in teacher quality and its impacts. Along with calls to formalize teacher education and the assessment of teaching quality, the differences between experts and novices helped further the depiction of teachers as professionals. In the more than 20 years since its publication, teaching has been identified as the most significant factor influencing learning, defined by standards, and broadly challenged by alternative certification. Still Berliner's developmental model accurately captures the prevalent teacher education experience of learning to teach.

The city seen anew: Becoming-teacher

May & Semetsky (2008) portray proposals like Berliner's as limiting practitioners to the 'inescapable horizon' of a pre-determined education of identities: no matter what the potential for new practice, promoting copies of teachers precludes the emergence of creative solutions to problems that arise. To see beyond this horizon, they climb on the shoulders of the French philosopher, Gilles Deleuze. Everyone remembers his or her first crashing encounter with the ideas of Deleuze. My own came as I helped map a site for the Polynesian Voyaging Society's educational centre on the beach across the harbour from downtown Honolulu. The designer, my son, proposed creating a series of transitional spaces through which voyagers would move back and forth between the open, nomadic spaces of the pelagic environment they lived in while at sea and the highly structured – Deleuze terms this *striated* – urban environment they encountered whenever on shore.

The educational implications were intriguing; perhaps these ideas could help reconceptualise the experience students had navigating between their free and independent lives outside of school and the highly structured school and classroom environments. At my son's suggestion I picked up a copy of *A Thousand Plateaus* (Deleuze & Guattari, 1987) and dove in. But it was not going to be so simple; from the very first words, the text was opaque. As I laboured to parse the 'plateaus', I began to appreciate how Polynesian navigators must feel: weeks spent in highly personal interactions among a very small crew on the open ocean, then suddenly coming ashore and subject to all the unwritten rules of social interaction in a large impersonal urban environment. Though excited at the possibilities, I was unprepared for the challenge I would face accessing the thinking behind these ideas. Deleuze, Ronald Bogue (2008) declares, is a polymath whose thought ranges widely across disciplines and time. The scope of those ideas is indeed astonishing. I explored at length *rhizomes, nomads, capture, refrains, smoothness, wolves, wasps, Bodies Without Organs, disjunctive syntheses*, and many other diverse yet interconnected concepts Deleuze deploys to construct his own philosophical 'image of thought'.

My disorientation was not unique, however. For one thing, Deleuze's style, especially within his extensive collaborations with Felix Guattari, 'appears a little mad, ideas and concepts seem to fly right off the page. For another, it is quite difficult to pin down just what his method or system is ...' (Buchanan, 2000, p. 40). Ansell Pearson (1997) posts this warning to those interested in learning more: 'To enter the labyrinth of his thought one must have courage for the forbidden where the strange and unfamiliar things of the future are more familiar than the so-called reality of the present' (pp. 2–3). Deleuze's project is a practice in concept formation that challenges '... the way that philosophy itself is written and formulated. Because of this, they [Deleuze and Guattari] draw both from new ideas and from those of a multiplicity of already existing disciplines' (Message, 1997):

> These engagements are at times fleeting and at times more sustained, and contribute to their strategy of preventing their position from stabilizing into an ideology, method, or single metaphor. In other words, they encourage philosophy to occupy the space of slippage that exists between disciplinary boundaries, and to question how things are made, rather than simply analysing or interpreting the taken-for-granted final result or image. (Message, 1997, p. 29)

St Pierre (2000) describes the slipperiness of her engagements with one of Deleuze's claims: 'I find this one of those provocative Deleuzean statements that seems straightforward but is best considered askew. If you go after it head on, it will unravel even as your understanding increases' (p. 283). Massumi invites the reader, in his Translator's Foreword to *A Thousand Plateaus*, to 'read it as a challenge' and to 'jump' with concepts that begin to 'pry open the vacant spaces that would enable you to build your life' (2002, p. xv).

Any attempts to pry open and rebuild images of educational practice are further complicated by the fact that Deleuze himself does not consider teaching or pedagogy at length in any work. But he does describe the critical role of thought in learning, and here I finally found a place to jump into the middle. In *Difference & Repetition* (1994), Deleuze challenges the 'Dogmatic Image of Thought", asserting: '... everybody knows and is presumed to know what it means to think' (Deleuze, 1994, p. 131). This dominating image invades our considerations and '... crushes thought under an image which is that of the Same and the Similar in representation, but profoundly betrays what it means to think and alienates the two powers of difference and repetition, of philosophical commencement and recommencement' (Deleuze, 1994, p. 167), subordinating learning to the product knowledge. In *A Shock to Thought,* Massumi (2002) describes Deleuze's notion of 'tracing':

> A tracing approach overlays the product onto the process, on the assumption that they must be structurally homologous. The assumption is that you can conceptually superimpose them to bring out a common logical outline. When this procedure is followed, product and process appear as versions of each other: copies. Production coincides with reproduction. Any potential the process may had had of leading to a significantly differently product is lost in the overlay of what already is (2002, p. xviii).

Deleuze, Bogue (2008) points out, questions the common assumption that:

> ... thought's goal in a world of recognition and representation is to eliminate problems and find solutions, to pass from non-knowledge to knowledge. Learning in such a world is simply the passage from non-knowledge to knowledge, a process with a definite

beginning and ending, in which thought, like a dutiful pupil, responds to pre-formulated questions and eventually arrives at pre-existing answers (2008, p. 6).

Learning envisioned as the Reproduction of the Same – a copying or tracing of the already known – allows for the correction of movements but not their initiation. Tracing implies some correct prior existence that is reconstructed, with 'truth' determined by fidelity and 'untruth' as error (Deleuze, 1994, p. 22). This characterization of learning fits well with the apprenticeship model described by Berliner and others and widely employed in many teacher education programs: novices are directed to copy more experienced colleagues until they have demonstrated the ability to faithfully reproduce those known practices.

Deleuze denounces such representational accounts of learning and teaching: 'Learning takes place not in the relations between a representation and an action (reproduction of the Same) but in the relations between a sign and response (encounter with the Other)' (1994, pp. 22–23). To liberate thought from the repeated replication of the known, Deleuze develops a critique of the Dogmatic Image of Thought, offering an alternative: 'thought without Image ... one which would have to renounce both the form of representation and the element of common sense' (1994, p. 132). He writes:

> Something in the world forces us to think. This something is an object not of recognition but of a fundamental *encounter*. ... In whichever tone, its primary characteristic is that it can only be sensed. In this sense it is opposed to recognition (1994, p. 139).

For Deleuze, these encounters act as shocks to thought, or, as Bogue writes: 'Only through a chance encounter with an unsettling sign can thought be jolted from its routine patterns ...' (2008, p. 3) or as he explains '... a disruption of ordinary habits and notions' (p. 7). Bogue goes on:

> By 'learning' Deleuze clearly does not mean the mere acquisition of any new skill or bit of information, but instead the accession to a new way of perceiving and understanding the world. To interpret signs is to overcome 'stock notions,' 'natural' or 'habitual' modes of comprehending reality. What often passes for learning is simply the reinforcement of commonsense notions, standard codes and orthodox beliefs. But the commonsense, conventional, orthodox world is ultimately illusory. Genuine learning, the learning through signs, takes us beyond the illusions of habit and common sense to the truths of what Proust calls 'essences' and Deleuze labels 'differences' (2008, p. 2).

Learning, for Deleuze, is not a movement from the unknown to the known, a retracing of the world in the individual. It is instead the exercise of the power of truth to 'disclose itself differently with each new encounter' (Colebrook, 2008, p. 41).

Encountering the Other

How do these ideas inform the practical act of teaching about teaching? How do they help us move beyond the limitations of the 'inescapable horizon' of the known described by May and Symetsky? Deleuze focuses on learning, referring to teaching only in passing. But his description of genuine learning, not as copying but as learning something new, tells us much of what we need to know. In perhaps the most straightforward of these passages, he disparages teachers who ask students to imitate or reproduce the models they are given:

> We learn nothing from those who say: 'Do as I do'. Our only teachers are those who tell us to 'do with me' and they are able to emit signs to be developed in heterogeneity rather than propose gestures for us to reproduce. (Deleuze, 1994, pp. 22–23)

Teaching, Deleuze might argue, is a collaborative experience, one in which signs are emitted, responses stimulated, and in their relationship encounters generated. May and Semetsky consider alternatives that promote creative possibilities:

> For Deleuze, education would begin, not when the student arrives at a grasp of the material already known by the teacher, but when the teacher and student together begin to experiment in practice with what they might make of themselves and their world (2008, p. 150).

Deleuze's 'experiment in practice' in most clearly explicated in *Difference and Repetition* where he borrows from Leibnitz the concrete example of learning to swim in the ocean:

> ... the movement of the response does not 'resemble' that of the sign. The movement of the swimmer does not resemble that of the wave, in particular, the movements of the swimming instructor which we reproduce on the sand bear no relation to the movements of the wave, which we learn to deal with only by grasping the former in practice as signs. ... When a body combines some of its own distinctive points with those of a wave, it espouses the principle of a repetition which is no longer that of the Same, but involves the Other – involves difference, from one wave and one gesture to another, and carries that difference through the repetitive space thereby constituted. To learn is indeed to constitute this space of an encounter with signs, in which distinctive points renew themselves in each other, and repetition takes shape while disguising itself. (Deleuze, 1994, pp. 22–23)

For learning to take place, genuinely new relationships between the learner and the signs he or she encounters must be created, relationships that are not limited by repetitions of the Same but always encounters with the Other. Each wave presents a new and different problem in which a new set of relationships between the swimmer and the sea must be created in response:

> Instead of being about transitions that something initiates or goes through, Deleuze's theory holds that things and states are *products* of becoming. The human subject, for example, ought not to be conceived as a stable, rational individual, experiencing changes but remaining, principally, the same person. Rather, for Deleuze, one's self must be conceived as a constantly changing assemblage of forces, an epiphenomenon arising from chance confluences of languages, organisms, societies, expectation, laws, and so on." (Stagoll, 2005, p. 22)

Likewise, each classroom event is not a repetition of some past teaching moment to be recognized and repeated, but a genuinely new combination of teachers, learners and ideas. Seen through a Deleuzean lens, teachers do not become experts as Berliner proposes, by tracing the practice of others until these actions become habitually replicated true to some dogmatic image of teaching. Learning to teach, like all learning, happens in an encounter with the Other. Practitioners must go beyond recognition of the same to engage life itself and all its differences: teaching involves encountering problems and exploring new solutions that act to change both teachers and learners. Novices do not at some point 'become' a teacher by crossing the border that insulates non-teachers from teachers; 'Becoming-teachers' emit signs that disrupt thought, enabling learners to encounter problems and create new assemblages of forces in response.

Disrupting thought in teacher education

Both images – the image of becoming a teacher by developmentally moving from novice to expert and the image of the Becoming-teacher articulating new relationships in each and every teaching event – pose significant challenges for teacher education. The developmental image, learning to see the classroom from the expert's perspective, requires more time and experience than the most current pre-service programs can afford to offer prior to certification, leaving the final stages up to certified novices to encounter on their own. More importantly, programs replicating expert practice offer few tools and strategies – aside from copying the experts – to keep novices engaged in their development long enough to survive the requisite years of experience.

But these are not the only challenges. The gap between preparation and practice is wide, and few teacher educators have established relationships with schools that enable candidates to have any specific idea, other than wide grade ranges like K-6, where they will begin their career. This reinforces a focus on the broad, general possibilities of teaching for a wide variety of potential situations. And, finally, teacher education programs typically spend significant time exploring theories and criticisms that Berliner argues are too sophisticated, subtle, and beyond the comprehension of beginning teachers in any case. If quality teaching develops with support over time, why do we persist in promoting theory over practice to any extent at all in the little time students have to develop their nascent skills?

The development of expertise model outlined by Berliner closely matches the orthodoxy of teacher education in one important way, however: most programs have adopted a developmental path through incrementally more sophisticated classroom experiences as their central strategy for learning to teach. The process of having novice beginners replicate the actions of experienced mentors underlies the near universal experience of student teaching, immediately before teachers are certified into professional practice.

If becoming a teacher requires tracing a fractured but identifiable trail, it benefits at least from widespread support and understanding. No such support exists in current practice or thought for the concept of Becoming-teacher derived from Deleuzean perspectives on learning, where the object is not a copying of expertise but the creation of multiple, new relationships between learners and ideas. Indeed, a teacher education program based on Deleuze's Image of Thought would be neither simple nor perhaps even recognizable.

> What escapes orthodox thought is difference, or the genuinely 'new,' which can only be engaged through an 'imageless thought'. Rather than arising from a conscious exercise of good will, genuine thought must be forced into action through the disruption of

ordinary habits and notions. The object of an imageless thought defies recognition, for 'the new—in other words, difference—calls forth forces in thought which are not the forces of recognition, today or tomorrow, but the powers of a completely other model, from an unrecognized and unrecognizable *terra incognita*' (Deleuze, 1994, p. 136, cited in Bogue, 2008). Such an object is understood not through representation but through explication, for the object is a sign, an internalized difference pointing toward something other than itself. (Bogue, 2008, p. 11)

Explicating how teacher education might deploy these ideas becomes an experiment in practice, as Deleuze would want it. But how might we go about prying our practices open and exploring the domain of problems for new possibilities, to create a Pedagogy of Becoming? Where might we jump in? Several thoughts come to mind.

One important step would be to identify and support opportunities for Becoming-teachers to engage with problems in practice. Problematizing the experience of learning to teach emphasizes both the learner and the ever-changing contexts in which they find themselves working, rather than the expertise of the teacher. As Bogue explains:

Rather than eliminating problems, the thought of difference is itself a thought of problems, and learning, rather than occupying the gap between non-knowledge and knowledge, is the process whereby thought explores the domain of problems (2008, p. 11).

Becoming-teachers require tools in order to engage with the domain of problems. The human and conceptual contexts of teaching and learning are both fluid and rapidly variable, much as the liquid environment surrounding Leibnitz's swimmer; each new encounter requires an experimental articulation between the teacher, learner, and concept. The lesson plan and observation report, used widely to guide beginning teachers, also serve to limit the horizon of teaching to a known set of expectations defined and controlled by experienced outsiders. Significantly, these external supports vanish once novice teachers move beyond the safety net of pre-service programs, leaving them unprepared for experimental inquiry into their own practice. Two strategies that help promote creative inquiry in teaching come to mind: both action research and lesson study explore the contexts of ongoing practice and are open to teachers of all levels of skill.

The critical goal is not to simplify the experience of those learning to teach, but to complicate their experience to the point where they are forced to think, forced to encounter the Other in ways that shock thought and disrupt habits. Learners should experiment with creating new approaches for new situations. Rather than becoming a teacher when one is deemed *competent*, those who teach would continue Becoming-Teacher with each new encounter with the Other, each new disruptive learning event.

Engaging novice teachers with the unique problems of practice in creative ways shifts the gaze of teacher education away from the comfortable steady flame of replicating expertise to the dim flicker of promoting creative difference. Interestingly, this shift serves to bring teacher education more closely into alignment with its own rhetoric of differentiation and individual learner needs. Why consider each student unique if we continue to measure against standardized expectations?

EDUCATION AND THE POLITICS OF BECOMING

Similarly, the time frame for Becoming-teacher shifts from the all too brief pre-service indoctrination to one that spans the career of a teacher. Learning to teach turns out to be the on-going exploration of new ideas and approaches, lasting long beyond the introductory pre-service period. This timeframe makes sense, yet we continue to limit our support for teachers to the few years of pre-service courses and perhaps a year or two of hit-and-miss mentoring. Again, our actions might better match our rhetoric if teacher education looked up from its unwavering attention on replicating good teachers who meet some external criteria of 'good' and sought ways to support the continuing growth of expertise, by helping each Becoming-teacher throughout their career.

This chapter opened with a discussion of pre-service students who identified themselves as teachers well before they began to teach, about the time they included themselves in the school narrative. Originally this was interpreted as a movement across the identity boundary from outside to inside. But a Deleuzean lens gives us a new conceptualization to explain the change in their discourse. Before teaching even one lesson, without one moment of copying more experienced teachers, these novices began to see themselves as teachers. They were posed a problem – creating a school portrait – a problem that forced them to reconsider their conceptions of teaching and schooling. During their investigation, their idea of 'teaching' expanded beyond an initial limited perspective of teachers working alone in classrooms with 30 children to include the many other actions and roles that teachers play in a school. Deleuze would call this expansion of connections, this making multiple, Becoming.

For those who teach teachers, the challenges of practice can seem overwhelming. How can abandoning our habitual teaching approaches in favour of creative experimentation in practice help us meet those challenges? I would argue the benefits are multiple and significant, but would like to point out just three at this time. First, we would be exploring strategies for understanding teaching that extend far beyond the limited frame of pre-service preparation. In fact we could abandon the notions of pre-service and in-service teaching identities altogether; they do little in reality except to exclude and limit based on external criteria and a developmental image of teaching. And most limited of all are teacher educators, who command one arena and rarely are seen in the other. Second, we would begin to focus our students (and ourselves) on how teaching really works, rather than limiting them to tracing the well-worn paths created by experienced experts with neither understanding nor creative joy. And third, we would be asking our students not to do as we do, but to do with us, as Deleuze puts it. We all would become members of a learning community that promotes meaningful teaching.

This is unfamiliar territory for teacher education, true, and problematizing practices are neither sufficient in themselves nor widely employed. They call into question our long-standing efforts to identify best practices and help others acquire the knowledge, skills and dispositions to replicate them. Rather they ask us to value the multiple *what could be's*, to push beyond the horizons of the known to the unknown new. In this strange territory we are forced to engage, to discover, to experiment in genuine ways with the ideas that lay at the very heart of teaching and learning, our bread and butter. To be honest, however, teacher educators have much to gain from exploring with our students what it means to enable Becoming-teachers; there is much to learn.

References

Ansell Pearson, K. (1997). Deleuze outside/outside Deleuze. In K. Ansell Pearson (Ed.), *Deleuze and Philosophy: The difference engineer* (pp. 1–23). London: Routledge.

Berliner, D.C. (1988). *The development of expertise in pedagogy.* The Charles W. Hunt Memorial Lecture presented at the Annual Meeting of the American Association for College of Teacher Education: Washington D.C. February 17–20, 1988.

Bogue, R. (2008). Search, swim and see: Deleuze's apprenticeship in signs and pedagogy of images. In I. Semetsky (Ed.), *Nomadic education: Variations on a theme by Deleuze and Guattari* (pp. 1–16). Rotterdam: Sense Publishers.

Buchanan, I. (2000). *Deleuzism: A metacommentary.* Durham, NC: Duke University Press.

Colebrook, C. (2008). Leading out, leading on: The soul of education. In I. Semetsky (Ed.), *Nomadic Education: Variations on a theme by Deleuze and Guattari* (pp. 35–42). Rotterdam: Sense Publishers.

Deleuze, G., & Guattari, F. (1987). *A thousand plateaus: Capitalism and schizophrenia* (Trans. Brian Massumi). Minneapolis: University of Minnesota Press.

Deleuze, G. (1994). *Difference and repetition.* (Trans. Paul Patton). New York: Columbia University Press.

Marble, S.T. (1997). Narrative visions of teaching. *Teaching and Teacher Education, 13*(1), 55–64.

Massumi, B. (2002). *A shock to thought: Expression after Deleuze and Guattari.* London: Routledge.

May, T., & Semetsky, I. (2008). Deleuze, ethical education, and the unconscious. In I. Semetsky (Ed.), *Nomadic education: Variations on a theme by Deleuze and Guattari* (pp. 143–158). Rotterdam: Sense Publishers.

Message, K. (2005). Black hole. In A. Parr (Ed.), *The Deleuze dictionary* (pp. 28–30). New York: Columbia University Press.

Semetsky, I. (2004). The role of intuition in thinking and learning: Deleuze and the pragmatic legacy. *Educational Philosophy and Theory, 36*(4), 433–454.

St Pierre, E.A. (2000). Nomadic inquiry in the smooth spaces of the field: A preface. In E. St Pierre & W. Pillow (Eds.), *Working the ruins: Feminist poststructural theory and methods in education* (pp. 258–283). New York: Routledge.

Stagoll, C. (2005). Becoming. In A. Parr (Ed.), *The Deleuze dictionary* (pp. 21–23). New York: Columbia University Press.

Latino families becoming-literate in Australia: Deleuze, literacy and the politics of immigration

David R. Cole

This article examines qualitative data from a two family case study in New South Wales. Both families are from South America and have recently moved to Australia. This study demonstrates that an understanding of the ways that the families are becoming literate in Australia necessitates moving beyond linguistic analyses of the changes that are occurring. The changes that are addressed constitute a politics of immigration, whereby the internal hopes and desires of the family make up an affective plane that transforms language learning. Such writing exemplifies the use of Deleuzian theory in the analysis of the literacy learning of the families, and shows how this rests on notions of the will to power, affect and the multiple nature of the self. The paper will use Masny's (2006) multiple literacies theory (MLT) to reconcile the politics of becoming involved with the immigration of the families and variant modes of expression.

Introduction

What does it mean to become literate? Certainly in the context of Australia, literacy has much to do with learning the English language to speak, read and write. Yet this study looks to broaden and expand upon such a focus, as learning the English language brings with it a host of divergent factors that include first language learning, cultural and social mores about education and specific contextual matters such as the ways in which the individuals and groups are being acculturated and schooled in Australia (Brown, Miller & Mitchell, 2006; Rennie, 2006). Furthermore, in contemporary society, reading and writing technology has moved on to include a plethora of mediated digital formats that the migrants also have to negotiate (see Kress, 2003). The expanded notion of becoming literate is represented here through the conjunction, 'becoming-literate', that implies a simultaneous convergence and divergence of factors involved with English language learning, rather than an outcome based understanding of what immigrants have to do to learn English or to fit in with the mainstream (cf. Dias, Arthur, Beecher, & McNaught, 2000). Becoming-literate is therefore a conceptual construction that does not simply involve the change from being illiterate to literate, but is a multi-directional and dimensional notion that is a convergent assemblage of parts that often chaotically collide in language learning spaces. These spaces may be schools, adult literacy classes, social situations, the home, work, or watching Australian media. Becoming-literate does not prioritise the subjectivity or agency related to individuals or groups English language learning, but draws social-cultural maps of the changes that are taking place in the families, and these maps are intended to indicate the directions in which the lives of the immigrants are moving (Ferdman, 1999) – both to demonstrate the physical reality of Latino family life in Australia and to show how their needs are evolving.

This notion of 'becoming-literate' relies on the socio-semiotic work of Deleuze & Guattari (1987) that appears in their second *Capitalism & Schizophrenia* opus, *1000 Plateaus*. Such socio-semiotics foregrounds becoming as a process that includes relationships with external factors of change simultaneous with those that are patterned in the construction of multiple selves such as self-determination, the will, motivation and attitude. This research paper, which is based on the Deleuzian notion of becoming, therefore importantly bisects the psychology of changes involved with literacy with those that may be constructed through understanding the sociology of the situation. The notion of becoming that one may derive from Deleuze (cf. Colebrook, 2002) is purposely designed to inhabit a different space from mainstream psychology or sociology, not to diminish either activity, but as a way of construing becoming as a potentially chaotic and indeterminate other that is crucially multiple.

In terms of education, the notion of becoming has been characterised as a type of constructivism (Semetsky, 2006), or micro sociology (Ringrose, forthcoming) that addresses the fluctuations of the self and other through learning. Yet migrant learning is also importantly open to the new social conditions that the immigrants have to understand and reconstruct from their perspective as they start to participate in contemporary Australian life. This change process implies that the Latino families' desires, intentions and actions are entwined with the ways in which capital is affecting them (see Bourdieu, 1997). In effect, they are redrawn as human capital through their move to Australia, and their reactions to the penetration of capital into their personal life will determine much of their future in the new society, including their educational horizons. This study of family literacies is therefore critically concerned with the politics of immigration and the ways in which it determines social life. The immigrants bring with them ways of coping with Australian conditions from their previous lives in South America. Yet they will also have to evolve new strategies for working with unfamiliar social and cultural factors, including divergent experiences of discrimination, isolation, racism, the English language and capital.

Two case studies

Two Latino families in western Sydney, NSW, were researched for a period of four months in 2010. These families were chosen through a series of social networks between the researcher/author and the research assistant. The research assistant was a bilingual South American who was chosen to work with the families in English and Spanish, as she would not take a non-interested position on the data. The case studies were constructed as pieces of social science (cf. Anyon, 2009), with open-ended interviews, observation, triangulation of the data where possible and full ethics approval for the project. Yet the writing of this article uses the poststructural positioning that educational research may derive from Deleuze and Guattari (see Hodgson & Standish, 2009). This positioning indicates that the two case studies are not structurally distinct data sets, solely one dimensional and purely qualitative in nature, or presented as being potentially representative of ideal or privileged Latino families. The writing of this report demonstrates the rhizomatic or schizoanalytic paradigm for social science that Deleuze and Guattari (1987, pp. 3–26) suggest. Subtle, sometimes disparate connections are henceforth made between data sets through examination and (re)presentation, and key aspects of the data are subsequently analysed for questions that relate to immanence, confluence and potentially conflictive affective change. This questioning is not to suggest that anything may now pass as poststructural social science, but that the combined consciousnesses of the researcher and writer are not imposed upon the data without intense scrutiny and analysis.

This writing is therefore pivotally suggestive of the often-relative power relationships that have happened in and through the research, and will attend to latent power relationships that are currently shaping the literacies of the two families in Australia. This work follows on from the discussions of qualitative analysis as they appear in Maxwell and Miller (2008), where the figure of Deleuze & Guattari's rhizome is positioned as encapsulating a poststructural extension of Hume's distinction between resemblance and contiguity as modes of association of ideas (1739). Saussure (1916), Jakobson (1956), and Barthes (1968) subsequently took up Hume's distinction as expressing the difference between paradigmatic and syntagmatic relationships. Deleuze & Guattari's (1987) rhizomatics adds another level of qualitative distinction to the analysis of the case studies, one that ultimately comes about through the specific writing of the report and provides a bridge between the multiplicities inherent in the data (i.e. life) and the linguistic and imagined sense of the analysis. The rhizome adds a non-spatial, anti-hermetic element to the work of research that is suggestive of inter-corporeal and transformative affect (see Cole, forthcoming). The qualitative data in this study is organised and presented through Deleuze & Guattari's rhizomatic lens:

i)   *La familia Flores*[1]

The first family that was researched are from Uruguay. They moved to Australia in 2007, and live in the Penrith district of Sydney. The family consists of a father, Raul, 42, a mother, Edith, 37, and they have two boys, Mati, 10 and Nico, 8. The mother had been born in Australia, but went back to Uruguay when she was 11 after her family decided that they missed South America. The family Flores came to Australia to seek greater economic opportunities, and to create a better future for their sons. They initially lived with Edith's brother, but had an acrimonious 'falling out' with him that has left a bitter scar. They currently rent a small flat in Penrith, the father works as a forklift driver in a local furniture warehouse; the mother has recently trained as an early childhood worker, but is presently unemployed. The two boys go to a local state-run primary school, and are engaging individuals who make friends easily, but are not interested in study. The mother is bilingual, and the father relies on her to translate from English to Spanish. Raul is struggling to learn English, has attended various adult language courses, though finds English pronunciation difficult, and does not consistently study English on his own. He misses his last job in Uruguay, which was as a chauffeur to the Dutch ambassador. He reminisces at length about this job, and speaks derisively about his current post in the warehouse.

The family keep in touch with their relatives in Uruguay on a daily basis via Skype and by using satellite telephone cards. The dominant language in the home is Spanish, though they are developing networks in English and Spanish. The boys speak English at school with Spanish accents, Mati is particularly sociable, and Edith has made friends with several English only speaking mothers at the school.

ii)   La familia Smith

The second family that were studied are from Chile. The father, Bob, 38 was born in Alabama, and met the mother, Reina, 42, who is from Valdivia, Southern Chile, on a scientific cruise. Reina had one daughter, Rose, 12, from a previous relationship, and the couple have a second daughter together, Violeta, 6. The family arrived in Australia in 2008, and came because Bob had been given a job with a company that sells and installs large scientific machines. His job involves the installation and set up of the machines. The parent company that controls this business has recently been replaced in a hostile corporate takeover that has caused family stress in terms of job security. Reina is a trained geologist, and wants to carry on with her studies or to get a job in this area, though she is currently doing only part-time courses such as permaculture to get out of the house. The family presently live in a rented house on a mountain that overlooks the Sydney basin. The eldest daughter is quiet and studious, and enjoys her new state high school. Rose speaks English with an American accent, as the family had previously lived in Texas, where Bob had also found work. Violeta is an incredibly energetic young girl, whom the family have recently moved to an alternative Montessori style school because she did not respond to the state school system. Reina chooses not to speak English if possible, both girls are bilingual and Bob speaks a little Spanish. Reina considers their time in Australia to be limited before they go back to Chile to live, though Bob openly contradicts this opinion as he states that he has little chance of finding suitable work in Chile. The family are beginning to develop networks of English and Spanish speaking individuals around their home.

Nomadic family literacies

Much of the work in this literacy knowledge field has come from the Unites States, where the immigration of Latino families is commonplace (see Tejeda, Martinez & Leonardo, 2000). Predominantly ethnographic, qualitative and narrative research methods have been deployed to understand the ways in which the families and their resultant literacies change once they arrive in their new country. These studies have looked at the success or otherwise of the migrant children in schools (Peterson & Heywood, 2007), the adult migrant literacies (Norton, 2006), bilingualism (Volk & de Acosta, 2001) and the ways in which the immigrants negotiate educational life in America by using Spanish (see Moll & Gonzalez, 2004).

The difference that this study brings to the knowledge area is that the two families of the case studies are set into motion as nomads even before they migrate to Australia. The knowledge of this study comes about because the research is grounded in the Deleuzian concept of becoming. Becoming lends the families a type of nomadism that is derived from *1000 Plateaus*. In *1000 Plateaus* social theory is mitigated through the behaviours of sedentary communality and nomadism. In and through sedentary accumulation and the consequent modes of living, the societies of Europe built up a form of organization that was vulnerable to attack from flighty and rapid nomadic invasion. The essential example of this is the Mongol hordes, which swarmed from Asia to assail medieval feudal Europe in the thirteenth century. Deleuze and Guattari (1987) contend that these nomads marked European history, not only as invaders, but also in terms of reorganised and renegotiated forms of warfare (Chambers, 1985). Previous to the invasions of the nomads, sedentary communities had been built around agrarian-serf types of accumulation that had dominated European society. Post-nomadic invasion Europe began to be based around expansionary capitalism. Braudel (1967) put the beginnings of the European market economy at around 1500; the point from Deleuze & Guattari (1987) is that the nomadism of the Mongols fundamentally changed the velocity and trajectory of European conquest over time through new social organization. The Europeans began to incorporate the nomadism of the Mongols in their armies, and in so doing left behind the aristocratic formalism of knights and serf-territories. In the place of land-locked feudalism, the Europeans set out in boats, and went to explore and conquer new territories. Armies became lighter, quicker, better organised and more able to adapt to new conditions. In short, Deleuze and Guattari sum up the influence of the nomad invasions on sedentary European society through the phrase, 'the war machine' (1987, pp. 351–423) which is a conjunction that explains the working of nomadism in defence orientated society.

The war machine could take us a long way from the Latino families becoming-literate in Australia. Yet the confluence of terminology here indicates the ways in which the Latino families have absorbed the lessons of the Mongols in their passage to Australia. Such learning is not a result of coming from South America, but happens in the change from one place to another, or by becoming 'other-than' (e.g. Cole, 2009) according to Deleuze. The nomadism of this study is about the 'othered' and 'othering' movement of two families' literacies, and indicates particular characteristics that relate to the findings of the case studies.

● *Economic literacies*

Both families have come to Australia for economic reasons. The Flores family is convinced that the poverty of South America is insurmountable and growing. Australia is on the other hand a rich country, where there is a good chance to make money. The Smith family came due to Bob's new job, which he describes as the best that he has ever had. The tax system, benefits, the price of groceries and presents for the children all take up a lot of thought and conversation of the two families. They are also aware that they are placed in a market system in Australia, where qualifications, skills and labour are priced. The Flores family adheres more closely to economic rationalism, whereas Reina in the Smith family does question this financial sea change in thought and language. She prefers to consider notions of community and values as they relate to her home in Chile, and she has reproduced these ideas as a shield in her new home in the mountains outside of Sydney. The Flores family are preparing to be actively engaged in entrepreneurial enterprises, such as trying to set up a mobile coffee-van, which they see as a possible way out of economic servitude. The children are not directly involved in these economic literacies, but act as receptors and consumers of the ideas, for example, the Flores boys are fascinated by video games; Violeta has mountains of toys that are piled up on the lower floor of their house. The research assistant noticed a marked increase in tension in the Smith household during the hostile corporate takeover and the consequent possible loss of income.

- *Bureaucratic literacies*

Parallel and overlapping the economic literacies, the families have had to engage with new bureaucratic systems as a consequence of moving to Australia. The health system, the benefit and rebate system, housing, the tax systems and visa/citizenship statuses are all designed with application forms and evidence for claims that the Latinos have to negotiate. In the Flores household, Edith has been put in charge of these literacies due to her English ability, and she feels this responsibility is a burden. Bob looks after the bureaucratic affairs in the Smith family, but is unsure whether or not to apply for permanent residency with the resultant lowering of tax and improved health coverage, due to the complexity of the process. These bureaucratic literacies are daunting for Spanish speakers as the application forms and associated technical documents contain a large array of new vocabulary and notions that do not exist in South America. Again, the children do not directly partake in these literacies, but feel the results of the tension and frustration that these systems can produce. In particular, the bureaucratic literacies have produced an imbalance in the Flores family, in that Edith feels under pressure to understand the bureaucratic system fully in order to apply in the correct way for available benefits. In the Smith family, the bureaucratic literacies have a latent power effect on the family, due to the understanding that their current work visas give them a continuing inferior status in Australia that they must eventually negotiate.

- *Emotional literacies*

Deleuze & Guattari (1987) use the notion of affect rather than emotion, but on a normative level, and with reference to the two case studies, the families have both had to deal with huge emotional upheavals. For example, the Flores boys miss their dog that they left behind in Uruguay – there is a picture of him, prominently placed in the cramped front room of their flat. Reina's mother has the early onset of Alzheimer's disease, and Reina feels that she should be back in Chile helping to care for her. Her eldest daughter, who misses the family connections and close, communal lifestyle in Chile, perhaps mostly keenly feels Reina's emotional literacy. Bob was in the US military for ten years before he met Reina, and is used to coping on his own, and in fact seems to enjoy the isolation of their mountain home. The Flores family are in an ambiguous situation with respect to emotional literacies. They compensate for the distance between themselves and their family in Uruguay by using Skype and telephone communication. They are also positioning themselves as potential trailblazers for more family members to come to Australia and to leave behind the difficult South American situation. The two boys are perhaps most affected by the Flores emotional literacies and demonstrate this by consistently acting in a childish manner.

EDUCATION AND THE POLITICS OF BECOMING

- *Adaptive literacies*

This subtle aspect of the family nomadic literacies, works underneath the other literacies as a powerful contiguous and disjunctive force. An example from the Flores family happened in a supermarket, where they experienced disgruntled annoyance from another shopper in the checkout queue. They had misunderstood the boxing arrangements, and because they were discussing this in Spanish, the next shopper decided to intervene on their behalf. An argument ensued, the family consequently learnt about shopping line etiquette in Australia, and the possible ways in which using Spanish in public places can be interpreted. The difference between the Flores family and the Smith family, is that Reina is not actively engaging in adaptive literacies (and their potential conflicts). She is fully capable of doing so, yet her embedded thought that she will soon be going back to Chile makes her less open to these potential lesion and displacement points. Reina's daughters and husband are more congruent and aligned with adaptive literacies.

These four literacies that the case studies have discovered are not exhaustive and cross over in various complicated ways. In contrast to studies that have placed cultural discontinuity as being a prime mover in immigrant literacy learning (e.g. Markose & Hellsten, 2009), this study represents the nomadic literacies as being simultaneous, emergent and continuous, yet indicating forms of entwined otherness. In Deleuze & Guattari's (1984) first work on *Capitalism and Schizophrenia*, the Oedipal family comes in for close attention, and is disrupted as a source of molar power. The nomadic approach that is used in their second volume sets the family amongst a series of interconnected qualitative flows or multiplicities. These flows had already started before the South American immigrants came to Australia, and live in their memories, actions and dreams. The four literacies as listed above show the ways in which the families are crossing over and 'becoming other' in Australia. They also represent a map of affect that sits within the literacies to create and be created by atmospheres that inhabit the same spaces as the families. The representation of the nomadic family literacies does not valorise or prioritise the family as a particular unit of organization, but shows the ways in which the families are changing and fully permeated by relative power concerns (see Masny, 2005).

Language as surface effect (MLT)

How do these nomadic family literacies translate into linguistic phenomena? Diana Masny (2009) has explained this aspect of the study in her work on Multiple Literacies Theory (MLT). Masny has explored the development of writing amongst school age children working in more than one language in Canada. She has found that the act of writing is a surface effect that results from a series of loosely connected accidents. For example, a first language Spanish speaking girl in Canada, who is also manipulating Portuguese with her father and French at school, will linguistically skip between the three syntactical systems when writing (Masny, 2009). The girl also demonstrates a strong emotional content in her writing, and relates much of what she articulates to her powerful family environment. In the terms of the nomadism of this study, the girl is negotiating between emotional and adaptive literacies through her

39

writing, whilst performing within bureaucratic literacies in terms of the designated French curriculum at school. Masny interviewed the girl and shows how the imagination of the child is fully activated in and through these writing activities, that are in many ways the final acts of entwined thought processes. The girl shows how she is associative in her thinking and is able to make imaginative leaps when talking about her writing, as she explains that much of the sense of her language comes from extra-terrestrials (2009, pp. 25–27). The point here is that being tri-lingual is 'othered' in mainstream schooling, and the child feels that her sense of language comes from a far off galaxy, very different from her present reality. In terms of MLT, the surface effect of language has been produced after the 'othering' environment at school has been experienced and internalised. The girl reacts to the French mainstream with recourse to the emotion of her maternal Spanish, which is for her safe and homely. In terms of this study, Reina's daughter Rose demonstrates otherness at school when asked about Australian citizenship during a routine reading comprehension exercise (Figure 1):

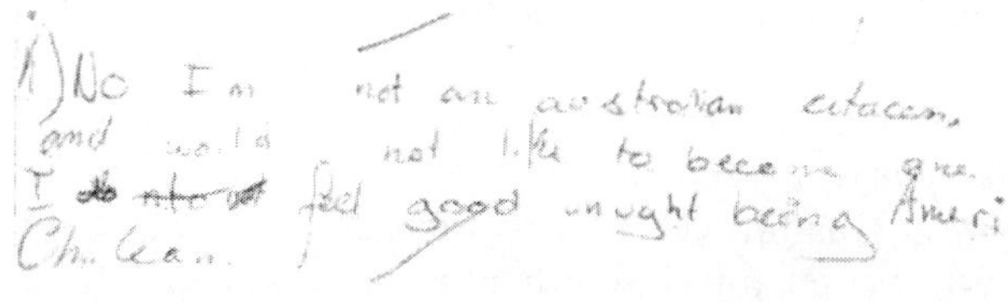

(No, I'm not an Australian citizen, and would not like to become
one be I feel good enough being American Chilean.)

Figure 1. Rose's response to a question in school about becoming an Australian citizen.

The teacher has raised the topic of citizenship through the classroom pedagogy and reading comprehension, and this action has had deep ramifications for Rose. In Figure 1, she has expressed her desire not to become Australian; in the terms of nomadic family literacies this reaction is related to the emotional, adaptive and bureaucratic literacies. The emotional and adaptive literacies are activated via the mention of Australia as home, and the ways in which Rose and Reina miss Chile. The bureaucratic literacies in this figure involve the curriculum that is being followed and the ways in which citizenship education is integrated into mainstream knowledge. The teacher may or may not have been aware of Rose's sensitivities as she is a quiet and inward girl. Yet giving her this exercise has stirred up profound memories and thoughts about the transitioning into Australia, where she currently feels out of place. In terms of MLT, the unconscious is full of qualitative detail (cf. Cole, 2010) that swirls and buckles with the forces of the nomadic family literacies. The writing in Figure 1 suggests a point of rupture that comes through the words, and leads to a maelstrom of indeterminate affect. Rose positions herself as an American-Chilean, and in doing this she removes herself from Australia, and through this gap she may possibly find happiness. In contrast, Mati's English writing book does not demonstrate any personal commentary, but a wealth of cartoon doodles (Figure 2):

EDUCATION AND THE POLITICS OF BECOMING

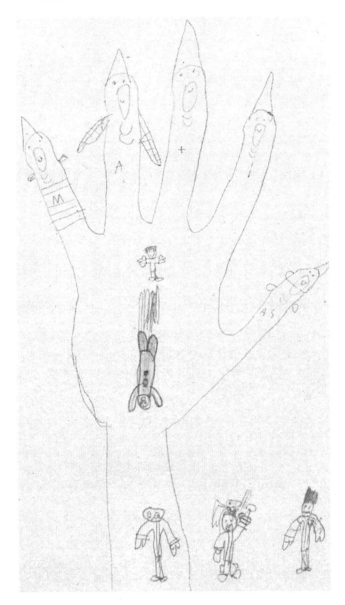

Figure 2. Doodle in Mati's English writing book.

The becoming-literate in the nomadism of the Flores family comes through Mati's doodles in terms of emotion and identification. Mati loves watching cartoons and playing video games, he is highly sociable and wants to fit in with the other children. His school writing as a surface effect of these forces is stilted and conformist. In contrast, his doodles are expressive and represent a through-line to the ways that he is learning in Australia. In terms of MLT, the inculcation of cartoons, video games and peer socialisation in Mati's life has created a means of expression that reproduces these effects through drawing. His cartoons show us the ways in which the multiple literacies come together through doodling, yet also remain distinct. The cartoons depict little action figures holding guns, diving and standing upright, ready to engage with the viewer. Mati's unconscious plays with emotional and adaptive literacies through these cartoons, whereas the bureaucratic literacies of the mandated curriculum reproduce power effects such as finishing the exercise or correctly answering a question. Mati sees power for himself in watching cartoons, playing video games and in making friends. The schoolteacher wants Mati to write in a way that he finds far less interesting. A rupture point has therefore been created between cartoon watching, playing video games and making friends, and his school-based literacy. This rupture point leads to affect, that is visible in Mati's temperamental emotional states and unstable powers of concentration at school. In this case, one might discern how one child's careful doodles are indicative of the affect produced through nomadic family literacies.

The politics of becoming

This study may be understood as a series of overlapping frames. One frame is shaped by the nomadic family literacies, another through language as surface effect or MLT. The third frame comes about due to the politics of becoming involved with the research project. Deleuze (1987) stated that his notion of becoming was derived from Nietzsche's will to power, and this pivot runs through the research, both in terms of the aspirations of the two families and the rationale for investigation. In the US, the politics of immigration involving Latino families crossing the border has created a broad polemic, and defines a south-north axis upon which people, money and goods travel. In Australia, the Latinos have mostly come by plane; this migration has been largely ignored politically as attention has been focused on boat arrivals and the north-south axis from Asia to Australia. This research therefore opens up a new front for discussion by examining the ways in which the Latino families are becoming-literate in Australia. Their respective wills to power are indicative of a set of changes that are happening to them as they settle and merge into the Australian populace. These immigrant changes may be spoken about and discussed, creating a dialogue and political discourse for education. The characteristics of the politics of becoming that emerged from the two case studies were:

1. *Money*
   Both families were very concerned about money. The economic problems in South America and the perception that Australia is a rich country are important drivers for both families. This aspect of the case studies translates into education through the ways in which the families are able to support their children's progress or otherwise. The Flores family in particular did not seem to be readily supportive and considered educational materials for the boys to be an unnecessary expense.

2. *Networks*
   The Latino families are making networks of friends and contacts in their respective locations. This part of the changes that are happening to them sits

within the shadow of the friends and families that they have left behind. South American society relies on these networks, and the families are attempting to reproduce these relationships in Australia by having barbecues, going to social events and proactively talking to neighbours. In educational terms, this networking translates into the social necessity of turning the school into a learning community. The Latinos flourish in networks of connective identities, and this aspect of social life is not strong in some parts of urban Australia. The Latino families sense and act on this separation, which translates into the politics of the situation through oscillations in perceived and real exclusion and inclusion, closeness and distance.

3. *Status*

The question of one's place in society is important for the Latinos. The two families relate this question to income and work, and Raul often reminisces about his important role as a chauffeur in Uruguay. Reina adds an interesting twist to this element of the politics of becoming as she considers herself and her family to be part of an indigenous community. Bob has Native American ancestry and she identifies with indigenous Chileans. Reina therefore associates indigenous heritage with dignity, values and the position of her family as being antagonistic to colonials; and such positioning has important ramifications for living in Australia. Educators need to be sensitive to status concerns when addressing the Latinos.

4. *Fun*

Beyond the serious elements of the politics of becoming as listed above, the Latinos have a profound sense of fun. This fun underlies much of what they want to do in Australia. For example, dancing is almost obligatory in every South American celebration, yet in Australia dance is not so centrally placed in one's life. There is an underlying flirtatiousness that mediates much of South American society that hardly exists in Australia. The South Americans are therefore likely to interpret standoffish behaviour as lacking in affection, as they are used to physical ties being demonstrated. Latinos can be caught out in educational situations by the strict moral rules around touching and physicality in Australian schools.

These four characteristics of the politics of becoming cross over and change given the fluctuations of life. The Latino immigrants are caught in this power matrix; yet can escape from it in unexpected and singular ways (Cole & Hager, 2010). For example, this research project has included giving the families tokens to buy books for their children, and this act works through the politics of becoming of the families by positioning the university as aiding their cause. The related associations of research, the university, education and the Australian system are joined through the bureaucratic literacies of the nomadic families, and merge into the politics of becoming through money and status. The families feel privileged to be part of this research, and the chance to purchase free books for their children is one less expense to worry about. These case studies found less direct expressions of discrimination and prejudice than expected; rather, the four elements of the politics of becoming straddle the lives of the families like the marbling in an elaborate cake. Perhaps this is because the recent immigration of the Latinos fits in with previous post-war waves of Mediterranean Greeks and Italians, who are now accepted parts of Australian culture (Collins, 1991). The Spanish accents when speaking English do mark out the Latinos to an extent, yet their friendly and sociable manner eases paths to inclusion in multicultural Australian life.

Conclusion

The politics of immigration that this research has discovered involves the specific lives of two Latino families, and their settlement in western Sydney. In tandem with all qualitative research, one should be sceptical about the generalisation of these findings. Yet the Deleuzian platform for this paper gives the researcher and analyst new tools to understand and articulate the facts of qualitative data. By focusing on the multiple literacies that run through the stories of the two families, one is able to extract planes of emergent data that interact and clash through their representation in such an article format. Deleuze's precise political framing of his ideas has been much debated in the scholarly literature (Garo, 2008), yet here it does extend to colouring the politics of immigration. For example, the Deleuzian framing does not make one focus exclusively or preferentially on issues of social justice. Rather, the 'real life' of the immigrants comes through the paper as a definite, shifting backdrop for any analytic remarks that have been made above. Deleuze (1987) was concerned about the normative power of his work, and this concern meant that he rarely sided with one simple position in a political debate.[2] He therefore retains his politics as fluid and fluctuating, able to pick up on and use either side of a political debate in a novel and creative way. Doing social research through a university is not value neutral, yet by employing Deleuze's philosophical position, one is able to attend to many of the power markers in research that could potentially pinpoint or demarcate the research participant as 'other'. The Deleuzian position, if applied, should help the immigrants and educationalists with literacy learning projects in Australia due to the explanations of their otherness.

Acknowledgement
This paper has come about due to an internal UTS research development grant.

Notes
1. All names that appear in this article are self-selected pseudonyms.
2. The famous exception to this was when Deleuze commented about the injustices that have been committed against the Palestinian people in *Le Monde*.

References

Anyon, J. (2009). *Theory and educational research: Towards critical social explanation.* New York and London: Routledge.

Barthes, R. (1968). *Elements of semiology* (Trans. A. Lavers & C. Smith). New York: Hill and Wang.

Bourdieu, P. (1997). The forms of capital. In A.H. Halsey, H. Lauder, P. Brown & A.S. Wells (Eds.), *Education, culture, economy and society* (pp. 46–58). Oxford: Oxford University Press.

Braudel, F. (1967). *Capitalism and material life: 1400–1800* (Trans. M. Kochan). New York: Harper and Row.

Brown, J., Miller, J., & Mitchell, J. (2006). Interrupted schooling and the acquisition of literacy: Experiences of Sudanese refugees in Victorian secondary schools. *Australian Journal of Language and Literacy, 29*(2), 150–163.

Chambers, J. (1985). *The devil's horsemen: The Mongol invasion of Europe.* New York: Athenaeum.

Cole, D.R. (2009). Indexing the multiple: An autobiographic account of education through the lens of Deleuze & Guattari. In D. Masny & D.R. Cole (Eds.), *Multiple literacies theory: A Deleuzian perspective* (pp. 119–133). Rotterdam: Sense Publishers.

Cole, D.R. (2010). Multiliteracies and the politics of desire. In D.R. Cole & D.L. Pullen (Eds.), *Multiliteracies in motion: Current theory and practice* (pp. 124–139). London & New York: Routledge.

Cole, D.R. (Forthcoming). The actions of affect in Deleuze: Others using language and the language that we make. In D.R. Cole, & L.J. Graham (Eds.), *The power in/of language, Special Issue of Educational Philosophy & Theory.*

Cole, D.R., & Hager, P. (2010). Learning-practice: The ghosts in the education machine. *Education Inquiry, 1*(1), 21–40.

Colebrook, C. (2002). *Deleuze.* New York: Routledge.

Collins, J. (1991). *Migrant hands in a distant land: Australia's post-war immigration* (2nd edn). Sydney and London: Pluto Press.

Deleuze, G. (1987). *Dialogues with Claire Parnet* (Trans. H. Tomlinson, & B. Habberjam). London: Athlone Press.

Deleuze, G., & Guattari, F. (1984). *Anti-Oedipus: Capitalism and schizophrenia* (Trans. R. Hurley, M. Steem, & H.R. Lane). London: The Athlone Press.

Deleuze, G., & Guattari, F. (1987). *A thousand plateaus: Capitalism & schizophrenia II* (Trans. B. Massumi). London: The Athlone Press.

Dias, C.J., Arthur, L., Beecher, B., & McNaught, M. (2000). Multiple literacies in early childhood: What do families and communities think about their children's early literacy learning? *Australian Journal of Language and Literacy, 23*(3), 230–247.

Ferdman, B.M. (1999). Ethnic and minority issues in literacy. In D. Wagner, R. Venezky & B. Street (Eds.), *Literacy: An international handbook* (pp. 95–101). Colorado: Westview.

Garo, I. (2008). Deleuze, Marx and revolution: What it means to 'remain Marxist'. In J. Bidet & S. Kouvelakis (Eds.), *Critical companion to contemporary Marxis* (pp. 605–624). Leiden: Brill.

Hodgson, N., & Standish, P. (2009). Uses and misuses of poststructuralism in educational research. *International Journal of Research & Method in Education, 32*(3), 309–326.

Hume, D. (1739/1978). *A treatise of human nature* (2nd Ed., L.A. Selby-Bigge). Oxford: Oxford University Press.

Jakobson, R. (1956). Two aspects of language and two types of aphasic disturbances. In R. Jakobson & M. Halle (Eds.), *Fundamentals of language* (pp. 55–82). S-Gravenhage: Mouton.

Kress, G. (2003). *Literacy in the new media age.* London: Routledge.

Markose, S. & Hellstén, M. (2009). Explaining success and failure in mainstream schooling through the lens of cultural continuities and discontinuities: Two case studies. *Language and Education, 23*(1), 59–77.

Masny, D. (2005). Multiple literacies: An alternative OR beyond Freire. In J. Anderson, T. Rogers, M. Kendrick & S. Smythe (Eds.), *Portraits of literacy across families, communities, and schools: Intersections and tensions* (pp. 171–184). Mahwah, NJ: Lawrence Erlbaum.

Masny, D. (2006). Learning and creative processes: A poststructural perspective on language and multiple literacies. *International Journal of Learning, 12*(5), 147–155.

EDUCATION AND THE POLITICS OF BECOMING

Masny, D. (2009). Literacies as Becoming: A child's conceptualizations of writing-systems. In D. Masny & D.R. Cole (Eds.), *Multiple literacies theory: A Deleuzian perspective* (pp. 13–31). Rotterdam: Sense Publishers.

Maxwell, J.A., & Miller, B. (2008). Categorizing and connecting strategies in qualitative data analysis. In P. Leavy & S. Hesse-Biber (Eds.), *Handbook of emergent methods* (pp. 461–477). New York: Guilford Press.

Moll, L., & Gonzalez, N. (2004). Engaging life: A funds-of-knowledge approach to multicultural education. In J. Banks & C. Banks (Eds.), *Handbook of research on multicultural education* (2nd edn.) (pp. 699–715). San Francisco: Josey-Bass.

Norton, B. (2006). Not an afterthought: Authoring a text on adult ESOL. *Linguistics and Education, 17*(1), 91–96.

Peterson, S.S., & Heywood, D. (2007). Contributions of families' linguistic, social, and cultural capital to minority-language children's literacy: Parents', teachers', and principals' perspectives. *The Canadian Modern Language Review, 63*(4), 517–538.

Rennie, J. (2006). Meeting kids at the school gate: The literacy and numeracy practices of a remote indigenous community. *Australian Educational Researcher, 33*(3), 123–140.

Ringrose, J. (Forthcoming). Beyond discourse? Affective assemblages, heterosexually striated space, and lines of flight online and at school. In D.R. Cole, & L.J. Graham (Eds.), *The power in/of language, Special Issue of Educational Philosophy & Theory*.

Saussure, F. de (1916/1986). *Course in general linguistics*. La Salle, IL: Open Court.

Semetsky, I. (2006). *Deleuze, education and becoming*. Rotterdam: Sense Publishers.

Tejeda, C., Martinez, C., & Leonardo, Z. (Eds.). (2000). *Charting new terrains of Chicana(o)/ Latina(o) education*. Cresskill, NJ: Hampton Press.

Volk, D., & de Acosta, M. (2001). Many differing ladders, many ways to climb: Literacy events in the bilingual classrooms, homes and community of three Puerto Rican Kindergartners. *Journal of Early Childhood Literacy, 1*(2), 193–224.

Living, learning, loving: Constructing a new ethics of integration in education

Inna Semetsky

> The paper positions education and learning in the context of Gilles Deleuze's ethico-political philosophy oriented to becoming-other amidst experiences and events. Deleuze's unorthodox affective epistemology is inseparable from ethics in terms of real-life consequences at the level of practice. The paper presents the critical and clinical analysis of experiential events as texts comprising a mode of the informal pedagogy in terms of creating new concepts, meanings, and values for experience. The logic of sense foregrounds ethical evaluations of experience with regard to multiple directions we might take in novel situations, which disrupt common sense with problems that do not yet yield answers as univocal and unidirectional solutions. The paper conceptualizes a model of the new ethics of integration as a follow-up to the ethics of care in education informed by the relational self-other dynamics and moral interdependence.

Introduction

This paper will critically examine Gilles Deleuze's ethico-political paradigm in the context of educational theory and educational philosophy. The paper will take the concept of 'learning' outside the walls of the traditional classroom and will reposition it in the middle of our practical life and socio-cultural experiences. As we learn from our experiences, we become embedded in life-long ethical education that contributes to our growth and development or, in Deleuze's words, 'becoming-other' in the midst of experiential, problematic and shocking, events. According to Deleuze, it is an experiential shock to thought that makes us think and learn from experience; thus to become-other when we create in practice a new meaning for a particular experience.

Becoming-other thus differs in principle from the outlived model of moral or character education. Real-life events become unorthodox 'texts' that we should 'read' critically and creatively so as to learn from them, thus transgressing formal instruction as a prevalent educational mode. Deleuze's philosophy focuses on shared deterritorialization, that is, transformations and changes as pertaining to both learning and teaching; as such it may be considered tending towards an ethical position of 'caring' as it pertains to moral education.

EDUCATION AND THE POLITICS OF BECOMING

Building on Nel Noddings' (1984) ethics of care, the paper suggests that real-life events, such as 9/11 and the Iraq and Afghanistan wars do produce shock to thought. As such they can become a means for creating a new pedagogy of concepts, meanings and values. The paper also conceptualizes the new ethics of integration paramount for our global age permeated by political conflicts of values at socio-cultural levels. Teachers, at both pre-service levels and in the form of professional development, should be exposed to the fundamentals of this new ethics – comprising such values as living, learning and loving – on the basis of an educational theory grounded in Deleuze's philosophy.

Deleuze's pedagogy of the concept

The potential of Gilles Deleuze's philosophical thought for educational theory and practice is currently being widely explored (e.g. Masny & Cole, 2009; Semetsky, 2004, 2006, 2008, 2010a, 2010b). A philosophical site, for Deleuze, transgresses the boundaries of individual consciousness towards the multiplicity of social, artistic, ethical, political and affective dimensions. Deleuzian philosophy is a sort of constructivism irreducible to classical syllogisms of deductive logic and the binary opposites that result in the unequivocal moral algebra of 'good' vs 'evil' or 'right' vs 'wrong'. A concept, as an integral part of Deleuze's philosophy (which is defined as uniquely a creative process of inventing novel concepts in *praxis,* in experience) is a vehicle for expressing the singularity of an event which is always already embedded in the social and political *milieu.*

In this framework, our *lived* experiences constitute informal lessons comprising as such what can be called a *school of life.* Experience is rendered meaningful – that is, becomes a *learning* experience – not by grounding empirical particulars in abstract universals but by active experimentation on ourselves in real life. Several of Deleuze's philosophical works were written together with practising psychoanalyst Felix Guattari (Deleuze & Guattari, 1987, 1994) such a collaboration representing an approach to knowledge as shared, distributed and situated, hence making philosophy (traditionally an intellectual enterprise) inseparable from socio-cultural issues, political decisions, and practical experiences.

Deleuze positions the origins of philosophical thinking at the level of practice. What he calls a thought without image, that is, a model of thinking that spills over the individual and dogmatic Cartesian *Cogito* is necessarily a mode of learning grounded in experience, in life. Thinking is oriented towards the evaluation of one's current, here-and-now, mode of existence, of actual *living*, and 'beneath the generalities of habit in moral life we rediscover singular processes of *learning*' (Deleuze, 1994, p. 28; emphasis added). The learning process cannot be confined to a formal classroom. It is the singularity of an informal experiential situation, rather than a mode of direct instruction, that contributes to our learning and the construction of new knowledge. It is this new knowledge acquired in experience that will have constituted human subjectivity as becoming.

Deleuze's complex epistemology is inseparable from ethics in terms of anticipated practical consequences and values 'that are yet to come' (Deleuze & Guattari, 1987, p. 5) thus implicitly addressing the 'untimely' or future-oriented dimension of philosophical thought, which is presently a pressing issue in educational research, theory and practice (Gidley & Inayatullah, 2002; Inayatullah, Milojevic, & Bussey,

48

2005; Semetsky, 2006). A newly created concept is a limit case of the experimental inquiry or the outcome of a learning process that goes beyond recognition to a fundamental encounter with the unknown and the yet-unthought. It cannot be otherwise because learning presupposes an encounter with something as yet unknown, or even shocking in its perplexity, and in order to make sense for this experience we will have to create new meanings and concepts in practice. In French the word *Sens* means both meaning and direction; Deleuze's 'logic of sense' (Deleuze, 1990) evaluates ethical questions with regard to multiple directions we might take when embedded in the midst of practical experiences. It is the invention or creation of concepts that is defined by Deleuze in terms of the very *pedagogy* of the concept that 'would have to analyse the conditions of creation as factors of always singular moments' (Deleuze & Guattari, 1994, p. 12); such a singularity representing 'a unique event which merges now with that which renders it possible' (Deleuze, 1995, p. 185).

As such, Deleuze's *pedagogy of the concept* represents an important example of 'expanding educational vocabularies' (Noddings, 1993, p. 5) in the concrete context of the often conflicting experiences constituting contemporary culture. For Deleuze, a concept is always full of critical, creative and political power that brings forth values and meanings. The relevance for education is paramount: Deleuze and Guattari were adamant that while 'the three ages of the concept are the encyclopedia, pedagogy, and commercial professional training, only the second can safeguard us from falling from the heights of the first into the disaster of the third' (Deleuze & Guattari, 1994, p. 12). It is the pedagogy of the concept that must educate us in becoming able to feel, to know, and to conceive, that is, to create novel conceptual understanding of the multiplicity of events in our *lived* experience which is inseparable from affects produced by bodily actions.

An intensive capacity 'to affect and be affected' (Deleuze & Guattari, 1987, p. xvi) is always social and disrupts existing moral codes with its rigid opposition of good and evil. As Deleuze commentator Michael Hardt says, society functions on

> ... its power to be affected. The priority of the right or the good does not enter into this conception of openness. ... What is open ... is the expression of power: the free conflict and the composition of the field of social forces. (Hardt, 1993, p. 120)

Affects, for Deleuze, take priority over syllogistic moral judgments. Affective forces express our innermost intense and as yet a-conceptual feelings among which Deleuze tends to prioritize love: he presents the immanent evaluations of experience in the affective language of '"I love" ... instead of "I judge"' (Deleuze, 1989, p. 141).

Thinking through affects brings an element of non-thought into a thought; such a forceful, as if physical, intensity of an encounter with an affect marks the passage between the experiential states of the body, which is defined by Deleuze, borrowing from Spinoza, as both physical and mental, corporeal and incoroporeal. Accordingly, the body's power is being changed. Deleuze specifies the body's power as a capacity to multiply and intensify connections. Conflicting real-life experiences are characterized by their *difference*; philosophical thinking, then, is conceptualized as the quasi-empirical, practical, mapping of such a difference. An experiential encounter with affect is pre-conceptual or unconscious. Learning from experience demands 'to bring [the] assemblage of the unconscious to the light of the day, to select the whispering voices, to gather ... secret idioms from which I extract something I call my Self (*Moi*)' (Deleuze & Guattari 1987, p. 84). The becoming of human subjectivity takes place in experience, in life, and often exceeds propositional language 'spoken' by the conscious subject but proceeds in the mode of silent discourse (Semetsky, 2010b), via 'silent spaces' (Gidley, 2009, p. 550).

A non-conscious component of learning is currently posited significant at the level of holistic practices comprising education and human development (e.g. de Souza, 2009; 2010; Semetsky, 2009a). For Deleuze, a rational Cartesian conscious-ness as the sole constituent of thought is insufficient because what is yet 'unthought' is equally capable of producing practical effects at the level of human experiences. Deleuze considered '*an unconscious of thought* [to be] just as profound as *the unknown of the body*' (Deleuze, 1988, p. 19; italics in original). When we encounter something in real experience which is so intense that it forces us to think – to reflect on this very experience – this encounter is not yet conceptually present to us. We are permeated by affects that we simply feel at the level of the body.

This very encounter can only be 'grasped in a range of affective tones: wonder, love, hatred, suffering' (Deleuze, 1994, p. 139). It is affect that provokes erotic desire (love) for knowledge in the form of the experimental creation of our conceptual understanding that blends critical (reflective) and clinical (value) elements together. Such is Deleuze's pedagogy of concepts. Even as a concept inhabits our experience (for Deleuze and Guattari it is a *living* concept) in its *virtual* or as yet unconscious form; still the ethical task remains 'to set up ... to extract' (Deleuze & Guattari, 1994, p. 160) the very 'sense' of this empirical event as the newly created concept in our *actual* practice. It is affect – desire and love – that brings forth 'the New: creativity, emergence' (Deleuze, 1989, p. 147).

The process of becoming as living, learning and loving is creative and 'ethical ... as opposed to morality' (Deleuze, 1995, p. 114). Tapping into 'the virtual and immanent processes of ... becoming' (Ansell Pearson, 1997, p. 4) is equivalent to 'affectivity' (1997, p. 4), and the process of becoming is always filled with affect, desire, love, Eros. Ian Buchanan remarks (in Semetsky, 2008) that Deleuze qualified education as an erotic, voluptuous experience, perhaps the most important one can have in life. Educational researcher Elizabeth St Pierre quotes Deleuze explaining an intensive way of reading as 'reading with love' (Deleuze, 1995, p. 9 in St Pierre, 2008), with affect: it is affect that produces becoming.

For Deleuze, education would begin not when the student arrives at a grasp of the material already known by the teacher, but when both of them together begin to experiment in practice with what they might make of themselves and the world. This, I contend, necessarily presupposes a developed ability of a particular literacy as a necessary addition to the variety of literacies that, in the framework Multiple Literacies Theory (Masny, 2005/2006), enable us to perceive and read the world as an experiential and experimental 'text'. Accordingly, reading and interpreting our experiences is what leads to their re-valuation; and it is because of the *ethical dimension* encompassing plural values 'subsisting', as Deleuze would say, in experiential milieu in their virtual form, that I refer to this specific literacy as *ethical*.

Being ethically literate, in the framework of Deleuze's philosophy, would amount to an inquiry into who we might become. We will ask this question on the basis of recognizing (as Spinoza did before Deleuze) that we have no real idea of who we might become because we do not yet know *what abody can do* and how it (body) might act in the midst of novel experiences. Philosophy, therefore, rather than focusing on the classical theoretical question of being, is devoted to the practice of becoming and, specifically, becoming-other.

Becoming-other presupposes breaking out of our old outlived habits and attitudes so as to creatively 'bring into being that which does not yet exist' (Deleuze, 1994, p. 147) by means of creating novel concepts informed by percepts and affects. Pedagogy of the concept presents the multiplicity of concepts, meanings and values as the *a-posteriori* products of understanding and evaluating our practical experience! Experience is concrete rather than abstract: it is our empirical reality, our very praxis. It makes what Deleuze would call a continuous experimentation on ourselves our informal *school of life* permeated by events and affects that thereby transform *static* being into *dynamic* becoming and meaning-making as embedded in our *lived* experience.

Never mind the subject-matter or isolated disciplines permeating contemporary formal curriculum: it is the same relational dynamics that underscores our learning to swim and/or learning to speak a second language. Says Deleuze:

> Learning to swim or learning a foreign language means composing the singular points of one's own body or one's own language with those of another shape or element, which tears us apart but also propels us into a hitherto unknown and unheard-of world of problems. (Deleuze, 1994, p. 192)

It is the re-valuation of experience, of our very actions, that constitutes learning.

New values are to be created because life is not a straightforward affair but presents problems whose multiple solutions constitute an open field of inquiry: it is how we might explore a particular situation by critically reflecting on the problem – rather than jumping upon a pre-reflective linear solution as a univocal answer – that would give a specific value to a singular experience. Deleuzian 'critical and clinical' (Deleuze, 1997) philosophy presents values as future-oriented vs pre-given, that is, plural values that are as yet to (be)come when we re-valuate experience in practice. This approach to the re-valuation of experience is strongly pragmatic and partakes of John Dewey's educational philosophy (Semetsky, 2006). Dewey, almost a century ago, explicitly equated the educative process with a meaningful life and contended that if 'education ... is identical with the operation of living a life which is fruitful and ... significant, the ... ultimate value which can be set up is just the process of living itself' (Dewey, 1916, p. 248).

Deleuze's emphasis on the clinical aspect as complementary to critical, both embedded in informal learning from life-experiences, sharply contrasts the ethical dimension of his philosophical thought with fixed moral codes. If moral values are pre-given and ratified by common sense, the Deleuzian ethical dimension pushes in the opposite direction. Deleuze uses the term *common sense* in a technical fashion, to refer to the identity (that he rejects) that arises when the faculties (in the Kantian formulation) agree with one another. Instead, we must disrupt our common sense with practical problems that do not yet yield answers as univocal solutions but invite a free flow of thought in a critical and self-reflective manner. For Deleuze, 'once one ventures outside what's familiar and reassuring, once one has to invent new concepts for unknown lands, then methods and moral systems break down' (Deleuze, 1995,

p. 103). A given moral standard simply does not enter Deleuze's discourse because the pedagogy of the concept presupposes 'the event, not the essence' (Deleuze & Guattari, 1994, p. 21). Event is always an element of becoming, and becoming is unlimited.

Acknowledging a particularly narrow approach to education, Deleuze described it as students' discovering solutions to the questions posited by teachers. In this way students lack the power to re-construct and re-valuate the 'given' problems themselves, but it is the construction of problems, for Deleuze, that is of paramount importance to one's sense of freedom. Our creative potential depends on the freedom of thought and on vital experiences in order to be realized. Or, using Deleuzian language, the virtual has a potential of becoming-actual. Only if and when 'thought is free, hence vital, nothing is compromised. When it ceases being so, all other oppressions are also possible, and already realized, so every action becomes culpable, every life threatened' (Deleuze, 1988, p. 4). In a democratic society, as Deleuze understands it, the power of thinking should be exempt from 'the obligation to obey' (Deleuze, 1988, p. 4).

Deleuze provides the following poignant vision anticipating the spread of the institutions of perpetual training and lifelong learning:

> One can envisage education becoming less and less a closed site differentiated from the workplace as another closed site, but both disappearing and giving way to frightful continual training, to continual monitoring of worker-schoolkids or bureaucrat-students. They try to present it as a reform of the school system, but it's really its dismantling. (Deleuze, 1995, p. 175)

Schooling as such is just a part of the whole institutional – and institutionalized – systematic organization as 'the widespread progressive introduction of a new system of domination' (p. 182). In the same way that large corporations have replaced small factories, schools are being replaced by the abstract concept of continuing education. By turning exams into continuous assessment, education itself is 'turning ... into a business' (Deleuze, 1995, p. 179).

In this manner, organized schooling itself becomes the means to provide a continuous stream of human capital for the knowledge economy. If and when human capital replaces *humans,* then, as Deleuze argues, individuals become *dividuals,* a market statistic, part of a sample, an item in a data bank. Creative movements along the *lines of flight* (Deleuze's neologism) can however disrupt the prevailing order of things by producing multiple becomings that are always already collective and social. As Deleuze (2000) says, we are made up of relations and experience makes sense to us only if we understand in practice the relations between several conflicting schemes of real experience. In fact, novel concepts are to be invented or created in order to make sense out of singular experiences and, ultimately, to affirm this sense. For Deleuze, to affirm means to acquire joy and 'to unburden: not to load life with the weight of higher values, but *to create* new values which are those of life, which make life light and active' (Deleuze, 1983, p. 185).

Like Dewey, who said that an individual experience is never 'some person's; it [is] nature's, localized in a body as that body happened to exist by nature' (Dewey, 1925/1958, p. 231), Deleuze too is firm on the question of the impersonality of event, that is, on its greater collective, socio-cultural or natural notwithstanding, dimension.

Event is a multiplicity and as such is profoundly social and collective therefore 'irreducible to individual states of affairs, particular images, [or] personal beliefs' (Deleuze, 1990, p. 19). One – in whose body an event is temporarily, culturally, politically, historically, and geographically localized – is to be worthy of this event. For this purpose, one has to attain an ethical responsibility or, as Deleuze says, 'this will that the event creates in us' (Deleuze, 1990, p. 148).

The continuing debate regarding the methods of ethics appears unending: philosophical discourse is firm on the fact that 'since Socrates [philosophers] have sought ... criteria for distinguishing between right and wrong and between good and evil' (Baron, Pettit, & Slote, 1997, p. 1). What is common to the mainstream approaches, however, is that they are framed by the reasoning of an independent rational moral agent that presents ethical categories in the form of 'either-or' dualistic opposites. For Deleuze, however, the affective logic breaks free from the constraints of either-or reasoning. It is based on 'shared deterritorialization' (Deleuze & Guattari, 1987, p. 293) that becomes possible because of Deleuze's ingenious conjunction 'and' as the basis for the logic of multiplicities embedded in the relational dynamics of becoming. Deleuze emphasizes the connection between two logical terms A and B: 'A *and* B. The AND is ... the path of all relations' (Deleuze, 1987, p. 57).

It is the conjunction 'and' that enables interaction between the otherwise dualistic opposites, such as self and other, or subject and object, or teacher and student, and connects them in a rhizomatic network of relations so that both are transformed by mutual experience. Becoming-other is described as

> ... an extreme contiguity within a coupling of two sensations without resemblance or, on the contrary, in the distance of a light that captures both of them in a single reflection. ... It is a zone ... of indiscernibility ... This is what is called an *affect*. (Deleuze & Guattari, 1994, p. 173)

Because of its affective dimension, the concept cannot be limited to its verbal expression grounded in propositional language. A concept 'does not belong to a discursive system and it does not have a reference. The concept shows itself' (Deleuze & Guattari, 1994, p. 140) at the level of ethical action amidst the very materiality of experiences and events.

Becoming-other via affects, via experiential encounters, presupposes our critical reflection on these encounters and events during which we can become-other through the re-valuation of experience via creating new meanings, concepts and values. The unconscious ideas 'hiding' in the virtual field of becoming need a means of expression other than words and sentences; they can take the form of legible images and symbols that we can read and interpret so as to makes sense of, and create meaning for, our experiences. For Deleuze, 'Sense is essentially produced' (Deleuze, 1990, p. 95). The unconscious, which is over and above its personal dimension, is conceptualized by Deleuze and Guattari as Anti-Oedipal. Irreducible to Freudian master-signified, it always deals with social and collective frame and is 'a productive machine ... at once social and desiring' (Deleuze, 1995, 144). In contrast to solely theoretical knowledge, it is desire or affect that educates the human psyche by means of its active participation in life-experiences in the process of creative subject-formation as this subject's becoming.

EDUCATION AND THE POLITICS OF BECOMING

It is *phronesis* as practical *wisdom* (cf. Gidley, 2009; Semetsky, 2009b) of living one life that characterises, for Deleuze, ways of living or modes of existence. A genuine educator in the framework of Deleuze's philosophy who indeed puts their ethics into practice can be described as 'an inventor of new immanent modes of existence' (Deleuze & Guattari, 1994 p. 113) that can include becoming-minor, becoming-revolutionary, becoming-democratic, and sure enough becoming-pedagogical; always already becoming-other. Such philosophical method as creative and ethical 'would affirm life instead of a [theoretical] knowledge that is opposed to [practical] life. Thinking would then mean ... inventing new possibilities of life' (Deleuze, 1983, p. 101; emphasis added).

Because of the number of significant experiential events in human life and culture, novel concepts must be continuously created as the means of their revaluation in practice. Deleuze's experiential and experimental 'epistemology' is inseparable from ethics in terms of values 'that are yet to come' (Deleuze & Guattari, 1987, p. 5). Due to a developed ethical literacy, the creation of concepts and values is a process that is at once living, learning, and – as permeated by affects that instigate our very becomings – loving!

From the ethics of care to the ethics of integration

Educational philosopher Nel Noddings introduced *caring* as a feminine alternative to character education (Noddings, 1984, 2002). Her ethics of care is in sharp contrast with paradigmatic moral education because what is fundamental to it is a self-other interdependent *relation* rather than an individual moral agent independent from others. She remarks that the contradictory and paradoxical attitudes we often take toward others constitute one of the great mysteries of human life. Borrowing the term *confirmation* from Hasidic philosopher Martin Buber, she suggests it as an integral part of the ethics of care in education. The idea of confirmation appears to be close to the very meaning of Deleuzian becoming-other, as if establishing in practice Buber's famous *I-Thou* relationship analogous to the intensive and affective relation between ourselves and others without which no becoming-other could take place.

The idea of becoming-other, as well of confirmation, emerges from our awareness of moral interdependence, that is, self-becoming-other by means of entering into another person's frame of reference and taking upon oneself the other perspective. In the context of education, to become capable, explicitly or implicitly, of becoming-other, means to confirm the potential best in both oneself and another person. Importantly, the idea of moral interdependence expands from individual lives to the mutual interactions at the cultural and political levels of various religious, ethnic, and national groups. Noticing that the reference point for moral education is traditionally located within the norms of local or religious communities, Noddings acknowledges the rapidly changing world and the inadequacy of the traditional approach. In this age of globalisation, care theory becomes a powerful resource that allows us to approach the world via *relations* and *caring* because in the framework of care theory it is a relation (and not an individual agent) that is ontologically and ethically basic.

Positing the important and timely question of how an ethic of care can be applied globally, Noddings (2010) argues that even nations and other large institutions can work under a care-driven conception of justice where it is 'caring-about' that serves the function of a motivational foundation for justice. The main aim of moral education in this context is to strive to bring up people who would be successfully engaging in caring relations both inside and outside formal educational settings. Noddings presents modelling, dialogue, practice, and confirmation as the pillars necessary for supporting this model of education in the context of personal, political, and cultural domains.

Ethics is never given a-priori in terms of some moral code of behaviour or how well our own values might fit some higher moral ideal. Instead values and meanings are created in experience in accordance with Deleuze's pedagogy of concepts and the affective logic analyzed in the preceding section. Ethical education oriented towards becoming-other thus differs in principle from the outlived model of character or civic education as well as from moral education as faith-based and grounded in religion. It is a micropolitical *milieu* permeated with affective and ethical dimensions of care, trust and love that creates the conditions for the actualization of virtual potentialities, thereby becoming what Noddings would have presented as an *excellent* system of education and which purports 'to open opportunities – never to close them' (Noddings, 1993, p. 13). The verb 'to open' is significant and can be applied to the open minds or open borders alike. Indeed, for Deleuze it is precisely 'an open society [that is] a society of creators' (Deleuze, 1991, p. 111).

The model of schooling based on the creative pedagogy of the concept will have to bring in the events of real life with all its messy experiences in the middle and muddle of uncertainties, fluxes, and fragilities. Real events in human culture thus become experiential 'lessons' to learn from. Noddings' opened her 2006 book *Critical Lessons: What our schools should teach* by pointing out that when the United States invaded Iraq in 2003, many public school teachers were forbidden to discuss the war in their classrooms thus missing an opportunity to exercise critical thinking in regard to this and other related controversial events even as such a restriction on free discussion appears to be simply outrageous in a liberal democracy. The opportunity to learn from significant events was thus closed!

Reflecting on the event of September 11 that was a predecessor to the Iraq war, French social theorist and critic Jean Baudrillard (2002) commented in his analysis of the spirit of terrorism on the shift into the symbolic sphere where an initial event becomes subjected to unforeseeable consequences. Such a singular event – like the destruction of the Twin Towers – propagates unpredictably, causing the chain of effects 'not just in the direct economic, political, financial slump in the whole of the system – and the resulting moral and psychological downturn – but the slump in the value-system' (Baudrillard, 2002, pp. 31–32) as well.

Baudrillard points out that not only terrorism itself is blind but so were the real towers: 'no longer opening to the outside world, but subject to artificial conditioning' (2002, p. 43): air conditioning, or mental conditioning alike. Yet any problematic situation in real life that requires our learning as practical problem-solving and meaning-making – that is, creating a new concept – is of the nature of an experienced event that immanently forms 'an intrinsic genesis, not an extrinsic conditioning'

(Deleuze, 1994, p. 154). The ruthless destruction of the towers represents that 'the whole system has reached a critical mass which makes it vulnerable to any aggression' (Baudrillard, 2002, p. 33) and which propagates and amplifies itself in a series of subsequent events such as Iraq or Afghanistan wars.

The moral reasoning that justified the wars was based on binary logic based on irreconcilable opposites, hence having resulted in partial (cf. Neumann, 1969) ethics which is still deeply ingrained in individual and collective consciousness as well as in education. The problem of teacher preparation becomes pressing, especially if we intend to move from partial ethics to holistic, in fact to make education itself holistic and experiential. How can schoolteachers be prepared to conduct lessons based on real-life events, that is, lessons functioning in both critical and clinical (in the framework of Deleuze's philosophy) modes? Lessons on current events rarely appear in the standard curriculum, but assuming that they did, to what extent would such imaginary lessons have been critical, clinical, and self-reflective?

Noddings is adamant that teaching should become a specific profession employing Renaissance people who will have had a broad knowledge not only of disciplines and 'subject matters' but also of perennial philosophical questions. Teacher preparation courses would indeed emphasize connections, and not only to other disciplines but also, and more importantly, to the common problems of humanity so as to create meaning for those problems, to make sense out of them! However, even if classical ethical theories are included in teacher preparation courses (and more often than not they are not included at all) the adequacy of those theories becomes doubtful in the current era of multiculturalism and globalization that demonstrates the conflict of values on the global scale.

Conclusion

It is our learning from experiences and real-life events in their socio-cultural and political contexts – that is, becoming ethically, culturally (micropolitically), and ecologically literate – that should help us in overcoming the dualistic split between self and other, to integrate 'the other' completely. This is what I call the ethics of integration! The ethics of integration is a precursor, using Deleuze's term, to the inclusive education. Integration presupposes, first of all, a Deleuzian conjunction 'and' between our conscious understanding of the other and the unconscious prejudices, outlived habits of thought or deeply engrained comfort zones that comprise our 'old' subjectivity. As embedded within the Deleuzian process of becoming-other, it is the ethics of integration that can create the conjunction 'and' between I and Thou, between Self and Other in our very praxis: self-becoming-other. Deleuze's process of becoming partakes of the evolution of consciousness as the practice through which individuals can be transformed and both personal and collective consciousness intensified and expanded (cf. Gidley, 2009; Peters & Freeman-Moir, 2006; Semetsky, 2009b, 2010b).

Undoubtfully, the ethics of integration, as building on the ethics of care, should 'challenge deeply held beliefs or ways of life' (Noddings, 2006, p. 1) and should create new understanding, new meanings in accord with Deleuze's pedagogy of the concept and his relational logic of affects. Teachers should be exposed to the fundamentals of Deleuze's philosophy and ethics starting as early as at pre-service level and also in the form of continuous professional development so as to incorporate it in their

EDUCATION AND THE POLITICS OF BECOMING

classrooms. It is clear that classical ethical theories based on rigid oppositions between self and other, good and evil, right and wrong that, in accord with Cartesian dualism, can never be reconciled, became quite inadequate, and especially in the context of a 21st-century global culture permeated by clashing value systems as well as political and economic upheavals and uncertainties. Very much in a Deleuzian spirit, Noddings (2006) comments that well-educated teachers should help students in understanding that knowledge cannot be adequately described as a set of easily retrievable answers to unambiguously stated questions. Instead, much real knowledge consists of being able to develop capacities to figure things out, to be unafraid to inquire, to experiment in practice and connect with others, confirming the best in our actual and potential relationships.

I propose that the ethics of integration, as a follow-up to the ethics of care, should emphasize the relations and interdependence, at the ontological, psychological, socio-cultural and ecological levels alike. Noddings' ethical theory 'rejects the notion of a truly autonomous moral agent ... As teachers, we are as dependent on our students as they are on us' (Noddings, 1998, p. 196). Deleuze and Guattari would have agreed: they commented (in characteristic language) on the 'communications of milieus, coordination between heterogeneous space-times' (Deleuze & Guattari, 1987, pp. 313–314) – each block of space-time representing heterogeneous elements (in our context, self and other) – yet, nonetheless 'each of which serves as a motif for another' (Deleuze & Guattari, 1987, pp. 313–314). This metaphor is helpful in articulating the affective dynamics of the process. Being a motif for each other affects *what a body can do*, a body itself described as a block of space-time, a dynamic *becoming.*

Real-life events, such as 9/11 and the Iraq and Afghanistan wars, do produce shock to thought because they break down 'the sedentary structures of [familiar] representation' (Deleuze, 1994, p. 37; emphasis added). They produce uncertainty, a bifurcation point and, importantly, as Deleuze (1990) points out, such uncertainty cannot be reduced to a cognitive doubt of the Cartesian *Cogito* who can subsequently achieve personal certainty by means of clear and distinct ideas. The ideas, for Deleuze (and it is important to repeat this) are as yet unconscious. It is the experiential becoming that forms a transversal line, which alone defies a 'fundamental distinction between subrepresentative, unconscious and aconceptual ideas/ intensities and the conscious conceptual representation of common sense' (Bogue, 1989, p. 59) because it is along this very line that we become aware of many unconscious factors in our experiences. We can *learn* from experience by virtue of transcending this experience in our empirical practice; such is Deleuze's method of transcendental empiricism due to which 'beneath the generalities of habit in moral life we rediscover singular processes of learning' (Deleuze, 1994, p. 25).

For Deleuze, it is an *objective* uncertainty which is derived from the singular structure of the event insofar as it moves in two directions at once, and insofar as it fragments the subject following this double direction. It is easy, under the circumstances, to remain a docile body within the dominant order of *being.* Such order is ruled by dogmatic political philosophy based on

> ... universality, method, question and answer, judgment,... a court of reason, a pure 'right' of thought ... The exercise of thought ... conforms to ... the dominant meanings and to the requirements of the established order. (Deleuze, 1987, p. 13)

EDUCATION AND THE POLITICS OF BECOMING

But it is the singularity of a shocking event that also produces the very conditions for creative *becoming* because, for Deleuze, 'a creator who isn't grabbed around the throat by a set of impossibilities is no creator' (Deleuze, 1995, p. 133). The experiences that produce shock to thought are conducive to learning and ethical education. Sure enough, what is there left to learn, as Patton (2000), commenting on Deleuze's philosophy and its relation to political thought, asks, if all 'knowledge is [reduced to] a form of *recognition*' (p. 19)? We learn from experience by evaluating it, because it is our experience saturated with affects that functions as the informal pedagogy of the concept and enables us to put into practice the ethics of integration informed by the values of living, learning and loving. The aim implicit in education thereby becomes the very 'intensification of life' (Deleuze & Guattari, 1994, p. 74) in the mode of our affective becoming and learning from events as cultural, informal, lessons in human lives.

References

Ansell Pearson, K. (1997). Deleuze outside/Outside Deleuze. In K. Ansell Pearson (Ed.), *Deleuze and philosophy: The difference engineer* (pp. 1–22). London: Routledge.

Baron, M.W., Pettit, P., & Slote, M. (1997). *Three methods of ethics*. Oxford: Blackwell.

Baudrillard, J. (2002). *The spirit of terrorism/Requiem for Twin Towers* (C. Turner, Trans.). London: Verso.

Bogue, R. (1989). Deleuze and Guattari. London & New York: Routledge.

Deleuze, G. (1983). *Nietzsche and philosophy* (H. Tomlinson, Trans.). New York: Columbia University Press.

Deleuze, G. (1987). *Dialogues* (with Clair Parnet), (H. Tomlinson, & B. Habberjam, Trans.). Minneapolis: Minnesota University Press.

Deleuze, G. (1988). *Spinoza: Practical philosophy* (R. Hurley, Trans.). San Francisco: City Lights Books.

Deleuze, G. (1989). *Cinema 2: The time-image* (H. Tomlinson & R. Galeta, Trans.). Minneapolis: Minnesota University Press.

Deleuze, G. (1990). *The logic of sense* (M. Lester, Trans.). New York: Columbia University Press.

Deleuze, G. (1991). *Bergsonism* (H. Tomlinson, Trans.). New York: Zone Books.

Deleuze, G. (1994). *Difference and repetition* (P. Patton, Trans.). New York: Columbia University Press.

Deleuze, G. (1995). *Negotiations, 1972–1990* (M. Joughin, Trans.). New York: Columbia University Press.

Deleuze, G. (1997). *Essays critical and clinical* (D.W. Smith, & M. Greco, Trans.). Minneapolis: University of Minnesota Press.

Deleuze, G. (2000). *Proust and signs* (R. Howard, Trans.). Minneapolis: University of Minnesota Press.

Deleuze, G., & Guattari, F. (1987). *A thousand plateaus: Capitalism and schizophrenia* (B. Massumi, Trans.). Minneapolis: University of Minnesota Press.

Deleuze, G., & Guattari, F. (1994). *What is philosophy?* (H. Tomlinson, & G. Burchell, Trans.). New York: Columbia University Press.

de Souza, M. (2009). Promoting wholeness and wellbeing in education: Exploring aspects of the spiritual dimension. In M. de Souza, L. Francis, J. O'Higgins-Norman, & D. Scott (Eds.), *International handbook of education for spirituality, care and wellbeing* (pp. 677–692). Dordrecht, The Netherlands: Springer Academic Publishers.

de Souza, M. (2010). The roles of conscious and non-conscious learning in impeding and enhancing spirituality: Implications for learning and teaching. In M. de Souza & J. Rimes (Eds.), *Education and spirituality: Australian perspectives*. Melbourne: Australian College ofEducation.

EDUCATION AND THE POLITICS OF BECOMING

Dewey, J. (1916/1958). Democracy and education. In J.A. Boydston (Ed.), *John Dewey, The middle works, 1899–1924* (Vol. 9, pp. 1–370). Carbondale and Edwardsville, IL: Southern Illinois University Press.

Dewey, J. (1925). *Experience and nature.* New York: Dover Publications.

Gidley, J.M. (2009). Educating for evolving consciousness: Voicing the emergency for love, life and wisdom. In M. De Souza, L. Francis, J. O'Higgins-Norman, & D. Scott (Eds.), *International handbook of education for spirituality, care and wellbeing* (pp. 533–561). Dordrecht, The Netherlands: Springer Academic Publishers.

Gidley, J., & Inayatullah, S. (Eds.) (2002). *Youth futures: Comparative research and transformative visions.* Westport, CT: Praeger.

Hardt, M. (1993). *Gilles Deleuze: An apprenticeship in philosophy.* Minneapolis: University of Minnesota Press.

Inayatullah, S., Milojevic, I., & Bussey, M. (Eds.). (2005). *Educational futures: Neo-humanism and transformative pedagogy.* Taipei: Tamkang University Press.

Masny, D. (2005/2006). Learning and creative processes: A poststructural perspective on language and multiple literacies. *International Journal of Learning, 12*(5), 149–156.

Masny, D., & Cole, D.R. (Eds.) (2009). *Multiple Literacies Theory: A Deleuzian perspective.* Rotterdam: Sense Publishers.

Neumann, E. (1969). *Depth psychology and a new ethic.* Great Britain: Hodder and Stoughton.

Noddings, N. (1984). *Caring: A feminine approach to ethics and moral education.* Berkeley: University of California Press.

Noddings, N. (1993). Excellence as a guide to educational conversation. In H. Alexander (Ed.), *Philosophy of education society yearbook* (pp. 5–16). Illinois: Urbana.

Noddings, N. (1998). *Philosophy of education.* Boulder, Colorado: Westview Press.

Noddings, N. (2002). *Educating moral people: A caring alternative to character education.* New York & London: Teachers College Press.

Noddings, N. (2006). *Critical lessons: What our schools should teach.* Cambridge University Press.

Noddings, N. (2010). Moral education in an age of globalization. In I. Semetsky (Ed.), *Local pedagogies/Global ethic,* Special issue, *Educational Philosophy and Theory, 42*(4), 390–396.

Patton, P. (2000). *Deleuze and the political.* London & New York: Routledge.

Peters, M.A., & Freeman-Moir, J. (Eds.) (2006). Edutopias: New utopian thinking in education. Rotterdam: Sense Publishers.

Semetsky, I (Ed.) (2004). Deleuze and education. Special issue, *Educational Philosophy and Theory,* 36: 3.

Semetsky, I. (2006). *Deleuze, education and becoming.* Rotterdam: Sense Publishers.

Semetsky, I. (Ed.) (2008). *Nomadic education: Variations on a theme by Deleuze and Guattari,* Rotterdam: Sense Publishers.

Semetsky, I. (2009a). Deleuze pure and applied: Becoming-ethical/traversing towards ecoliteracy. In D. Masny & D.R. Cole (Eds.), *Multiple Literacies Theory: A Deleuzian perspective* (pp. 93–104). Rotterdam: Sense Publishers.

Semetsky, I. (2009b). Whence wisdom? Human development as a mythic search for meanings. In de Souza, M., L.J. Francis, J. O'Higgins-Norman & D. Scott (Eds.), *International handbook on education for spirituality, care and wellbeing* (pp. 631–652). Dordrecht, The Netherlands: Springer Academic Publishers.

Semetsky, I. (Ed.). (2010a). *Semiotics education experience.* Rotterdam: Sense Publishers.

Semetsky, I. (2010b). The folds of experience, or: Constructing the pedagogy of values. In: I.Semetsky (Ed.), *Local pedagogies/Global ethics,* Special issue, *Educational Philosophy and Theory, 42*(4), 476–488.

Semetsky, I. (2010c). Silent discourse: The language of signs and 'becoming-woman'. *SubStance #121,* Special issue. *Spiritual Politics After Deleuze, 39*(1), 87–102.

St Pierre, E.A. (2008). Deleuzian concepts for education: The subject undone. In I. Semetsky (Ed.), *Nomadic education: Variations on a theme by Deleuze and Guattari* (pp. 183–196). Rotterdam: Sense Publishers.

'It's all about relationships': Hesitation, friendship and pedagogical assemblage

Sam Sellar

> This paper examines the relationships between hesitation, friendship and pedagogy. It develops three main arguments: (a) first, that feelings of hesitation can unsettle our self-assurance in what we know, activating new problematics; (b) second, that this unsettling may become pedagogical under certain conditions; and (c) third, that friendship provides such conditions, potentially spurring creative processes of thought and learning. In response to secondary school teachers' claims about their teaching and relationships with students, the paper employs hesitation as a methodological strategy for thinking beyond established understandings about pedagogy. The concept of *pedagogy as assemblage* is elaborated, drawing on the work of Deleuze and Guattari, and friendship is then conceived as a *joyous encounter* and mode of *intellectual hospitality*. These concepts enable description of the affective contexts in which the destabilisation of knowledge about ourselves and our worlds might provoke learning, in response to problems that are newly sensed in hesitation.

Introduction: Feeling hesitant

It's always unsettling when I reach for my car keys and realise my pocket is empty. Before the implications of the discovery can unfold, there is a moment of hesitation when my confidence in the way I imagined things to be falls away. I was sure that I had my keys and was heading home, but all of a sudden I'm jolted out of the narrative of my unfolding plans. In discussing events that undermine our belief in what we 'know', Isabelle Stengers (2005a, p. 996) suggests that these moments involve 'a passing fright that scares self-assurance'. This scare can open up spaces of questioning; spaces in which we are affectively engaged through a sense of fright or shock (Massumi, 2002, p. 36). Prior to the hesitation I knew what would happen next, but now I have been drawn into a more experimental disposition: What now? Hesitation involves a breakdown in our habitual patterns of cognition, forcing us to engage in deliberation and analysis (Varela, 1999).

In contrast to this quotidian example of lost keys, Stengers' (2005a) is concerned with events in which political voices become imbued 'with the feeling that they do not master the situation they discuss' (p. 996). This feeling marks a loss of confidence, a sense that one's power to know and act has been diminished. Stengers argues that these events force us to question "'What are we busy doing?" making an interstice in the soil of good reasons we have for doing so' (p. 996). However, ' . . . interstices close rapidly. Worse still, silencing the fright often results in confirming our many reasons with an additional baseness that does away with the hesitation' (p. 996). In this case, fright is pushed aside in order to quickly reassemble good reasons and restore a sense of mastery. Beyond the initial shock, not much changes. But, Stengers suggests, these events might also provoke transformation if we allow them to focus our attention on potentials in the event for the emergence of new understandings and new arrangements of things.

It is this pedagogical potential in hesitation that I want to explore in this paper. There are significant learning opportunities in moments of hesitation, when our self-assurance is unsettled and we are forced to reappraise the world and make sense anew. But doing so in substantive ways depends on whether we affirm or negate these events. That is, a loss of self-assurance that registers as fright might present different possibilities to one that registers as joy, which I will later align with a particular conception of friendship. To begin discerning some of the differences between hesitating in fright or friendship, it is useful to consider the hesitant body from the *ethological* perspective that Deleuze (1988a) draws from his reading of Spinoza: that is, by understanding it in terms of its capacities for affecting and being affected.[1] From this perspective, a body is composed of other bodies in relation. It is 'a nexus of variable interconnections, a multiplicity' (Gatens, 1996, p. 165). Bodies are composite *and* enter into composition with other bodies:

> When a body 'encounters' another body, or an idea another idea, it happens that the two relations sometimes combine to form a more powerful whole, and sometimes one decomposes the other, destroying the cohesion of its parts . . . as conscious beings, we never apprehend anything but the effects of these compositions and decompositions: we experience *joy* when a body encounters ours and enters into composition with it, and *sadness* when, on the contrary, a body or an idea threaten our coherence. (Deleuze, 1988a, p. 19)

Compatible relations with other bodies 'give rise to joyful affects which may in turn increase the intensive capacity of the body', while incompatible relations diminish capacities and produce sad affects (Gatens, 1996, p. 169). That is, the capacity of the body is not given once and for all; it depends on its encounters with other bodies. These encounters change the state of the body, which is felt as affection and 'accompanied by a variation in capacity' (Massumi, 2002, p. 15). For example, when we discover our keys are missing, a sense of diminishment may arise as our body immediately senses its reduced power to act as intended, and this decrease in capacity registers as a brief scare, or perhaps a sinking feeling in our stomach. In contrast, a sense of increased capacity to act arises when the body apprehends new and productive compositions with other bodies. In this case, the encounter would give rise to joyous affects and, I will argue, conditions in which the interstices created in hesitation might remain open long enough that we come to understand the world differently.

There is a potentiating dynamic at work in events of hesitation, from which either pedagogical transformation or a reinforcement of established understandings might follow. This dynamic suspends the narrative line of our conscious experience, problematising the ways things are while activitating the potential for them to become otherwise. This is a process of *virtualization*: a

> ... change of identity, a displacement of the center of ontological gravity of the object considered. Rather than being defined principally through its actuality (a solution), the entity now finds its essential consistency within a problematic field. (Lévy, 1998, p. 26)

In reaching for my keys I embody a solution to the problem of how to get home, but the felt shock of finding them missing reactivates this problem. In shock the body viscerally registers the dynamic of virtualization as intensity or affect:

> Viscerality ... is a rupture in the stimulus-response paths, a leap in place into a space outside action-reaction circuits. Viscerality is the perception of suspense. The space into which it jolts the flesh is one of an inability to act or reflect, a spasmodic passivity, so taut a receptivity that the body is paralyzed until it is jolted back into action-reaction by recognition. (Massumi, 2002, p. 61)

This jolting back into action can result, as Stengers proposes, in a confirmation of established reasons and purposes for acting, or it can unfold a new line of thought, a process of learning. I am interested in the question of whether, through affirming the potential that hesitation holds for new compositions, we might recognize suspensions of action and reflection as opportunities for learning rather than crises of self-assurance that demand a reassertion of knowledge and mastery?

The paper comprises three main sections. The first presents empirical data in a narrative form and recounts a sense of hesitation I experienced when collaborating with teachers and other researchers in a large action-research project: the *Redesigning Pedagogies in the North* (RPiN) project. During the early stages of the project, teachers claimed that their pedagogies were 'all about relationships'. However, our research team initially heard little that sounded pedagogical in these claims, but were also criticized by some teachers for misrepresenting their work. In the second section I take my hesitations during this moment in the project as a methodological starting point for an alternative reading of teachers' emphases on relationships, drawing on Deleuze and Guattari's (1987) concept of assemblage to articulate an understanding of pedagogy that is literally 'all about relationships'. In the final section of the paper I consider how thinking about pedagogy as assemblage enables us to think differently about the role that friendship plays in intellectual production. Indeed, I argue that friendship provides an affective context in which hesitation might be productively translated into a pedagogical encounter.

Relationships: Talking with teachers about pedagogy in 'the north'

I want to begin in the middle of a dialogue between RPiN teachers and researchers, which took place during a series of roundtables. These were convened in a recently built community centre, servicing a new housing estate 15 kilometres north of the centre of a major Australian city. This region is often homogenously referred to as the 'northern suburbs', or simply 'the north'. However, this particular estate is newer and more affluent than areas even further north, where an exodus of manufacturing industries over recent decades has left many communities struggling with the harsh effects of multi-generational unemployment. The community centre houses a library,

EDUCATION AND THE POLITICS OF BECOMING

as well as lecture theatres, computer pools and teaching rooms used by staff and students from the adjacent university—an interstitial space where community learning and institutional education rub shoulders. It was an appropriate location for project meetings between researchers from the university and 30 teachers from nearby areas. In this region student engagement and retention are long-standing problems and the RPiN project aimed to support collaborative development of new pedagogies and curricula, which might enable schools to connect more strongly with students and their communities.

The second project roundtable began with a plenary session in which researchers provided feedback on recent visits to teachers in schools. During one of these visits a small group of researchers, including myself, met with a teacher who was critical of the way the research team had represented teachers and teaching in 'the north'. When introducing the rationale for the project at the first roundtable, the research team had characterized teachers as travelling into and out of 'the north' on a daily basis, leading to disconnection from the knowledge and practices that have currency in students' community lives outside of school. In quite blunt terms, this particular teacher challenged us to listen more carefully to those like her, who had grown up in this region and who had a strong connection to the place and its communities. This challenged our sense of who we were working with and why or how they would benefit from our expertise. It was a decisive moment in the project for me; one that caused me to hesitate, unsettling any sense of mastery I had as a researcher working with teachers to redesign their practice. This hesitation continued to resonate over the coming months.

After the plenary session, the group split up to discuss the teachers' reflections on interviews with colleagues that they had been asked to conduct in preparation for the roundtable. In one breakout room a researcher prompted teachers to begin by sharing what they felt was most important about teaching in 'the north'. One teacher responded:

> I guess the first thing I put down, which is the most important thing for me, is teaching in the north I think you have to develop positive relationships before you can get anything else. That would be my first and most important thing I've got on my list.

Some other teachers enthusiastically agreed and 'ticked that off' their lists too. The researcher asked whether everyone had listed 'relationships' and the whole group replied with an emphatic 'yes'. In another room, one teacher remarked that 'one of the things that pops out is 'before the rest of the group finished the sentence in unison: ... relationships'! The importance of relationships was repeatedly noted across each of the small group discussions.

Teachers had also brought along artefacts that represented what is most meaningful about teaching in 'the north' and later in the day small groups reconvened to discuss them. One teacher shared a photo album with pictures of students, other teachers and school events. Her photo was in the centre. She described the challenge of arranging her photographs in a way that showed the connections between her teaching and the complex network of people and places in which it is situated: 'I meant to do this quite differently, but I thought "No, it's going to be too huge" because I wanted to actually have radiating lines, and then have different aspects, and

64

I thought "I'll just put it in together"'. In another group a young teacher spoke with emotion about a poster she had created:

> The one thing that I guess is important to me, and it's something we've all been saying continuously, is relationships, and I didn't know how to bring relationships in, so what I have just made here, at my school I find my relationships are with my students ... And basically that's all I've done on here, I've put photos and things that were significant ... I'll let people have a look at it. It's much easier to have a look at it than explain it I guess. *I couldn't really put it in words.*

Teachers in other rooms also struggled to translate their valued relationships into articulate descriptions of practice. Some described the importance of 'positive relationships' and winning the trust of students; others explained how relationships facilitate students' engagement with the curriculum or provide a supportive context for explicit teaching and assessment. At some points the discussion extended into questions of friendship. One teacher claimed that 'you can still be a teacher, friend, and all that sort of stuff with it being a healthy relationship too'. Other teachers were less sanguine about friendship:

> The word 'relationship' is really what covers the whole thing, very much so, and I don't think the relationship ... has to be a buddy-buddy, friend relationship, and I think it's a relationship where you have to push and cajole and care, and all the rest of it, but it's not just being a friendly relationship.

While this particular teacher makes a distinction between friendship and relationships that involve placing academic demands on students, across their discussions teachers described their pedagogical relationships in diverse, complex and ambivalent ways.

From this point in the project teachers tended to rally around the claim that pedagogy is 'all about relationships'. However, the researchers struggled to hear an educational dimension to this claim and worried over teachers' apparent inability to talk about pedagogy in articulate ways. As a research team we staged an intervention. In the following project meeting we moved to reframe the emphasis on relationships in more strongly educational terms, and some of us went on to develop conceptual resources to help teachers talk more explicitly about their pedagogies.

A few months later the fourth project roundtable brought teachers and researchers back to the community centre. In one of the breakout rooms a researcher revisited the initial discussion about relationships and its subsequent reframing by the research team:

> Think back to the second roundtable when we were talking a lot about the importance of relationships with students, and how everybody put that, how that was an important aspect of it, and yet last time ... I heard you were talking about how you can't just leave it as a relationship, you've got to make it an *educative relationship*. You're not just there to know them, you actually have to turn it into something that's connected to education as well, and that that's an issue for us.

This is the narrative that had emerged among researchers: teachers had identified the importance of relationships, this was complicated by researchers who argued for a more 'educative' conception of relationships, and it was now the task of a unified 'us' to address this problem of how relationships with students could be parlayed into pedagogical encounters. But this narration, particularly the implication that relationships are somehow distinguishable from the real work of teaching and learning, met with hesitation from our teacher colleagues.

For example, one teacher queried whether there is a more immediate connection between relationships and learning than was supposed in the research team's account: 'but don't you find also that relationships aid the learning process ... a lot of those kids are disengaged and if they have a relationship with the teacher they're more willing to actually go with the curriculum'. Another teacher expressed caution in the face of the positions being adopted by both teachers and researchers:

> I think we need to be really careful that we don't try and pin down one thing as the magic part ... I don't think there is one magic answer to this ... we can talk about relationships, about establishing relationships, there is no answer to that. We can talk about structuring lessons and breaking down content and all sorts of methodologies, but I don't think there's one magic influence there either. I think what we're talking about is that willingness of teachers to be flexible in lots and lots of different ways.

This caution raises the question of whether talk about relationships, which trips easily off the tongue, as well as the research team's urging for more detailed talk about teaching and learning *per se*, both obscure something more important, something which cannot be easily captured because it manifests in 'lots of different ways'.

This hesitation among some teachers resonated with my own. I increasingly felt that something in the teachers' claims was not being heard and was instead being reframed through positions that we, as a research team, had brought to the project. Stengers (2005a, 2005b, 2008) argues for the methodological importance of such hesitation, grounded in empirical situations and events that challenge our application of pre-existing theoretical frameworks and rationalities. This approach involves a *political ecology* (see also Massumi, 2002, p. 255) 'that gives the situations we confront the power to have us thinking, feeling, imagining, and not theorizing about them ... giving to the world the power to change us, to "force" our thinking' (Stengers, 2008, p. 57). This is the approach that I want to take here, allowing the hesitation provoked during this moment in the RPiN project to force a new line of thinking between the positions adopted at that time by the teachers (it's all about relationships) and the research team (it's more than relationships); positions that potentially elide something more important in what the teachers sought to describe.

Pedagogy: Teaching and learning as a process of assemblage

In the interstices opened by this hesitation I want to ask two questions: First, what conditions are necessary to allow this hesitation to force a new line of thinking? And second, in what directions might this thinking proceed? I'll begin with the second question, in order to elaborate a conception of pedagogy that supports a response to the first. In thinking about pedagogical relationships it is important to heed the notion that there is no one 'magic part': pedagogy is complex. Indeed, a number of the RPiN teachers encountered difficulties in representing the relational nature of their work, struggling to 'put it in words' and feeling overwhelmed when thinking about the 'radiating lines' that connect all the different parts. This suggests the need for conceptual resources that resist the oversimplification of teaching and learning. Indeed, I will argue that we might understand the emphasis on relationships not as pointing simply to interpersonal relationship between 'teacher' and 'learner', but to forces at play during encounters between complex bodies. How might we understand these encounters and bodies?

Lusted's (1986) highly influential article *Why Pedagogy?* is an obvious place to start. As is well known, Lusted defines pedagogy as 'the transformation of consciousness that takes place in the interaction of three agencies—the teacher, the learner and the knowledge they together produce' (p. 3). This triadic conception of pedagogy-as-relationship 'foregrounds exchange between and over the categories, it recognises the productivity of the relations, and it renders the parties within them as active, changing and changeable agencies' (p. 3). In this account, pedagogy is the means through which knowledge 'is produced in the process of interaction . . . between teacher and learner at the moment of classroom engagement' (p. 4). That is, knowledge is a product of a relationship with others. Indeed, Lusted argues that the importance of pedagogy as a concept lies in the attention it draws to this relational '*process* through which knowledge is produced' (p. 2).

Extending from Lusted's work, Green's (1998) discussion of post-critical pedagogies provides another set of resources that help to account for the complexity of this process. Green proposes that pedagogy 'refers specifically to teaching *and* learning, as dynamically interrelated although not necessarily identical or iso-morphic activities' (p. 179). Further, he suggests that pedagogy 'is best conceived as "teaching *for* learning", with teaching understood not as the *cause* of learning but rather as its *context*' (p. 179). This causal separation of teaching from learning complicates any easy distinction between what teachers and learners do together and what is learnt from these encounters. Indeed, Ellsworth (2005) argues that the learning which takes place during pedagogical encounters both precedes and exceeds what becomes known:

> Pedagogy teaches but it does not know how it teaches. We come to a knowing only as we emerge from a realm of sensation/movement that is ontologically prior to cognition. We come to the time and space of speaking about learning only after it has already taken place in a time and space that language cannot name. Language *follows* that which it would name. (2005, p. 167)

Lusted, Green and Ellsworth each provide useful resources for understanding both the relational nature of pedagogy and the difficulty RPiN teachers encountered when trying to translate this into language. However, I want to extend from these resources to think about pedagogy in terms of *assemblage*.

The concept of assemblage (*agencement*) developed in the work of Deleuze and Guattari (1986, 1987), and extended in secondary commentaries (e.g. DeLanda 2006; Patton, 2000), describes the production of composite entities or phenomenon. That is, assemblages are both things and processes. Deleuze and Guattari conceive of assemblages as multiplicities, which have also been characterised as rhizomes (Deleuze & Guattari, 1987), 'meshworks' (DeLanda, 1999), or 'intensive networks' (Bonta & Protevi, 2004). Phillips (2006) cautions against 'common sense' readings of the concept, arguing that it does not simply refer to 'a collection of things', but rather the idea of dynamic 'unities composed by bodies in connection' (2006, p. 109). That is, the concept of assemblage enables the 'in-between' processes of change and becoming to be drawn into clearer focus:

> Assemblage can be seen as a relay concept, linking the problematic of structure with that of change and far-from-equilibrium systems. It focuses on process and on the dynamic character of the inter-relationships between the heterogenous elements of the phenomenon. It recognizes both structurizing and indeterminate effects: that is, both flow and turbulence, produced in the interaction of open systems. (Venn, 2006, p. 107)

The concept helps to overcome certain limitations of theories that emphasise structure or 'actual' things, by drawing attention to 'the irruption of the unexpected or unpredictable' (from the transcendental field that, for Deleuze, is 'virtual') and the 'co-relating of phenomena across different fields, for example . . . the affective and the cognitive' (Venn, 2006, p. 107). Analysing the relation between the affective and cognitive dimensions of teaching and learning has become an important site of research for pedagogy studies (e.g. Ellsworth, 2005; Probyn, 2004; Watkins, 2006, 2007; Zembylas, 2007a, 2007b).

However, employing the concept of assemblage does not simply redress the difficulty of talking about the elusive relational process of teaching-and-learning. Translating such processes into stable conceptions entails a risk of ossifying the very movement that one is trying to describe. Marcus and Saka (2006) warn that 'whoever employs [the concept of assemblage] does so with a certain tension, balancing, and tentativeness where the contradictions between the ephemeral and the structural, and between the structural and the unstably heterogenous create almost a nervous condition for analytic reason' (p. 102), a tension borne 'of trying to stabilize an object or subject state that is inherently elusive' (p. 106). Following Phillips (2006), it is perhaps more apt to use the concept of assemblage as 'an imaginative resource for framing objects and operations of the social sciences' (p. 109). From this perspective, I do not seek to render the elusive process of pedagogy entirely comprehensible in terms of assemblage, but do suggest that it can help us to think about it in productive ways.

A detailed exegesis of 'assemblage theory' (Delanda, 2006) is beyond the scope of this paper, so I will focus on two key characteristics here. First, assemblages are composite entities/processes constituted through relations between different parts. These relations produce a synthetic whole without fusing components together in a manner that would change the assemblage from a heterogeneous network to a homogenous entity. That is, an assemblage is a sum greater than its parts but these parts maintain a degree of autonomy. DeLanda (2006) explains:

> The reason why the properties of a whole [assemblage] cannot be reduced to those of its parts is that they are the result not of an aggregation of the components' own properties but of the actual exercise of their capacities. These capacities do depend on a component's properties but cannot be reduced to them since they involve reference to the properties of other interacting entities. Relations of exteriority guarantee that assemblages may be taken apart while at the same time allowing that the interactions between parts may result in a true synthesis. (2006, p. 11)

Second, parts of an assemblage may enter into relations with parts of other assemblages, and to the extent that this changes the capacities of the parts it will also change the nature of the assemblages in which they participate. For example, teachers and students can be understood as assemblages in their own right. When parts of these assemblages enter into relation a third assemblage emerges. If this new set of relations effects a transformation of the teacher-assemblage or learner-assemblage, to 'simultaneously organize and disorganize a variety of understandings' (Simon, 1992, p. 56), it might be considered a pedagogical assemblage.

However, the teacher and learner are not 'totally' implicated in the pedagogical encounter. Parts of them connect and change while other parts do not. That is, bodies are not affected by other bodies *in toto,* but rather 'bit by bit' (Bignall, 2010). Bignall explains that 'encounters are not simply events describing the meeting of whole bodies as they come into contact, but more precisely involve a multitude of engagements taking place at the many particular sites of the affections that describe a body' (p. 86). From this perspective, teaching and learning involves relationships between synthetic entities (e.g. teacher and learner) through which parts of these entities connect, effecting a change in capacity of the connecting parts and, to some degree, the broader synthetic entities involved. This is a conception of pedagogy that *is* all about relationships. For example, the classroom teacher is embedded in a network of connections: connections with students, parents, other teachers, communities, policies, technologies, architecture etc. Changes in or across this network, whether produced as a result of 'teaching' *per se* or by any number of other factors such as policy changes or a significant event, will traverse the parts-in-connection, altering their capacities and potentially producing learning in unpredictable ways. And rather than simply seeing the teacher or learner as *entering* into these relationships, we can also see them as constituted *from* the changing networks of relationships in which they are embodied. As Ellsworth suggests, learning takes place in a realm that precedes capacities for reflection and description, which emerge at the level of synthetic entities. In a sense then, this is a sub-personal conception of pedagogy, the experience of which eludes easy translation into language and conscious thought.

However, while this approach provides a conceptual language that extends from and takes account of the claim that pedagogy is about relationships, it does so in a somewhat abstract sense: the RPiN teachers' did not describe their teaching in the philosophical terms of assemblage theory. Indeed, their descriptions were characterised by an affective investment in the *quality* of these relationships. Allowing teachers' claims to force our thinking requires more than an account of pedagogy as assemblage. It also requires thinking about the affective quality of the relationships that constitute these assemblages and how this relates to learning. To pursue this, I want to return to the question of what conditions are necessary for hesitation to give rise to learning or, in the terms just set out, what conditions potentiate pedagogical assemblages? I want to propose that friendship, in a particular sense, has an important role to play in pedagogical assemblages and, in turn, in creating conducive conditions for learning when our encounters with others produce hesitation.

Friendship: A micropolitics of pedagogical assemblages

Friendship has occupied an ambivalent place in thinking about pedagogy, particularly in relation to teachers' work in classrooms. Indeed, beyond the obvious risks of unprofessional conduct when befriending students, friendship can be a source of tension between different aspects of teachers' practice. For example, there was some support among RPiN teachers for friendship being part of 'healthy' teaching and learning, but there was also a sense of caution, reflecting a broader scepticism that appears deeply ingrained in 'teacherly' common sense. For example, many beginning teachers are advised 'not to smile until Easter' and are often warned that they are not the students' friend. Indeed, Weinstein (1998) found that many pre-service teachers feel torn between establishing rapport with and caring for students on the one hand, and maintaining control in the classroom on the other: 'wanting to be nice, but having to be mean'. The participants in Weinstein's study identified interpersonal relationships as the primary means through which they care for students (ahead of pedagogical and classroom management strategies), while management strategies were believed to be the primary means of establishing order (ahead of interpersonal relationships and pedagogy). The analytical framework of this study, like common sense advice to separate the interpersonal from the pedagogical, implies that friendship and pedagogy are distinct and potentially conflicting types of relationship.

However, such distinctions rest on an understanding of friendship as a relationship between 'whole' persons. That is, the teacher is either the students' friend or they are not, and because teaching clearly calls for relationships with students that are not solely about friendship, the latter is often considered preferable. Further, in terms of Lusted's (1986) definition of pedagogy as the relationship between the three agencies of teacher, learner and knowledge, this notion of friendship appears to involve only two of them: teacher and learner. This is problematic given that the pedagogy is fundamentally dependent on the third—knowledge—and makes it difficult to think of friendship in combination with the other types of encounter. However, this approach to thinking about pedagogy and friendship does not account for the complex interrelations of forces, perceptions and sensations that traverse assemblages: 'an entire world of unconscious micropercepts, unconscious affects, fine segmentations ... There is a micropolitics of perception, affection, conversation, and so forth' (Deleuze & Guattari, 1987, p. 213). I am interested in friendship as a dynamic that operates across this micropolitical terrain: a sub-personal or impersonal modality of friendship.

Friendship of this kind involves a particular type of affection and is not limited to 'total' connections between 'whole' persons. O'Sullivan (2004, p. 20) argues that Deleuze's ethological perspective, outlined above, 'offers a powerful framework for thinking friendship' in terms of compositions between compatible bodies that give rise to joyous affects. These joyous encounters are 'partial' insofar as some aspects of the bodies-in-relation may connect compatibly with some aspects of others, while other parts may remain unaffected or even be affected in incompatible ways. In this sense, friendship is not an 'all or nothing' relationship. As Bignall (2010) argues, 'one must not simply strive to unite with bodies that one perceives to be wholly sympathetic and similar, but more precisely with the sympathetic facets that comprise one's social milieu' (p. 87).

As a joyous affection, friendship can also be understood as a dynamic of thought that arises from encounters between compatible ideas. An ethological perspective does not admit a dualism between body and mind because, as Watkins (2006, p. 272) explains, Spinoza's concept of affection 'is framed by a psychophysical parallelism ...

affect has both a corporeal and cognitive dimension'. Spinoza conceives of the mind as 'the idea *of* the corresponding body' (Deleuze, 1988a, p. 86), such that 'there is a correspondence between the affections of the body and the ideas of the mind, a correspondence by which these ideas represent these affections' (p. 87). As a result, 'all that is action in the body is also action in the mind' (p. 88). We can have ideas of joyous affections while encounters between ideas can give rise to joyous affects. It is in terms of this parallelism that we can understand Deleuze and Guattari's (1994) claim that friendship is intrinsic to philosophy: that 'the philosopher is the concept's friend; he is the potentiality of the concept' (p. 5). Deleuze and Guattari understand philosophy as the creation of concepts, a creation that involves a 'competent intimacy', 'a sort of material taste and potentiality' (p. 9) similar to that which a carpenter exercises in drawing out form from a piece of wood. Such drawing-out involves the carpenter assessing the capacities of the wood and becoming sensitive to how it can connect with his tools and with his imagination in compatible ways.

To illustrate this relationship between friendship and intellectual production, I want to briefly consider Kaufman's (2001) notion of *intellectual hospitality*. Kaufman examines the intellectual friendships of Bataille, Blanchot, Deleuze, Foucault and Klossowski, which are manifest in the 'laudatory essays' they wrote about one another. The intellectual friendships between these philosophers involved a transformative dynamic through which, Kaufman (2001) argues, 'the very identity of the interlocutor is at stake. It would entail a willingness to give up one's grounding as a person into a movement of thought that is groundless' (p. 131). This is an impersonal friendship that traverses thought. As Kaufman suggests:

> These thinkers obey impersonal rules of hospitality—hospitality to the other as a form of thought and not as a person … a new form of intellectual hospitality, a mode of being in common that is not a form of correcting or out-mastering the other, but rather a way of joining with the other in language or in thought so that what is created is a community of thought that knows no bounds, a hospitality that liquidates identity, a communism of the soul. (Kaufman, 2001, p. 141)

Deleuze's (1988b) writing on Foucault is a case in point. Rather than simply critiquing or supporting Foucault's work, Deleuze finds ways to join with it and take it in new directions. As a result, it becomes difficult to attribute this movement of thought to a distinct person.

Albrecht-Crane (2005) provides a more concrete example of intellectual hospitality in her meditation on pedagogy as friendship. She describes a coursework essay in which one of her students demonstrated his knowledge of poststructuralist theory while 'hoping' that the theory was untrue, because it contradicted his conservative religious faith. Likening the student's unusual response to a friendly 'wave', Albrecht-Crane acknowledged his engagement with her teaching and extended an invitation to continue the conversation. This exchange gave both teacher and student occasion to hesitate; however, an affective sense of friendship provided conditions in which this hesitation could provoke new lines of thought for both, rather than reinforcing an oppositional stance between 'critical' teacher and 'conservative' student. This friendship was not borne from a close interpersonal relationship, but from a gesture in the student's writing. Stivale (2000) explains how, for Deleuze, friendship emerges from gestures of this kind:

EDUCATION AND THE POLITICS OF BECOMING

> Each of us is apt to seize upon a certain type of charm in another, or our perception of another's charm—for example, in a gesture, in a thought, in a certain modesty. Thus in penetrating to the vital roots of perception, this charm creates a friendship, constituting an indelible effect through our perceiving someone who suits us, who teaches us something, opens us, awakens us, rendering us sensitive to an emission of signs. (2000, p. 11)

In this sense, an affective context of friendship, forged 'bit by bit' across pedagogical assemblages, can produce impersonal communities of thought through a sense of intellectual hospitality. Further, this modality of friendship provides conditions in which a loss of self-assurance might open the way for creative thinking and learning with others: friendship as a productive context for intellectual creation that is spurred by, and can sustain, the hesitation and dissensus that is crucial to thought (Deleuze, 1994).

The professional communities created through the work of the RPiN project brought together teachers and researchers over a three-year period, to think, research and write together. At times, encounters between participants involved such senses of intellectual hospitality. Indeed, in this paper I have sought to extend hospitality to the teachers' thought as a methodological strategy for opening up new lines of conceptual development in response to their claims that pedagogy is 'all about relationships'. This intellectual hospitality is one strategy for making sense of and responding to the hesitation experienced when struggling with teachers over how to represent their work; one disposition that can be nurtured during the jolt back into action-reaction circuits after we have hesitated. Indeed, I want to suggest that it is a particularly productive strategy for translating hesitation into a pedagogical encounter.

Conclusion

This paper has sought to develop three main arguments: first, that feeling hesitant can unsettle our self-assurance in what we know, giving rise to a process of virtualization that activates new problematics; second, that this unsettling can become pedagogical in the appropriate context; and third, that friendship, understood as a joyous encounter between compatible bodies, provides one such context. I began by considering how hesitation opens spaces of questioning in which we might either seek to reassert existing positions or allow ourselves to be forced into thinking as we respond to a new set of problems. Second, I employed my own hesitation as a methodological strategy for engaging with empirical data and allowing it to provoke new lines of conceptual development. Drawing on Deleuze and Guattari's (1987) concept of assemblage, I sought to pursue a conceptualization of pedagogy that was adequate to this event, preparing the way for a particular reading of the role that friendship can play in potentiating pedagogical assemblages. That is, friendship conceived as a joyous encounter between compatible bodies and ideas, as a form of intellectual hospitality, implicates certain of our affective connections with others in movements of thought and learning. Indeed, the sense of intellectual hospitality that emerged at times during the collaborations between teachers and researchers in the RPiN project provided a context in which each were forced to think and to be changed by their participation. Moreover, as Albrecht-Crane (2005) suggests, the same dynamic has value in the context of classroom-based pedagogical relationships

EDUCATION AND THE POLITICS OF BECOMING

between teachers and students. Friendship, then, has an important pedagogical role to play when it creates conditions in which we might both connect with others, at least in part, and allow these connections to change our understandings of ourselves and our worlds.

Acknowledgement

Led by a research team from the Centre for Studies in Literacy, Policy and Learning Cultures (University of South Australia), RPiN was partly funded by the Australian Research Council (LP0454869) as a 'linkage' project with industry partners: the Northern Adelaide State Secondary Principals Network; the Australian Education Union (SA Branch); and the South Australian Social Inclusion Unit.

Note

1. While I will refer specifically to human bodies here, this ethological approach can be used to analyse all manner of bodies: human, nonhuman, social, political, chemical, biological, etc.

References

Albrecht-Crane, C. (2005). Pedagogy as friendship: Identity and affect in the conservative classroom. *Cultural Studies, 19*(4), 491–514.

Bignall, S. (2010). Affective assemblages. In S. Bignall & P. Patton (Eds.), *Deleuze and the postcolonial* (pp. 78–102). Edinburgh: Edinburgh University Press.

Bonta, M., & Protevi, J. (2004). *Deleuze and geophilosophy*. Edinburgh: Edinburgh University Press.

DeLanda, M. (1999). Deleuze, diagrams, and the open-ended becoming of the world. In E. Grosz (Ed.), *Becomings: Explorations in time, memory, and futures* (pp. 29–41). Ithaca, NY & London: Cornell University Press.

DeLanda, M. (2006). *A new philosophy of society: Assemblage theory and social complexity*. London & New York: Continuum.

Deleuze, G. (1988a). *Spinoza: Practical philosophy* (R. Hurley, Trans.). San Francisco: City Lights Books.

Deleuze, G. (1988b). *Foucault* (S. Hand, Trans.). Minneapolis, MN & London: University of Minnesota Press.

Deleuze, G. (1994). *Difference and repetition* (P. Patton, Trans.). New York: Columbia University Press.

Deleuze, G., & Guattari, F. (1986). *Kafka: Toward a minor literature* (D. Polan, Trans.). Minneapolis, MN & London: University of Minnesota Press.

Deleuze, G., & Guattari, F. (1987). *A thousand plateaus: Capitalism and schizophrenia* (B. Massumi, Trans.). Minneapolis, MN & London: University of Minnesota Press.

Deleuze, G., & Guattari, F. (1994). *What is philosophy?* (H. Tomlinson & G. Burchell, Trans.). New York: Columbia University Press.

Ellsworth, E. (2005). *Places of learning: Media, architecture, pedagogy*. New York & London: RoutledgeFalmer.

Gatens, M. (1996). Through a Spinozist lens: Ethology, difference, power. In P. Patton (Ed.), *Deleuze: a critical reader* (pp. 162–187). Oxford: Blackwell.

Green, B. (1998). Teaching for difference: Learning theory and post-critical pedagogy. In D. Buckingham (Ed.), *Teaching popular culture: Beyond radical pedagogy* (pp. 177–197). London: University College London.

Kaufman, E. (2001). *The delirium of praise: Bataille, Blanchot, Deleuze, Foucault, Klossowski*. Baltimore and London: The Johns Hopkins University Press.

Lévy, P. (1998). *Becoming virtual: Reality in the digital age* (R. Bonnono, Trans.). Plenum Publishing Corporation: New York and London.

EDUCATION AND THE POLITICS OF BECOMING

Lusted, D. (1986). Why pedagogy? *Screen, 27*(5), 2–14.

Marcus, G.E., & Saka, E. (2006). Assemblage. Theory. *Culture and Society, 23*(2–3), 101–106.

Massumi, B. (2002). *Parables for the virtual: Movement, affect, sensation.* Durham and London: Duke University Press.

O'Sullivan, S. (2004). Friendship as community: From ethics to politics. *"Takkekortet: The written acknowledgement* (pp. 20–21). Arhus, Denmark: Rum46.

Patton, P. (2000). *Deleuze and the political.* London & New York: Routledge.

Phillips, J. (2006). Agencement/Assemblage. *Theory Culture and Society, 23*(2–3), 108–109.

Probyn, E. (2004). Teaching bodies: Affects in the classroom. *Body & Society, 10*(4), 21–43.

Simon, R. (1992). *Teaching against the grain: Texts for a pedagogy of possibility.* New York & London: Bergin & Garvey.

Stengers, I. (2005a). Deleuze and Guattari's last enigmatic message. *Angelaki: Journal of the Theoretical Humanities, 10*(2), 151–167.

Stengers, I. (2005b). The cosmopolitical proposal. In B. Latour & P. Weibel (Eds.), *Making things public: Atmospheres of democracy* (pp. 994–1003). Cambridge, MA & London: The MIT Press.

Stengers, I. (2008). Experimenting with refrains: Subjectivity and the challenge of escaping modern dualism. *Subjectivity, 22*(1), 38–59.

Stivale, C. (2000). The folds of friendship: Derrida-Deleuze-Foucault. *Angelaki: Journal of the Theoretical Humanities, 5*(2), 3–15.

Varela, F. (1999). *Ethical know-how: Action, wisdom, and cognition.* Stanford, CA: Stanford University Press.

Venn, C. (2006). A note on assemblage. *Theory Culture and Society, 26*(2–3), 107–108.

Watkins, M. (2006). Pedagogic affect/effect: Embodying a desire to learn. *Pedagogies, 1*(4), 269–282.

Watkins, M. (2007). Disparate bodies: The role of the teacher in contemporary pedagogic practice. *British Journal of Sociology of Education, 28*(6), 767–781.

Weinstein, C. (1998). 'I want to be nice, but I have to be mean': Exploring prospective teachers' conceptions of caring and order. *Teaching and Teacher Education, 14*(2), 153–163.

Zembylas, M. (2007a). *Five pedagogies, A thousand possibilities: Struggling for hope and transformation in education.* Rotterdam: Sense Publishers.

Zembylas, M. (2007b). The specters of bodies and affects in the classroom: A rhizo-ethological approach. *Pedagogy Culture & Society, 15*(1), 19–35.

Uprooting music education pedagogies and curricula: Becoming-musician and the Deleuzian refrain

Elizabeth Gould

> Based on the British choralism movement of the nineteenth century, the historical legacy of music education in Canada and the US is one of social control. By the twentieth century, North American music educators used choral singing and music listening to teach music literacy skills to groups assumed to be in need of 'improvement': the working class, immigrants, and school-age children. Deploying so-called good music to improve moral character and instill national pride, their goal was to create docile citizens content with their place in society and committed to hard work. Exclusions, stereotyping, and arbitrary standards in music education still construct acceptable musics and musical behaviours along lines of race, gender, class, and sexuality that support the status quo and maintain social order. Uprooting music education practices from these manifestations of the Deleuzian refrain that constrains the profession opens spaces for transformative musical and educational potentialities.

Music instruction in Canadian and US schools is typically characterized by a small number of pedagogical approaches that imply and apply specific curricula and musical materials. For elementary general music instruction, music educators tend to rely on personalized combinations of teaching methodologies associated with composers Zoltán Kodály, Carl Orff, and Émile Jaques-Dalcroze, each of whom in the first half of the twentieth century developed a unique perspective for teaching music. Secondary general music classes typically combine the teaching of music history and theory with composition using alternative notational strategies, and performance activities. Meanwhile, performance-based classes at both elementary and secondary levels usually utilize a diagnostic teaching approach by which the teacher (conductor) leads a student ensemble in singing or playing instruments, diagnoses performance errors, prescribes remediation, and checks for 'understanding', which is to say, accurate performance. Notable exceptions to these approaches do exist, of course, as music educators gradually respond to diverse student populations and turn toward approaches associated with informal learning and popular music, but these pedagogical approaches are exceptional more because of their paucity than their success.

Since it was first introduced in Canadian and US schools during the nineteenth century, the purpose of music education has been to elevate moral character and bring (good) music to students (Green & Vogan, 1991; Keene, 1982/2009). Initially comprised of curricula focused on singing and reading and notating music at all levels (in the service of moral uplift and social integration), school music curricula expanded by the twentieth century to include listening, moving, playing instruments, and knowing music history and theory. The goal of the still mostly performance-based instruction associated with these curricula has been to mold students into musicians, to hopefully become-musician, whether as producers or consumers. The effect, however, molds students into worthy citizens of the nation-state, what philosopher Gilles Deleuze would refer to as State music education. These music-citizens typically read standard notation at a basic level, sing or play modestly, and know minimal music history and theory. Meanwhile, continuing exclusions, stereotyping, and standards construct legitimate music and music roles along lines of race, gender, class, and sexuality. Within systems of exclusion and control, music education pedagogies and curricula focus on what Deleuze and Guattari (1987) refer to as the *refrain* (as opposed to music).

The Deleuzian refrain consists of musical materials that stabilize and create a territory. For musicians, it includes territories of genre and stylistic practices and conventions on which music performances and compositions stabilize. For music educators, the Deleuzian refrain includes territories of music concepts and performance skills on which pedagogies and curricula stabilize. Delineating these territories for students is what music educators 'do'. In this doing, however, 'the potentiality of the "fascist" danger [of] music'[1] (p. 302) is actualized through various forms of musical, social, pedagogical, and curricular control, circumventing movement that would deterritorialize the Deleuzian refrain from established concepts, forms, and practices. The problem of music and music education, then, is the Deleuzian refrain. Conceiving music pedagogies and curricula in terms of music rather than the Deleuzian refrain moves the focus of music pedagogies and curricula to sonorous potentialities of 'creative and active' expression between students, teachers, and music. This movement opens spaces for confronting music teaching and learning in a politics of becoming that 'voices' students and teachers with music in pedagogical and curricular collaborations of becoming-musician. Beginning with a brief historical overview of how music education in Canada and the US continues to be implicated in discourses of social control, I describe Deleuze's concept of music as deterritorializations of the (Deleuzian) refrain, and argue that music education practices and discourses of music (as opposed to the Deleuzian refrain) hold dynamic potentialities to vitalize music and education pedagogies and curricula in terms of all those who teach, learn, and make music through them.

Exclusions, stereotyping, and standards in music education

A variety of processes, based for the most part on stereotyping, are in place in music education that result in exclusions of musical roles (ways of music-making, or musician-ing), musics, individuals and social groups. Indeed music education historically has been deeply implicated in social control of purportedly inferior or 'needy' social groups through religious, civic, and colonialist discourses of salvation. So-called educational and musical standards are only the most recent discourse of controlling not only what is taught and learned in school music education, as well as how it is taught and learned, but who teaches and who learns it, designating and naming in the end, who is musical and who is not.

By the mid-nineteeth century, music instruction in Britain, on which much North American music education is modeled, had already proven effective as a means of social control. John Hullah, considered to be 'the most celebrated music educator' (Olwage, 2005, p. 26) of the time, held mass singing classes as a means of 'improvement' for London's poor, disadvantaged, and working classes with the goal of making them industrious and loyal patriotic citizens. Using James Curwen's[2] tonic sol-fa system of associating syllables (do, re, mi, fa, sol, la, ti) with music pitches, Hullah is credited with teaching some 50,000 children of the working classes to sing and read music as part of a music education movement that came to be known as 'choralism'. While music may have been a means of entertainment and enjoyment for the upper classes, for the lower classes, participating in choral music practices was integral to both uplifting and civilizing them—while discouraging labour unrest and worker uprisings. Indeed, choralism was so successful in controlling disenfranchised groups in England that later in the nineteenth century it was implemented wholesale as a means to counter the so-called 'Black peril' perceived to be threatening white colonizers and missionaries in British colonial South Africa (Olwage, 2005).

In the US and Canada during the late eighteenth and first half of the nineteenth centuries, more or less formal music instruction was undertaken first by ministers and later by itinerant musicians, most of whom came from Britain and Europe, in what was known as 'singing schools' in order to improve congregational singing in church and individual moral character outside of it. Choral societies, employing the same general goals, emerged throughout the nineteenth century, even as music was introduced for much the same reasons into the curricula of many North American public schools. Indeed, by the end of the nineteenth century, public discourses in Canada and the US imbued music with capacities that could not only reform society, but could also instill in citizens humanitarian and patriotic values (Ahlquist, 1997; Donakowski, 1977; Eaklor, 1982, 1994; Levine, 1988; Musselman, 1971; Whitesitt, 1997).[3]

During the Progressive Era around the turn of the twentieth century, in part as a function of the settlement house movement, public attention and concern turned specifically to recent immigrants and members of the working underclass living in cities. Music reformers, as they were known, acted on the belief that *good music* would bring comfort to people in need and induce them to change what was framed as the wretched circumstances of their lives. Led by 'a small group of professional music teachers', these music reformers, 'a loose coalition of musicians, composers, music critics, industrialists, journalists, social workers, civic leaders, and women's clubs' (Campbell, 2000, p. 260), championed what they characterized as good music as a means to ease the transition of immigrants into white, Christian North American society, as well as to alleviate their—and the poor's—purported moral and social shortcomings. Although never precisely defined, good music certainly included music of the Western art music canon, and most decidedly excluded jazz and ragtime, what was thought of at the time as 'degenerate' music associated with Black Americans. With the help of professional organizations such as the Music Supervisors National Conference (the precursor of MENC: The National Association for Music Education), so-called good music was provided to those designated in need through free and low-cost concerts performed in outdoor public venues by community bands and orchestras. In addition to members of the underclass, and immigrants and their children living in or near urban social settlement houses, other audiences targeted for concerts of 'good music' included all students attending public schools, factory workers, prisoners, and military personnel. Through discourses of pity and salvation, and convinced that the social problems and moral inadequacies falsely associated with immigrants and the poor would destabilize society and promulgate social unrest, music reformers thus made 'aesthetics ... social policy' (Campbell, 2000, p. 262). Their motivations, grounded in traditional liberal theory, included compassion and concern for social, cultural, and political *others* uneasily juxtaposed with terror and trepidation of them.

> In the end, music reformers forever spiraled in an ideological circle, doubling back on themselves as they struggled to combine their own deep concern for those less fortunate with their equally abiding desire to reinforce their own values, their own moral vision, and their own definition of democracy. (2000, p. 262)

The ultimate goal of music reformers and music education in general during much of the first half of the twentieth century, then, was to assimilate newcomers and the poor into the great American melting pot or Canadian mosaic, while asserting white, Christian middle-class values and ideals of nationhood.

In music education currently, vestiges of these discourses remain in far more subtle and nuanced forms. Jazz styles of the first half of the twentieth century are institutionalized in school music curricula, and with the Fox television show, *Glee*, show choirs that initially proliferated with jazz programs in the 1970s, are making a strong comeback. Multicultural music (commonly referred to as 'world music') and concerns about diversity comprise an increasingly large proportion of contemporary music education discourses (see for instance, Burton & McFarland, 2009; Jordan, 1992; Moore, 2009; Quesada & Volk, 1997; Volk, 1993). Patricia Shehan Campbell alone has developed a veritable juggernaut of research and resources related to these areas (see, for instance, Campbell, 1991, 1996, 2004), as well as a plethora of co-authored texts, perhaps most notably the online electronic book, *Cultural Diversity in Music Education: Directions and Challenges for the 21st Century* (2010), and music resources, many of which are published through World Music Press and MENC: The National Association for Music Education.

Similarly, interest in composition and improvisation, pedagogical approaches based on creativity and/or discovery, and ongoing critiques of music education practices, discourses, and taken-for-granted pedagogical approaches along with their originators (Abramo, 2010; Benedict, 2009; Regelski, 2002) comprise a slowly increasing proportion of music education research.[4] Nevertheless, music students and teachers, teaching materials, instrument selections, and occupations mostly remain stratified by gender and/or race (see for instance, Abeles, 2009; Gould, 2003; Gustafson, 2008; Hawkins, 2007; Kinney, 2010; Koza, 2003; Stewart, 1991; VanWeelden & McGee, 2007). Structural obstacles that constrain change to ongoing exclusions include audition processes and evaluation criteria, music repertoire, and of course, music and education standards, all of which function within and are expressions of discourses related to who is and who is not musical, as well as what is and what is not good music (Benedict, 2006, 2007; Branscome, 2005; Horsely, 2009;

Laird, 2009; Popkewitz & Gustafson, 2002). Concerns raised by this research may be addressed by conceiving music and musicality in light of potentialities offered by Deleuzian concepts of becoming and difference.

The Deleuzian refrain

As a philosopher concerned with the interesting, the remarkable, and the important (May, 2003), Deleuze's (and Guattari's) concept of music provides challenging and provocative ways of thinking as performing, composing, conducting, teaching, and learning music. A 'double articulation [music] brings together a block of content (the refrain) and a form of expression (becoming)' (Buchanan, 2004, pp. 15, 16) in an 'active, creative operation which consists of deterritorializing the refrain' (Deleuze & Guattari, 1987, p. 300). The Deleuzian concept of *refrain* is similar to, but not the same as, a musical refrain or chorus sung or played between contrasting musical sections (typically verses) as a 'little return', what musicians know as *ritournelle* (p. 302). Like the chorus of a song (the return of familiar musical material),[5] the Deleuzian refrain constitutes a moment of stability in chaos. In addition to tunes we might hum when we are afraid, examples of the Deleuzian refrain include folk songs, national anthems, sacred hymns, even bird songs—as all function to delineate a territory (Murphy & Smith, 2001). It is comprised of musical materials: 'properly musical content, the ... content proper to music' (Deleuze & Guattari, 1987, p. 299), and delineates sites not only to which music returns (music compositions that serve a specific purposes such as national anthems, or sections of music compositions such as the chorus in a song), but sites to which musicians of all kinds (performers, composers, conductors) and music educators and students return (music genres and styles and pedagogies and curricula, respectively), as well.

The Deleuzian refrain is comprised of three aspects, expressed succinctly, 'A point of stability, a circle of property, and an opening to the outside' (Bogue, 2003, p. 17). With the first aspect the Deleuzian refrain functions as a territorializing force that coheres and stabilizes music structurally and relationally through, for example specific recognizable forms such as song form (chorus/verse/chorus), and the interaction of melodies and harmonies moving (resolving) toward anticipated points of rest. In terms of the second aspect, the content of the Deleuzian refrain delineates a territory that may be conceived as the musical materials and practices of any particular style or genre, notwithstanding Deleuze and Guattari's (1987) emphasis on Western art music. With the last aspect, musical materials of the refrain 'open onto a future', and join cosmic forces as a means to launch forth, 'hazard[ing] an improvisation' (p. 311) that nonetheless reterritorializes through processes of decoding and recoding structures and relations. To summarize,

> Sometimes [with the first aspect] one goes from chaos to the threshold of a territorial assemblage ... Sometimes [with the second aspect] one organizes the assemblage ... Sometimes [with the third aspect] one leaves the territorial assemblages for other assemblages, or for somewhere else entirely ... And all three at once. Forces of chaos, terrestrial forces, cosmic forces: all of these confront each other and converge in the territorial refrain. (1987, p. 312)

EDUCATION AND THE POLITICS OF BECOMING

Inasmuch as it 'is territorial, territorializing, and reterritorializing' (p. 300) the problematic field of music is the Deleuzian refrain, the opening and extending of which Deleuze and Guattari characteristically portray as an 'adventure'.

What music does, by contrast, is make the Deleuzian refrain 'a deterritorialized content for a deterritorializing form of expression' (p. 300). Creative and active, the Deleuzian refrain is deterritorialized as music when strict musical forms are opened up and exceeded; when melodies and harmonies do not resolve or conclude, escaping structural, formal, and aural (horizontal and vertical) relations through transversal lines of pure sonorous material (Murphy & Smith, 2001); when rhythm outplays meter as 'the Unequal or the Incommensurable' (Deleuze & Guattari, 1987, p. 313). For example, the rhythmic experiments of twentieth century composer Olivier Messiaen, known for his use of birdsongs in his music compositions, created openings to the cosmos, as he converted 'sound matter . . . capable of harnessing . . . unthinkable, invisible nonsonorous forces' (p. 343) in ways that seem to make audible cosmic time, such as the time of human evolution. Similarly, Edgar Varèse, known for his composition, *Ionisation* (1929–1931), the first work in the Western art music tradition composed exclusively for percussion instruments, as well as his use of electronic music sources, created with his music, 'A *sound machine* (not a machine for reproducing sounds), which molecularizes and atomizes, ionizes sound matter, and harnesses a cosmic energy' (Deleuze & Guattari, p. 343, emphasis in original). Varèse's sound machine not only makes processes of sound themselves audible, but it connects listeners with material and forces beyond sound. Both composers connected the so-called 'properly' musical with the extramusical, and their music demonstrates how the refrain is decoded or deterritorialized 'within an unfolding activity' (Bogue, 2003, p. 74) of music.

So 'what musicians [and by implication what music educators] do should be musical, it should be written in music' (p. 300), performed in music, heard, danced, read, taught, learned, and engaged in music as musicians and music educators decode or disrupt conventional, rooted (territorial) relations of the Deleuzian refrain. This occurs not only through compositional practices of composers but through a variety of music and educational processes connected with lived musical experience. As Deleuze and Guattari (1987) argue, LeRoi Jones (Amiri Baraka) demonstrates in his book, *Black People* (1963) that slaves deterritorialized the territorialized Deleuzian refrain of African work songs by resignifying them in terms of the conditions of their forced labour while in bondage in the US. Although the songs were reterritorialized by white men singing them in 'blackface' during minstrel shows later in the nineteenth century, black Americans deterritorialized them yet again beginning early in the twentieth century, along with songs and dances of whites, 'transforming and translating' (p. 137) the musical material into new (forbidden) dances and musical forms such as the blues. With this example, educators deterritorialize the Deleuzian refrain when they participate with students in confronting and engaging these historiographies and musics associated with them in ways that exceed received narratives of slavery, resistance, and oppression, extending the problematic field of education in music beyond internal, as well as external, boundaries of control.

Providing lines of flight as it disrupts and disengages, music cannot be the sole province of humans: 'the universe, the cosmos, is made of refrains' (Deleuze & Guattari, 1987, p. 309), even as the very stars are musicians. These are ancient ideas

80

among musicians, of course, expressed even in rationalist Western music through Pythagorus' music of the spheres which asserted that the spacing of the planets had the same ratios as the sounds produced by a plucked string, and Boethius' *musica mundane*, which described music of the universe and the natural world: 'The question [then] is more what is not musical in human beings, and what already is musical in nature' (p. 309). Found everywhere, music exceeds humans and human activity even as teaching and learning music exceed music, pedagogies and curricula. Music is in the world around us, in and as the singing of whales, the dancing of bees, the vibrations of tectonic plates. In the cosmos, it is beyond all this and what we have yet to imagine—or hear in processes of becoming. Thinking of music itself as a form of Deleuzian becoming provides a means to conceive and inform how we create, perform, teach and learn it.

Becoming relates to space and time between in terms of both (all) directions at once, eluding and eliding the present, as it 'does not tolerate the separation or the distinction of before and after, or of past and future' (Deleuze, 1990, p. 1). Pure becoming includes infinite assemblages that encompass entire spectrums of time, quantities, actions, thoughts, and results, even while transcending their limits. It is always double and never imitative. Rather than mimetic, becoming-*like* or becoming-*as* musician, or processual, becoming-*toward* (Colebrook, 2000) musician, becoming is perhaps most usefully conceived as becoming-*alongside* (Bogue, 2003) musician, where becoming is understood as 'an unspecifiable, unpredictable disruption of codes that takes place alongside' (p. 35), in this case, musicians and notions of musicality, what I think of as musician-ness. Because becoming expresses transformative potential, all becomings are 'fluid movements of creativity that subvert the dominant' (May, 2003, p. 149) structures and relations of control related to both education and music.

Perhaps most notably for this discussion, however, becomings are creative acts of difference in the Deleuzian sense of difference based not on identity (as in not-the-same-as), but difference in itself; difference in kind rather than quality (variation). While identities do not create difference (not-the-same-as), it is nevertheless on the ground of difference that identities are founded—even as difference is not located in those identities. Instead, difference unfolds in time, 'beneath and within the passing identities to which it gives rise' (May, 2003, p. 146), as becoming, where that which 'becomes is not [a] specific something or set of somethings, but the chaos which produces all somethings' (p. 147). As this form of becoming, music incites potentialities of becoming-musician beyond the Deleuzian refrain characteristic of music education that would specifically stereotype, limit, and exclude.

Deleuzian uprootings in music education

In their introduction to *A Thousand Plateaus* (1987), Deleuze and Guattari argue against the rootedness of tree logic, an '"arborescent model" of thought' (Massumi, 1987, p. xii), that is based on 'a logic of tracing and reproduction' (Deleuze & Guattari, 1987, p. 12). Incapable of moving thinking about music or education, for instance, arborescent thought uses '[b]inary logic and biunivocal relationships' (Deleuze & Guattari, 1987, p. 5) dependent on unities or identities that result from linearity and circularity. Further, it is characterized by concepts that have 'a shared, internal essence: the self-resemblance at the basis of identity' (Massumi, 1987, p. xi).

Rhizomatic thought, by contrast, is described in terms of the rhizome, a completely interconnected underground root system that grows sideways and moves horizontally and outward rather than vertically and upward like arborescent thought does. As an 'acentered, nonhierarchical, nonsignifying system' (Deleuze & Guattari, 1987, p. 21) with no end or beginning, the rhizome exists in the middle, the in-between, where things accelerate or intensify. Although it may be broken at any point, the rhizome creates new connections and continues to spread through other multiple lines 'of flight or deterritorialization' (p. 21). Rhizomatic movement in this space consists of comings and goings through 'multiple entryways and exits and its own lines of flight' (p. 21). Similarly, rhizomatic lines of flight connect the theoretical and political, include experiences from everyday life, conflate so-called high and low culture, and mix expressive modes, which describes the transdisciplinary nature of rhizomatic thought. Not only are ideas borrowed from one discipline to another, the hierarchies on which they are organized are deliberately subverted or deterritorialized (Braidotti, 1994, p. 37). Indeed, rhizomatic thought both accounts for change and is, itself, constituted as change. Its traces are mapped in ways that are 'always detachable, connectable, reversible, modifiable' (Deleuze & Guattari, 1987, p. 21), allowing for fluidity and multiplicity, as opposed to the linearity and hierarchical of arborescent thought.

Content and achievement standards in music education, government and/or school board mandated curricula, and over-reliance on pre-planned, pre-determined pedagogical approaches all function in terms of the Deleuzian refrain as points of stability. In combination, they delimit the content of the refrain's territorial music education, a profession in North America that conceives itself as continuously under threat. This 'siege mentality' is evidenced by the cultivation of corporate partnerships by MENC: The National Association for Music Education in the US as part of its near-obsessive focus on advocacy, as well as the exclusive advocacy activities of what is arguably the most influential music education organization in Canada, the Coalition for Music Education. Its stated mission is to 'promote the importance of music in our schools and in our lives'.[6]

It is perhaps not surprising that the music education profession in Canada and the US trends toward conventionality, ordinariness, safety, and most notably, exclusions, as it subjects musical materials—and people—to order, control, and systematic rules. Even excursions to the outside demonstrated by innovative teachers, teaching materials, and curricula directed toward student creativity and expression reterritorialize the Deleuzian refrain when, for instance, 'other music' (music of *others*) is used as a 'hook' to move students on to 'good music'; when 'other music' is taught through standard music education approaches involving traditional instru- mental and vocal performing techniques and performance practices; when 'other music' or student compositions and other creative musical projects are vehicles for teaching what music educators commonly refer to as the elements of music (melody, harmony, rhythm, timbre, texture, form). In other words, innovation stabilizes and territorializes the Deleuzian refrain when difference is deployed as identity or sameness.

Deterritorializations that shape musical materials of the Deleuzian refrain as music in processes of becoming-musician constitute the work of musicians and music educators. These processes are rhizomatic, which is to say interconnected rather than hierarchical, conjunctive rather than representational, constituted as alliances rather than allegiances. Rather than stable entities that undergo change, music students embody confluences of interconnected and constantly changing combinations of forces and flows that are physiological, auditory, and socio-cultural. They become-musician with educators through immersion in and apprenticeship to music—to processes of becoming-music that voice the auditory events of their imaginations in the context of their lived experiences of themselves, their schools and communities, the natural world, and the cosmos. Music educators and students deterritorializing the Deleuzian refrain transform and incite potentialities of all voices, engaging difference in itself through alchemies of 'a thousand tiny [revolutions]' (Deleuze & Guattari, 1987, p. 213). The creativity of becoming-musician through our encounters with and in music opens spaces for its proliferation as it releases the Deleuzian refrain.

Music is musical because it can; that is what it *does*, because it is inherently creative, because music itself is becoming, and so are we through it. Clearly, musicians and music educators engage in musical activities, just as teachers and students engage in music education, teaching and learning music even as we make music. Engaging becoming-musician in this way, transformatively through and as difference, creates 'a ubiquitous experimental *bricolage*' (Bogue, 2003, p. 69) without any grand design or goal, existing only to invent, to explore, to activate. As musicians and teachers interacting with students and music, we look for what more is in music and our musical encounters; for what we all bring to music and our engagements with music—in order to decode music and social relations as they exist and recode them in new and different configurations only to decode them again—as we create and are creative together in and through music.

Encounters with music and music education certainly involve more than music elements or materials of music, the Deleuzian refrain—wherever it may be grounded, however it is territorial, and whatever it territorializes. These encounters also include connections with people, their interactions, historical moments, emotional dimensions, and political becomings beyond identity-based collectives. Becoming-musician or claiming/producing subjectivity in and through music is comprised of interactions of becoming alongside musician, in all the myriad of ways musician may be enacted. Rather than imitating musician behaviours or roles, becoming-musician consists of instantiations of musician that embody and enact music, making becoming-musician, or musican-ness as creative as music itself.

Disruptions that create new—different—and transitory points of stability, transgress and delineate shifting innovative territories, and exceed them, extend music to and even beyond sonority itself. Releasing music 'in the Cosmos ... is more important than building a new system' (Deleuze & Guattari, 1987, p. 350), such as notational scores, lesson plans, curricula, and pedagogical methodologies. Systems like these are sedentary, rooted; they do not *do* anything. Music, by contrast, as adventuring in infinite personal, intellectual, and social ways by teachers and students, involves risk and unpredictability, as well as dangers: 'black holes, closures, paralysis of the finger and auditory hallucinations, Schumann's madness, cosmic force gone *bad*, a note that pursues you, a sound that transfixes you' (p. 350, emphasis in original). Educators may think of these dangers in terms of predetermined goals and objectives, governmental mandates, professional expectations, students' resistance, stereotypes and exclusions. And even though potentialities for becoming are always already inhered in our encounters with music and each other,

EDUCATION AND THE POLITICS OF BECOMING

even with assurances that 'the cosmic force [is] already present in the material', we also know that 'we can never be sure we will be strong enough, for we have no system' (p. 350). In response to this uncertainty, we cultivate '*active* acceptance of the inevitability of misunderstanding [difference]', and quite literally walk out on Peggy Phelan's (1993/2005, p. 174, emphasis in original) 'rackety bridge'. Precarious as it is, this bridge between, a swaying becoming-bridge, is the only site where deterritorialized teaching, learning, and music-making together can occur. Certainly difficult,

> ... The inevitability of our failure to remain walking *on* the bridge (when the storms come we keep rushing to the deceptive 'safety' of one side or the other) guarantees only the necessity of hope. (1993/2005, p. 174, emphasis in original)

It is this very hope, however, that propels us back out on the bridge, alongside becomings. We have only what we do, who and how we are, who and how we become as teachers, learners, musicians. Deleuze and Guattari (1987) suggest that we have 'only lines and movement'; and, they add, 'Schumann' (p. 350). I might proffer that educators have only encounters and music—deterritorialized interfaces of teaching and learning. And, I would add, students.

Notes

1. By which Deleuze and Guattari mean the refrain.
2. Curwen borrowed heavily from, adapted and popularized as his own Sarah Glover's Norwich sol-fa method (Bennett, 1984).
3. These discourses are not so different today. At the 2010 Race, Erasure, and Equity in Music Education Conference, hosted by the Consortium on Research on Equity in Music Education (CRÈME), keynote speaker Gloria Ladson-Billings spoke at some length about the 'humanizing' effects of music—as an argument not only for teaching it in schools, but for teaching it for those very effects which are assumed to be inherent in it. Her comments were met with rapturous applause from the audience comprised of mostly university music education professors and graduate students.
4. See, as well, websites of professional organizations such as Gender Research in Music Education-International (http://post.queensu.ca/~grime/), and the MayDay Group (http://www.maydaygroup.org/).
5. It is, of course, not by accident that the most memorable melodic material, commonly known as the 'hook' of most popular music is invariably the chorus (refrain).
6. See http://www.coalitionformusiced.ca/; also may be accessed (as of 13 July 2011) at the url, weallneedmusic.ca.

References

Abeles, H. (2009). Are musical instrument gender associations changing? *Journal of Research in Music Education, 57*(2), 127–139.

Abramo, J. (2010). Historically conceptualizing Orff Schulwerk: Recapitulation theory and völkish thought. Paper presented 22 October at the Race, Erasure, and Equity in Music Education Conference, Madison, WI.

Ahlquist, K. (1997). *Democracy at the opera: Music, theater, and culture in New York City, 1815–1860*. Urbana: University of Illinois Press.

Benedict, C. (2006). Chasing legitimacy: The US national standards viewed through a critical theorist framework. *Music Education Review, 8*(1), 17–32.

Benedict, C. (2007). Naming our reality: Negotiating and creating meaning in the margin. *Philosophy of Music Education Review, 15*(1), 23–35.

Benedict, C. (2009). Processes of alienation: Marx, Orff, and Kodály. *British Journal of Music Education, 26*(2), 213–224.

Bennett, P.D. (1984). Sarah Glover: A forgotten pioneer in music education. *Journal of Research in Music Education, 32*(1), 49–64.

Bogue, R. (2003). *Deleuze on music, painting, and the arts.* New York and London: Routledge.

Braidotti, R. (1994). *Nomadic subjects: Embodiment and sexual difference in contemporary feminist theory.* New York: Columbia University Press.

Branscome, E. (2005). A historical analysis of textbook development in American music: Education and the impetus for the national standards for music education. *Arts Education Policy Review, 107*(2), 13–19.

Buchanan, I. (2004). Introduction: Deleuze and music. In I. Buchanan & M. Swiboda (Eds.), *Deleuze and music* (pp. 1–19). Edinburgh, UK: Edinburgh University Press.

Burton, J., & McFarland, A. (2009). Multicultural resources. *General Music Today, 22*(2), 30–33.

Campbell, G.J. (2000). 'A higher mission than merely to please the ear': Music and social reform in America, 1900–1925. *The Musical Quarterly, 84*(2), 259–286.

Campbell, P.S. (1991). *Lessons from the world: A cross-cultural guide to music teaching and learning.* New York: Schirmer Books.

Campbell, P.S. (Ed.). (1996). *Music in cultural context: Eight views on world music education.* Reston, VA: Music Educators National Conference.

Campbell, P.S. (2004). *Teaching music globally: Experiencing music, expressing culture.* New York: Oxford University Press.

Campbell, P.S., Drummond, J., & Dunbar-Hall, P. (Eds.). 2010. *Cultural diversity in music education: Directions and challenges for the 21st century. eBooks.com*: the digital bookstore, http://www.ebooks.com/ebooks/book_details.asp?IID=298228, accessed 4 November 2010.

Colebrook, C. (2000). Introduction. In I. Buchanan & C. Colebrook (Eds.), *Deleuze and feminist theory* (pp. 1–17). Edinburgh: UK, Edinburgh University Press.

Deleuze, G. (1990). *The logic of sense.* (M. Lester, Trans., with C. Stivale, & C.V. Boundas). New York: Columbia University Press.

Deleuze, G., & Guattari, F. (1987). *A thousand plateaus: Capitalism and schizophrenia.* (B. Massumi, Trans.). Minneapolis and London: University of Minnesota Press.

Donakowski, C.L. (1977). *A muse for the masses: Ritual and music in an age of democratic revolution, 1770-1870.* Chicago: University of Chicago Press.

Eaklor, V.L. (1982). Music in American society, 1815-1860: An intellectual history. Unpublished Ph.D. dissertation, Washington University, St. Louis, MO.

Eaklor, V.L. (1994). The gendered origins of the American musician. *The Quarterly Journal of Music Teaching and Learning, 4/5*(4-1), 40–46.

Gould, E.S. (2003). Cultural contexts of exclusion: Women college band directors. *Research and Issues in Music Education, 1*(1), http://www.stthomas.edu/rimonline/vol1gould.htm. Accessed 9 November 2010.

Green, J.P., & Vogan, N.F. (1991). *Music education in Canada: A historical account.* Toronto: University of Toronto Press.

Gustafson, R. (2008). Drifters and the dancing mad: The public school music curriculum and the fabrication of boundaries for participation. *Curriculum Inquiry, 38*(3), 267–297.

Hawkins, P.J. (2007). What boys and girls learn through song: A content analysis of gender traits and sex bias in two choral classroom textbooks. *Research and Issues in Music Education, 5*(1), 1–8.

Horsely, S. (2009). The politics of public accountability: Implications for centralized music education policy development and implementation. *Arts Education Policy Review, 110*(4), 6–12.

Jones, L. (1963). *Blues people.* New York: William Morrow & Company.

Jordan, J. (1992). Multicultural music education in a pluralistic society. In R. Colwell (Ed.), *Handbook of research on music teaching and learning: A project of the Music Educators National Conference* (pp. 735–748). New York: Schirmer Books.

Keene, J.P. (1982/2009). *A history of music education in the United States.* Centennial, CO: Glenbridge Publishing.

Kinney, D.W. (2010). Selected nonmusic predictors of urban students decisions to enroll and persist in middle school band programs. *Journal of Research in Music Education*, *57*(4), 334–351.

Koza, J. (2003). *Stepping across: Four interdisciplinary studies on education and cultural practices*. New York: Peter Lang.

Laird, S. (2009). Musical hunger: A philosophical testimonial of miseducation. *Philosophy of Music Education Review*, *17*(1), 4–21.

Levine, L. (1988). *Highbrow, lowbrow: The emergence of cultural hierarchy in America*. Cambridge, MA: Harvard University Press.

May, T. (2003). When is a Deleuzian becoming? *Continental Philosophy*, *36*, 139–153.

Massumi, B. (1987). Translator's foreword: Pleasures of philosophy. In G. Deleuze, & F. Guattari, *A thousand plateaus: Capitalism and schizophrenia* (pp. ix–xv). Minneapolis and London: University of Minnesota Press.

Moore, J.E. (2009). Multicultural music education and Texas elementary music teachers: Attitudes, resources, and utilization. Unpublished Ed. D. dissertation, Lamar University, Beaumont, TX.

Murphy, T.S., & Smith, D.W. (2001). What I hear is thinking too: Deleuze and Guattari go pop. *ECHO: a music centered journal*, *3*(1), http://www.echo.ucla.edu/volume3-issue1/smithmurphy/index.html, Accessed 7 February, 2010.

Musselman, J.A. (1971). *Music in the cultured generation: A social history of music in America, 1870–1900*. Evanston, IL: Northwestern University Press.

Olwage, G. (2005). Discipline and choralism: The birth of musical colonialism. In A.J. Randall (Ed.), *Music, power, and politics* (pp. 25–46). New York and London: Routledge.

Phelan, P. (1993/2005). *Unmarked: The politics of performance*. London and New York: Routledge.

Popkewitz, T.S., & Gustafson, R. (2002). Standards of music education and the easily administered child/citizen: The alchemy of pedagogy and social inclusion/exclusion. *Philosophy of music education review*, *10*(1), 80–91.

Quesada, M.A., & Volk, T.M. (1997). World musics and music education: A review of research 1973–1993. *Bulletin of the Council for Research in Music Education*, *131*, 44–66.

Regelski, T.A. (2002). On methodolatry and music teaching as critical and reflective practice. *Philosophy of Music Education Review*, *10*(2), 102–123.

Stewart, C. (1991). Who takes music? Investigating access to high school music as a function of social and school factors. Unpublished Ph.D. dissertation. Ann Arbor, University of Michigan.

VanWeelden, K., & McGee, I.R. (2007). The influence of music style and conductor race on perceptions of ensemble and conductor performance. *International Journal of Music Education*, *25*(1), 7–17.

Volk, T.M. (1993). The history and development of multicultural music education as evidenced in the *Music Educators Journal*, 1967–1992. *Journal of Research in Music Education*, *41*(2), 137–155.

Whitesitt, L. (1997). Women as 'keepers of culture': Music clubs, community concert series, and symphony orchestras. In R.P. Locke & C. Barr (Eds.), *Cultivating music in America: Women patrons and activists since 1860* (pp. 65–86). Berkeley: University of California Press.

Policy prolepsis in education: Encounters, becomings, and phantasms

P. Taylor Webb and Kalervo N. Gulson

> We argue that the concept of a *policy prolepsis* is a category of becoming-policy that actualizes educational practices within spaces of desired policy initiatives and implementations. Policy prolepses represent a range of emergent policy ontologies produced through the interface of educational actors' senses of policy and their estimations of possible outcomes. We use Deleuze's (1990) *logic of sense* to argue that becoming-policy occurs in a pre-conscious space, and that this space is produced politically and used strategically for desired, yet ostensibly unformed, policy outcomes. Educational policy, then, is an ontological activity representing a myriad of policy outcomes through the management of semiotic desires and actors' inferences about these persuasive signs. The paper illustrates the practical idea of policy prolepsis by demonstrating how *policy apparitions* use fear in becoming-policy. Policy apparitions, then, are just one species of policy prolepses that utilize the affect of fear to manipulate educational actors' interpretations.

Prolepsis (n.) - *The representation of a thing as existing before it actually does or did so.*

Up until the 1980s, it was commonly assumed that education policy represented the implementation of solutions to educational problems, and that educational research should and could contribute to policy effectiveness (Simons, Olssen, & Peters, 2009). While in the 1990s and 2000s, critical policy studies in education challenged this view, it is the case that a techno-rational characterization of education policy still has a stranglehold on education policy makers and educational researchers. Techno-rationality in the development and implementation of policy is paralleled in educational policy research which is increasingly required to be *for* policy and the expected 'solutions' to indeterminate problems, and eventually, to be aimed at evaluating the efficiency and effectiveness of reforms (Rizvi & Lingard, 2009). Debates about policy have become claims and counterclaims about methodology and related issues of rigour and what counts as legitimate evidence (Wiseman, 2010).

Techno-rational approaches to policy development and research imply that variations in policy meaning, implementations, and outcomes are attributable to actor's incorrect interpretations, or imply a certain set of literacy skills in reading or decoding policy have atrophied (Cohen, 1990). As such, these approaches suggest that actors have misinterpreted a 'fixed meaning' of policy, thus assuming these meanings are objective, accessible, and complete. In this paper when we talk about policy interpreters we are referring to actors, or crudely, end-users of policy, in what Bowe, Ball, and Gold (1992) identify as the context of practice, or the realm of 'policy enactments' (Ball, Hoskins, Maguire, & Braun, 2010). We argue, in refrain of Ball (1994) and (Ball et al., 2010), that various levels of policy, including the complexities, ambiguities and ambivalences associated with making, delivering, receiving, resisting and/or transforming policy, require analyses of policy that acknowledge and work with problematizations[1] rather than reductions of complexities. This is to work with and within, what (Youdell 2011), following Deleuze and Guattari has termed the *education assemblage.*

Furthermore, and against the above backdrop, our departure point for this paper is to work from a critical policy studies orientation (Simons et al., 2009), to rethink and reorient a key claim made consistently in critical policy studies over the last 20 years. This contention is that policy is *not* a seamless process from development to implementation.[2] Like Ball (1994), we agree that policy is characterized by incompleteness, ad hocery and 'the "wild profusion" of local practice' (p. 10). Policy is always and only a contingent and provisional fixing. Part of these claims of the provisional lie in the idea of interpretation, that educational policy is involved with semiotics (Ball, 1990), including teachers as semioticians of curriculum policy (Rizvi & Lingard, 2009).

In refuting ideas of techno-rationality in analyses of (neoliberal) policy implementation, we do not relinquish politics. Like Youdell (2011), we believe that various forms of post-structural analyses of education –

> ... and the practices they espouse have received varying degrees of recognition and takeup in the mainstream of education theory and practice, and while for the most part they have been remained marginal, they have been legitimate, recognizable and speakable. (2011, p. 10)

What is of interest for us in this paper is that in the midst of this turbulence surrounding education policy, the concept *policy* remains untouched. It is the legitimacy of evidence, for example, that is contested, not what policy *is* (Cf., Ball, 1994), not whether policy can actually do the work for which it is claimed, and what effects are produced – and continually produced – in the name of policy. In this paper our understanding of education policy is informed from Ball's (1994) idea that 'policy is both text and action, words and deeds, it is what is enacted as well as what is intended' (p. 10). Throughout, we refer to policy documents, including: press releases, government decisions, legislation, formal authorizations, mandates, laws, speeches, white papers, reports, and curricula. We also refer to policy intentions that attempt to construct, prevent, and/or solve a 'problem' (Miller & Rose, 2008); send a (symbolic) message; resolve political tensions; and maintain the status quo (e.g., regulate, standardize, cement).

In this paper, then, we explore the ideas of policy ad hocery, indeterminacies, and so forth, using Deleuze's (1990) ideas of affect, encounters, and becomings. We are concerned about not only the epistemology of policy studies but also the ontology of policy and practice; an ontological politics, or a politics of becoming-policy. This paper introduces the concept of a *policy prolepsis* in education, and we argue that policy prolepsis is a category of becoming-policy that actualize educational practices within the spaces of desired, yet not fully developed, policy initiatives and policy implementations. Policy prolepses represent a range of emergent policy ontologies that are produced through the interface of educational actors' senses of policy and their estimations of possible policy outcomes. We use Deleuze's (1990) idea regarding the *logic of sense* to argue that becoming-policy occurs in a pre-conscious space, and that this space is able to be manipulated. Educational policy, then, is a diverse ontological activity representing a myriad of policy outcomes through the management of semiotic desires and actors' inferences about these persuasive signs.

Readers will note that we utilize Deleuze and Guattari's (1987) idea of *becoming* to form our conception of policy in terms of sense, through attention to affect, percept, and so on. As a site of scholarship, this paper links the idea of becoming to Deleuze's (1990) additional ideas about a *logic of sense*. Becoming, then, is a materiality of policy and subjectivity produced through the senses of those expected to implement it. Prolepses signal the way becomings are rhetorically figured. Deleuze and Guattari (1987) explained that,

> a line of becoming is not defined by points that it connects, or by points that compose it; on the contrary, it passes between points, it comes up through the middle ... a line of becoming has neither beginning nor end, departure nor arrival, origin nor destination... Becoming is the movement by which the line frees itself from the point, and renders points indiscernible: the rhizome, the opposite of arborescence; break away from arborescence. (pp. 293–294)

Our policy prolepsis intends to move thinking about policy as discourse or text (Ball, 1994), to indicate a certain materiality of the body, or a technology of self, that is intimately connected to policy texts and discourses. This is to begin to see policy as part of education's rhizomatic terrain, and to consider:

> ... how [education] ... renders particular educational subjects and how it provokes and corrals affectivities suggests a complex map of education that brings together forces, orders, discourses, technologies, practices and bodies; from the legislative functions of the state to the affective eruptions of the playground. (Youdell, 2011, p. 55)

In one sense, our policy prolepsis is a methodological strategy to identify constructions of 'professional' identities and provides methods to map styles of practice and styles of care. For example, teachers and practitioners can utilize the idea of a policy prolepsis to ascertain the particular ways education policy induces and prompts particular behaviours and desires. More importantly, a policy prolepsis can assist teachers develop ideas and practices for a care of the self that consciously uses the resistances, variegations, and uncertainties that arise when confronting the unrelenting semiotics of policy. Thus, one, though of course not the only, possibility, is that policy prolepses may become a powerful heuristic for teachers to transform the oft-used action research methodologies into a fieldwork of the self,[3] rather than, and only as, a particular methodology to regulate themselves and their practice against curriculum policy directives.

The paper illustrates the idea of a policy prolepsis by demonstrating how *policy apparitions* use fear in becoming-policy. Policy apparitions, then, are just one species of policy prolepses that utilize the affect of fear to manipulate educational actors' interpretations. These interpretations and inferences are produced politically and are used strategically for desired, yet ostensibly unformed, policy outcomes.

Policy prolepsis

> *Every orientation presupposes a disorientation.* (Hans Magnus Enzensberger, 1966, cited in Calvino, 1986, p. 23)

We discuss policy prolepses in relation to semiotics – processes involved with signification and communication of signs. We situate the concept of policy prolepses within rhetorical designata (semantic) and within cognitive interiorities (pragmatics). Our discussion develops two tightly entangled politics within education policy studies, separated only for analytical purposes: a politics of sense and a politics of time. We argue that policy prolepses rhetorically figure policy interpretations through sense making, and subsequently position subjects (e.g., teachers) and their practice in particular ways that are not apparent or recognized. We believe that the idea of policy prolepsis can assist others in their own analyses of educational policy and practice, and provide a way to discuss a larger *politics of becoming-policy*.

Semetsky (2006, citing Peirce, 1955) provides a definition of semiotics:[4]

> A sign can be anything that stands to somebody, a sign-user, for something else, its object, in some respect and in such a way so as to generate another sign, called its *interpretant,* to designate a sign, in agreement with the word representation describing *both* the dynamic process *and* the terminus of such a process, by which one thing stand for another. (p. 27)

We use the triadic model – interpretant, sign-user, representamen – to explain our concept *policy prolepsis.* However, rather than use the term 'representamen' to refer to the process and objects of a semiotics, we have selected the term *prolepsis* instead. The term prolepsis originates from rhetorical studies and our use of the term signals a *politics of becoming-policy* with rhetorically figured – and rhetorically figuring – signs.

Policy prolepses, then, are a category of becoming-policy, produced rhetorically and used politically, that shape policy interpretations and shape educational practices within the spaces of desired, yet incomplete, indeterminate, and ad hoc, policy initiatives and implementations. Policy prolepses demarcate a wide range of emergent policy ontologies and fragmented practices produced through educational actors' senses of policy and their subsequent interpretations of policy, including their calculations of policy outcomes.

Policy prolepsis and 'reading' affective tones

Deleuze (1990) argued that semiotic sign-encounters occur pre-consciously and thought and thinking *follow* a sensory-sign encounter. Within such a configuration, policy interpretations are second-level thoughts influenced from sensed-signs, perhaps better described as rationalizations of sign-perceptions. Deleuze (1994) described the process of affective sensing, or sign encounters, and its preceding role in thinking:

> Something in the world forces us' to think. This something is an object not of recognition, but a fundamental 'encounter'... It may be grasped in a range of affective tones: wonder, love, hatred, suffering, [fear]. In whichever tone, its primary characteristic is that it can only be sensed. In this sense it is opposed to recognition. (1994, p. 139)

The Deleuzean and Guattarian (1987) idea of affective sensing has been taken up by a number of scholars in education. For instance, Masny and Cole (2009) described creativity and alienation as powerful affective tones that organize and structure thought (p. 5).[5] In another example, Semetsky (2006) suggested that the idea of *intuition* is another way to understand how signs are sensed in addition, or in combination, with wonder, love, hatred, suffering, fear, etc. Figure 1 (below) represents policy prolepses in affective tones, where signs are affectively encountered *prior* to understanding or recognition, and that *influence* subsequent thought.[6]

Policy prolepses operate through affective tones, or affective sensings, that function without certainty, and indeed, on serendipity. In its opposition to recognition, policy prolepses are sign-encounters mediated through a *logic of sense* (Deleuze, 1990). The distinction between *encounter* and *recognition* destabilizes notions that policy has an established identity or fixed meaning. For example, researchers have examined how teachers make sense of, or understand, policy (e.g., Achinstein & Ogawa, 2006; Patterson & Marshall, 2001), and the ways teachers 'misinterpret' policy (D. Ball, 1990; Cohen, 1990). McLaughlin (1987) observed that teachers' policy interpretations "... often seemed quite idiosyncratic, frustratingly unpredictable, if not downright resistant ..." (p. 172). Given teachers' unique positions within phantasmic space, Schwille et al. (1983) noted that teachers –

> ... are better understood as political brokers than as [policy] implementers. They enjoy considerable discretion, being influenced by their own notions of what schooling ought to be as well as persuaded by external pressures. (1983, p. 377)

As we have noted elsewhere in our respective work, policy-signs of race and racism are powerful influences for thinking about schooling (Gulson, 2006, Gulson, 2011) and powerful influences on teachers' practices (Webb, 2001).

Furthermore, and with some affinity for work that demonstrates how policy practices are underpinned by complex and often contradictory premises (Ball, 2003), the distinction between *encounter* and *recognition* destabilizes ideas that policy interpretation is a conscious and rational process of 'reading' fixed policy meanings and developing 'correct' or 'incorrect' interpretations – in fact, policy interpretations are developed or 'read' through 'random collisions of affects' (Masny & Cole, 2009, p. 5). Policy and its meanings are indeterminate, contingent, paradoxical,

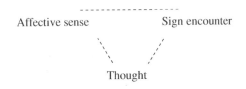

Figure 1. Policy prolepsis in affective tones.

contradictory, and disorienting (often deliberately) – 'every orientation presupposes a disorientation' (Enzenberger, 1966, p. x, cited by Calvino, 1986, p. 23). Notions of policy 'interpretations', then, are transformed into a politics of controlling affective registers of meaning, if not, attempts to control affects themselves. Policy prolepses, then, can be understood as the ways policy signs are rhetorically figured to influence those sensings and the ways educators make sense of policy, shape their practice, and eventually, create themselves in relation to perceived signs.

The politics of affective space: Phantasmic positionings

Policy prolepses are coded affectively (wonder, love, hatred, suffering, fear, humor, etc.) and rhetorically position subsequent policy interpretations and, eventually, position subjects themselves. Deleuze (1990) used the notion of *phantasm* to explain sign encounters and to explain how subjects are positioned in phantasmic space. Deleuze (1990) noted that phantasms are:

> ... constituted by simulacra which are particularly subtle and agile... capable of supplying the animus with visions... all of the images which correspond to desire... Not that desire is creative here; rather, it renders the mind attentive and makes it choose the most suitable phantasm from among all the subtle phantasms in which we are immersed. (p. 276)

Deleuze borrowed his ideas of phantasm and seduction from Laplanche and Pontalis (1964/1968). They noted how subjects are positioned by phantasms when they stated, 'phantasm is not the object of desire, it is a scene. In the phantasm ... the subject does not target the object or what stands for it; rather he figures there himself, caught up in the sequence of images' (p. 1868).

Kenneth Burke (1966) argued similarly, albeit more linguistically and explicitly dramaturgically, that affects function as *terministic screens*. Burke noted that affects were rhetorically figured and direct 'attention into some channels rather than others' (p. 45), and constructions of ' "reality" may be but the spinning out of possibilities implicit in our particular choice of terms' (p. 46). Likewise, Peirce (1955) anticipated a range of possible ontologies when he queried, 'consider what effects, that might conceivably have practical bearings, we conceive the object of our conception to have. Then our conception of these effects is the whole of our conception of the object' (cited by Semetsky, 2006, p. 27). Finally, Blackburn (1990) argued that affects are constantly "filling in space", producing a myriad of different ontologies, or becomings, when trying to categorize and understand signs. Blackburn (1990) noted, '[dispositions] might only bring us to the instancing of a power ... at some region of space explained by the instancing of some other power at some related region of space' (p. 62). Blackburn's (1990) *filling in space* provides our prolepsis with ways to discuss how subjects make sense of, or represent, the indeterminacies and contradictions of policy – subjects fill in these spaces affectively.

Educational researchers have identified ways affects shape policy interpretations. For example, Honan (2004) developed a 'rhizo-textual analysis' of policy texts, which explored the construction of the subject position *teacher* through teachers' sensings of policy. Honan explained how teachers understood policy through the affects of *independence, self-doubt, denial*, and *inadequacy*, and she illustrated how these sensings consequently shaped interpretations of policy and practice (pedagogy). Similarly, Roy (2003) developed the idea of 'aura' (based on his interviews with teachers) in similar ways to our notion of policy prolepsis[7] as a way to explain how teachers are rhetorically positioned through policy. Roy (2003) explained that an aura is 'an indirect acknowledgement of the presence of the absent' which 'leaves room for the [subject's] becoming in the encounter, of the possibilities of realizing unsuspected relationalities that striated space excludes in its reinforcing of rigid boundaries' (pp. 112–113). In his work, Roy (2003) noted how stress shaped teachers' senses of policy and their subsequent policy interpretations and, ultimately, their pedagogy.[8] The powerful endogamous/exogamous imagery of Delueze's (1988) *fold*, for example, could be used to further illustrate ways in which one's relation to oneself could be seen to take place in different settings, and to show how the self is folded in on endogamous parts of policy and how policy is folded onto exogamous elements of the body.

The politics of absences and presences: Policy prolepsis in time

A policy prolepsis generates various registers of interpretation. However, the significance of policy prolepses is that policy interpretations are never removed from their initial sensings of rhetorically figured signs and spaces – signs and spaces that figure thought, interpretations, practice, and subjects. Deleuze (1983) noted the time between a sensory-sign encounter and the subsequent thought produced when he stated, 'we are *awaiting* the forces capable of making thought something active, absolutely active, the power capable of making it an affirmation' (p. 108, italics added). Policy prolepses occur in time and identify the intermediary spaces between policy-sensings and subsequent policy interpretations – the wait-times, the *intermezzo*,[9] or, 'the waiting of that which is going to come about as a result, and also of that which is already in the process of coming about and never stops coming about' (Deleuze, 1990, p. 242). For our purposes, we want to link metaphor with materiality, and posit that time represents both an *absent space* of policy prolepses and spaces where/when policy interpretations are developed – the thinking about sensed-signs. We represent policy prolepses in time in Figure 2 (below) where we have placed our previous figure (Figure 1) within crude axes of temporal space.

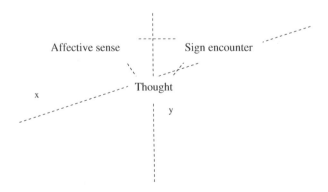

Figure 2. Temporal phantasms: Absent spaces in policy prolepsis.

Just as policy signs are figured rhetorically, absent spaces of policy prolepses are mutable and controllable. For instance, the mediatization of education policy produces unprecedented number of sign-encounters for educators (Rawolle, 2005). The mediatization of education policy also accelerates the circulation of policy-signs while seemingly simultaneously compressing space (e.g., geographical, in a verita-ble example of space-time compression (Cf., Harvey, 1989)) policy-signs traverse, or 'cross fields' (Lingard & Rawolle, 2004). Time can also be manipulated through the (all too) frequent distribution of multiple policies to educators (Honig, 2006).[10] Multiple policies reduce the time to meaningfully engage with them individually. As a result, multiple policies that are not accompanied with support structures to *increase time* position teachers to only 'read' policy as sign-encounters. In effect, multiple policies on teachers' desks ironically ventriloquize the message 'do not read' or 'only encounter' as a result of reducing teachers' time. In the end, the manipulation of time (reducing, accelerating) creates a myriad of affects, notwith-standing feelings of stress and inadequacy, which are prevalent affective orientations for policy prolepses (Honan, 2004; Roy, 2003).

The time of policy prolepses are spaces where/when sensings produce policy interpretations. Semetsky (2006) discussed these middle spaces and their relation-ships to thought. She noted:

> It is the very presence, that is, the included middle of the transversal link ... which does not rely on absolutes, but aims 'to bring into being that which does not yet exist' [Deleuze, 1994a, p. 147] ... that which is as yet imperceptible by means of laying down a visible map of some invisible territory or, in other words, creating a mediatory space between discursive and non-discursive formations. The very 'interstice ... between seeing and speaking' [Deleuze, 1988a, p. 87] is the place where thinking occurs. (pp. 33–34)

This is not the paper to cover the myriad of writings on space and education policy (Taylor, 2009; Thiem, 2009). What we want to highlight, however, is that Deleuze is noticeably absent in education policy studies that employ spatial approaches. This is somewhat remiss, for arguably Deleuze's work is premised on, and constitutes, a spatial philosophy of relationality and multiplicity (Buchanan & Lambert, 2005). As Murdoch (2006) notes, and this provides another way into what we are discussing,

> ... [m]ultiplicities conceive spatial forms through their generative capacities, and these depend on the emergent properties (or 'affects') that come into being as relations are formed between entities of various kinds. (p. 92)

Our phrase *absent space*, then, is used to signal the *intermediary* and *political* spaces involved in policy prolepses which are, of course, constantly present, or as Doel (2000) definitively asserted, 'space is immanent' (p. 125). Thus, we recog-nize the apparent contradiction in our conception of absent space; however, we hope readers afford us the semantic pleasure of *absence* even if we mean *invisibly present, hidden, not readily apparent,* or *ontologically forthcoming*. Likewise, *negative space* is an idea that is used in art and architecture and generally refers to the space around and in-between images and signs. Negative space is *apparent* when the space around a sign forms a counter space that produces additional signs.

Moreover, negative space, like our absent space, is synthetic and artists, architects, city planners, and policy authors, to name but a few, are skilled in their abilities to manipulate this space.

Policy apparitions: Examples of policy prolepsis and fear

In this last section, we briefly illustrate the idea of policy prolepsis by demonstrating how fear filled absent spaces of educational policy in our respective works (Gulson, 2011; Webb, 2009). While others have approached fear and policy with great precision (e.g., Berliner & Biddle, 1996; Ginsberg & Cooper, 2008), our examples intend to demonstrate how policy itself is a semiotic monster that *uses* perceptions of fear to assemble intended and unintended educational acts and subjectivities. For instance, Bullen, Fahey and Kenway (2006) discussed how risk economies are spectral images – ghosts – designed to mobilize action through fear and understood with Derridaean 'hauntology'. We use the idea of a *policy apparition* to signal the senses of ephemerality, uncertainty, doubt, and fear that inscribe cases of policy implementation. What follows, then, are two brief illustrations of policy prolepsis through the primary sense of fear; becoming-policy of school restructuring and accountability. The first example is concerned with how apparitions produce subjectivities, and the second example is concerned with identifying the assemblages of fear and uncertainty in policy apparitions.

In the first example, accountability polices instilled fear in teachers and described how teachers generated fabrications as spectral responses to the surveillance of pedagogy. Fear was produced in teachers through a fear of punishment and a fear of losing one's job. For instance, one participant noted:

> [Test] scores are published. They're on radio; they're in the news, on the television. They are in the newspapers – I'm hypersensitive to it, being it's my job [at stake], but they're everywhere. They're on the Internet. They compare the schools to different schools. (Webb, 2009, p. 106)

The fear instilled by accountability policy was transmitted onto teachers by circulating test scores (i.e., signs) through the media (i.e., time). More importantly, teachers created and used fabrications to refract the surveillance of pedagogy. As a result, teachers acknowledged their concomitant schizophrenia as a result of performing fabrications, to different audiences, a political response to accountability-policy-fear. Teachers noted how, and in which ways, their *selves* were changing as an assemblage of accountability fear, fabricated performances, and the swirling micropolitical pressure at the school. Thus, teachers were fearful and felt threatened, and responded to interpretations of policy that attempted reduce fear (Webb, 2009).

Our second example pertains to inner city public school restructuring policy in Sydney, Australia, that was initially released as a draft proposal for public feedback. We want to draw attention to the designation of this policy as a 'draft', and suggest this allowed for both absence (as in this is not really the policy) and apparition, that is these proposals may or may not be taken up. With the uncertainty of a draft policy, fear circulated through the city and the schools which operated in a local K-12 education market. We also want to note the ambiguity and uncertainty meant that what was encountered *and* manifested was fear of the non-White 'other' in the inner city, notably fear of Aboriginal students and parents. Aboriginal students were a central part of schooling in the inner city while simultaneously feared if they continued to be so. Some inner city schools were majority Aboriginal which carried with it the generation of non-Aboriginal fear of poor academic performance, violence and other forms of unsanctioned behaviour. One aspect of the draft policy proposal was to amalgamate these majority Aboriginal schools with a majority white student school. Apparitions of race and policy were thus always already becoming, that is as form, despite being in draft. The point we want to make from this brief example is that this draft operated as a policy apparition in which fear, Aboriginality and education markets were inexorably linked (Gulson, 2006, 2011).

Conclusion

In this paper we created and played with the idea of policy prolepsis as the process of forming multiple ontologies, that is the 'real', in relation to sense-encounters of policy. We wanted to reinforce ideas that policy inherently contains multiple, contradictory, incoherent, and fluid meanings and are always becoming through assembling senses. We also wanted to posit this paper as part of a rhizomatic politics (Youdell, 2011), for we believe that a policy prolepsis can be a powerful heuristic for critical policy researchers and teachers to better understand how policy positions problems, solutions, and more importantly, subjectivity. Policy prolepsis can be used to identify constructions of professional identities and map styles of practice. Teachers, practitioners, and policy researchers can use policy prolepses to identify the ways education policy induces and prompts particular behaviours and desires. More importantly, policy prolepses can assist 'end users' of policy to develop their relationships with themselves and develop ideas and practices for caring for the self. We believe these practices of the self, or becoming-teacher, may be different than those expected from policy. Specifically, becoming-policy can be identified by distinguishing it from a notion of policy as fixed in meaning (techno-rational policy analyses, official documents, of single meaning). This suggests that far from policy being a reflection of, and intervention into, order, policy is an always already failed attempt to manage chaos. Policy thus can be construed as always and only a matter of orientation that presupposes a disorientation.

A policy prolepsis may be our 'best guess' about the meaning of a policy, but the prolepsis is derived from wisps of textual, spoken, sensed, intuitive, and graphical instances of policy – policy rhetoric – and where policy meanings are hidden, indeterminate, ad hoc, contradictory and designed to provoke action in particular ways. The absent space of policy prolepses identifies phantasmic space as relational, recursive, material, intersticed, and temporal. Thus, policy prolepses are always becoming with 'neither beginning nor end, departure nor arrival, origin nor destination' (Deleuze & Guattari, 1987, p. 293). We attempted to illustrate this idea using the notion of policy apparitions, and we would like to remark in finishing that policy apparitions are but just one conceivable way to illustrate policy prolepsis. Depending on a myriad of affective tones, policy prolepses might resemble, for example, *policy seductions* (desire), *policy learnings* (wonder), *policy repulsions* (hatred), *policy hypnosis* (intuition), and *policy nostalgia* (sufferings).

Acknowledgements

We would like to thank Diana Masny and David Cole for developing this important issue. We would also like to thank the anonymous reviewers for their excellent comments and suggestions.

Notes

1. Here, we are using Michel Foucault's (1970) notion of *problematization* that Rabinow (2003) discussed, and which parallels Lather's (2009) ideas of 'getting lost' in/with educational policy studies.
2. This is a point also made in political science, e.g. Howlett & Ramesh, 1995.
3. And very much related to Pinar's (2004) ideas of currere and complicated conversations.
4. We have decided to not cite the original in order to highlight the important research that Inna Semetsky has done in the field of education and Deleuze studies.
5. Diana Masny has been developing Multiple Literacies Theory (MLT) to great effect for the past decade. Her influential book (2005) provided a number of contributors ways to link MLT to the thinkings of Gilles Deleuze, including co-editor David Cole.
6. Borrowed from Semetsky's (2006) similar schematic (p. 31).
7. And, perhaps, similar to Semetsky's (2006) idea of *intuition*.
8. Unfortunately, we cannot elaborate on the idea of teacher-becomings here; our goal is to make a contribution to educational policy studies with the work of Gilles Deleuze and ideas of spatial philosophy. However, Zembylas (2003, 2007) discussed the idea of teacher-becomings to some extent, and we engage with this intriguing area in some of our other work.
9. Semetsky (2006) noted that the *intermezzo* characterized much of Deleuze's thinking, whereas, the intermezzo is spaces in-between; spaces of becoming; spaces of waiting. Deleuze and Guattari (1987) would liken the intermezzo to a rhizome – "a rhizome has no beginning or end; it is always in the middle, between things, interbeing, intermezzo" (p. 25).
10. For example, policies of assessment, accountability, curriculum, including mathematics, literacy, etc.

References

Achinstein, B., & Ogawa, R.T. (2006). (In)Fidelity: What the resistance of new teachers reveals about professional principles and prescriptive educational policies. *Harvard Educational Review, 76*(1), 30–63.

Ball, D. (1990). Reflections and deflections of policy: The case of Carol Turner. *Educational Evaluation and Policy Analysis, 12*(3), 247–259.

Ball, S.J. (1990). *Politics and policy making in education: Explorations in policy sociology.* London: Routledge.

Ball, S.J. (1994). *Education reform: A critical and post-structural approach.* Philadelphia: Open University Press.

Ball, S.J. (2003). *Class strategies and the education market: The middle classes and social advantage.* London: RoutledgeFalmer.

Ball, S.J., Hoskins, K., Maguire, M., & Braun, A. (2010). Disciplinary texts: A policy analysis of national and local behaviour policies. *Critical Studies in Education, 52*(1), 1–14.

Berliner, D.C., & Biddle, B.J. (1996). *The manufactured crisis: Myths, fraud, and the attack on America's public schools.* New York: Basic Books.

Blackburn, S. (1990). Filling in space. *Analysis, 50*(2), 62–65.

Bowe, R., Ball, S.J., & Gold, A. (1992). *Reforming education and changing schools: Case studies in policy sociology.* London: Routledge.

Buchanan, I., & Lambert, G. (Eds.). (2005). *Deleuze and space.* Toronto: University of Toronto Press.

Bullen, E., Fahey, J., & Kenway, J. (2006). The knowledge economy and innovation: Certain uncertainty and the risk economy. *Discourse: Studies in the Cultural Politics of Education, 27*(1), 53–68.

Burke, K. (1966). *Language as symbolic action: Essays on life, literature, and method.* Berkeley: University of California Press.

Calvino, I. (1986). *The uses of literature.* London: Harcourt Brace & Company.

Cohen, D. (1990). A revolution in one classroom: The case of Mrs Oublier. *Evaluation and Policy Analysis, 12*(3), 311–329.

Deleuze, G. (1983). *Nietzsche and philosophy.* New York: Columbia University Press.

Deleuze, G. (1988). *Foucault.* Minneapolis: University of Minnesota Press.

Deleuze, G. (1990). *The logic of sense.* New York: Columbia University Press.

Deleuze, G. (1994). *Difference and repetition.* NY: Columbia University Press.

Deleuze, G., & Guattari, F. (1987). *A thousand plateaus: Capitalism and schizophrenia.* Minneapolis: University of Minnesota Press.

Doel, M. (2000). Un-glunking geography: Spatial science after Dr Suess and Gilles Deleuze. In M. Crang & N. Thrift (Eds.), *Thinking space* (pp. 117–135). London: Routledge.

Foucault, M. (1970). *The order of things: An archaeology of human sciences.* New York: Random House.

Ginsberg, R., & Cooper, B.S. (2008). Introduction: What's fear got to do with it? *Educational Policy, 22*(1), 5–9.

Gulson, K.N. (2006). A white veneer: Educational policy, space and 'race' in the inner city. *Discourse: Studies in the Cultural Politics of Education, 27*(2), 251–266.

Gulson, K.N. (2011). *Education policy, space and the city: Markets and the (in)visibility of race.* New York: Routledge.

Harvey, D. (1989). *The condition of postmodernity.* Cambridge, MA: Blackwell.

Honan, E. (2004). (Im)plausibilities: A rhizo-textual analysis of policy texts and teachers. *Educational Philosophy and Theory, 36*(3), 267–281.

Honig, M.I. (2006). *New directions in education policy implementation: Confronting complexity.* New York: State University of New York.

Howlett, M., & Ramesh, M. (1995). *Studying public policy: Policy cycles and policy subsystems.* Toronto: Oxford University Press.

Laplanche, J., & Pontalis, J.B. (1964). Fantasy and the origins of sexuality. *The International Journal of Psychoanalysis, 49*(1), 1–18.

Lather, P. (2009). 2007 Kneller Lecture, AESA Getting lost: Social science and/as philosophy. *Educational Studies, 45*(4), 342–357.

Lingard, B., & Rawolle, S. (2004). Mediatizing educational policy: The journalistic field, science policy, and cross-field effects. *Journal of Education Policy, 19*(3), 361–380.

Masny, D. (2005). Multiple literacies: An alternative OR beyond Freire. In J. Anderson, M. Kendrick, T. Rogers & S. Smythe (Eds.), Portraits of literacy across families, communities, and schools: Intersections and tensions (pp. 171–184). Mahwah NJ: Lawrence Erlbaum Associates.

Masny, D., & Cole, D.R. (2009). *Mutliple literacies theory.* Rotterdam: Sense Publishers.

McLaughlin, M.W. (1987). Learning from experience: Lessons from policy implementation. *Educational Evaluation and Policy Analysis, 9*(2), 171–178.

Miller, P., & Rose, N. (2008). *Governing the present: Adminstering economic, social and personal life.* Cambridge: Polity Press.

Murdoch, J. (2006). *Post-structuralist geography: A guide to relational space.* London: SAGE Publications.

Patterson, J.A., & Marshall, C. (2001). Making sense of policy paradoxes: A case study of teacher leadership. *Journal of School Leadership, 11*(5), 372–398.

Peirce, C.S. (1955). *Philosophical writings of Peirce.* New York: Courier Dover Publications.

Pinar, W. (2004). *What is curriculum theory?* Mahwah, NJ: Lawrence Erlbaum Associates, Inc.

Rabinow, P. (2003). *Anthropos today: Reflections of modern equipment*. Princeton: Princeton University Press.

Rawolle, S. (2005). Cross-field effects and temporary social fields: A case study of the mediatization of recent knowledge economy policies. *Journal of Education Policy, 20*(6), 705–724.

Rizvi, F., & Lingard, B. (2009). *Globalizing educational policy*. London: Routledge.

Roy, K. (2003). *Teachers in nomadic spaces: Deleuze and curriculum*. New York: Peter Lang.

Schwille, J., Porter, A., Belli, G., Floden, R., Freeman, D., Knappen, L. et al. (1983). Teachers as policy brokers in the content of elementary school mathematics. In L. Shulman & G. Sykes (Eds.), *Handbook on teaching and policy* (pp. 370–391). New York: Longman.

Semetsky, I. (2006). *Deleuze, education and becoming*. Rotterdam: Sense Publishers.

Simons, M., Olssen, M., & Peters, M.A. (2009). Re-reading education policies: Part 1: The critical policy orientation. In M. Simons, M. Olssen & M.A. Peters (Eds.), *Re-reading education policies: A handbook studying the policy agenda of the 21st century* (pp. 1–35). Rotterdam: Sense Publishers.

Taylor, C. (2009). Towards a geography of education. *Oxford Review of Education, 35*(5), 651–669.

Thiem, C.H. (2009). Thinking through education: The geographies of contemporary educational restructuring. *Progress in Human Geography, 33*(2), 154–173.

Webb, P.T. (2001). Reflection and reflective teaching: Ways to improve pedagogy or ways to remain racist? *Race, Ethnicity and Education, 4*(3), 245–252.

Webb, P.T. (2009). *Teacher assemblage*. Rotterdam: Sense Publishers.

Wiseman, A.W. (2010). The use of evidence for educational policymaking: Global contexts and international trends. *Review of Research in Education, 34*(1), 1–24.

Youdell, D. (2011). *School trouble: Identity, power and politics in education*. New York: Routledge.

Zembylas, M. (2003). Interrogating 'teacher identity'. *Educational Theory, 53*(1), 107–127.

Zembylas, M. (2007). Risks and pleasures: A Deleuzo-Guattarian pedagogy of desire in education. *British Educational Research Journal, 33*(3), 331–347.

Grotesque gestures or sensuous signs? Rethinking notions of apprenticeship in early childhood education

Linda Knight

> Deleuze asserts that education is a mass of signs. Children learn to decode these signs, albeit in randomized and individual ways, displaying great skill in decoding some signs but not others, and demonstrating different acuities with different clusters of signs. Deleuzian notions of apprenticeship, a fluid becoming to knowledges as formal education is encountered, operate at some distance to linear, culturally loaded apprenticeship concepts embedded in sociocultural theories. Conceptualizing education as gestures and signs, and apprenticeship as temporal rather than developmental, makes it difficult to try to quantify what is learnt. Deleuzian notions of apprenticeship, whilst troubling, can begin to dislodge teaching and learning conventions, particularly around accessing and responding. This essay explores drawing as education in Deleuzian terms.

Education might be conceptualized as a swarm of signs. Deleuze, in *Proust and Signs* (1964/2008) suggests that 'Everything that teaches us something emits signs' (p. 4). Plainly speaking, and in terms of school education, components such as the behaviours and instructions of a teacher, the school equipment and furniture, the school dress codes, and daily timetable, all give out myriad information suggestions to whomever encounters them. The quote from Deleuze suggests that anything which furthers knowledge or information acquisition relies upon our encountering a mass of signals, but that such signals are chaotic: overt, directional, as well as incidental, unpredicted; that is, they are not easily listed, anticipated or defined, and are not received identically. Children can become skillful in decoding much of this mass, this multitude of signs that they encounter during the time of their school education. This does not happen uniformly, however, because signs 'are organized in circles and intersect at certain points' (p. 4); not all signs flow forth in a uniform direction. The signs of learning emitted by a dress code, for example, may not exactly partner those signs of learning emitted by the chemistry laboratory equipment, or the signs of learning emitted by the school library. They may connect at certain points and may also operate in distinct separation. This can cause children to demonstrate different acuities with different clusters of signs. The points of connection and separation of these signs will also differ for each of them.

This Deleuzian notion of a fluid, intersecting apprenticeship, of a child becoming to some other/othered knowledges as they encounter an education filled with these myriad signs, operates at some distance to sociocultural concepts of apprenticeship (Kozulin et al., 2003; Vygotsky, 1978) that focus on anticipated, linear sequences of gaining culturally-loaded knowledge from more experienced others.

This paper offers a critique on aspects of Vygotsky's approaches to the educational learning of young children, and it places this in the contemporary Australian context. Concepts of apprenticeship, based on Deleuzian theories of signs, are discussed as a suggested alternative approach for early childhood education. The paper focuses on drawing as an exemplar of this alternative apprenticeship. This is because children require varied access to complex combinations of signs; however, they should also have opportunity to offer their *responses* in similarly diverse ways. It is important to advocate for a rethinking on how children might receive information *and* how they can disseminate and communicate that information.

Drawing is the focus here because it serves to exemplify how apprenticeship can be thought about as a creative process rather than as sequential or culturally driven. Particularly, drawing is discussed because it serves to exemplify Deleuzian concepts around intersecting clusters of signs and the relationship between time and learning, rather than age or development stage and learning.

Notions of apprenticeship

Notions and theorizations about apprenticeship in education emerge from different philosophical and sociological frameworks. Within a sociocultural framework, the Russian theorist Vygotsky (1978) claims that 'the system of signs restructures the whole psychological process and enables the child to master her movement. It reconstructs the choice process on a totally new basis' (p. 35). Here Vygotsky suggests that once signs are recognized, a new chapter begins – which suggests that the previous one ends, a boundary line is crossed. Vygotsky centralizes the human in that accruement, evidenced most when he states 'the child begins to master his attention, creating new structural centers in the perceived situation' (p. 35). This centralization paradoxically infers separation, of some void between the human and the Other. The human here is identified as having enough of a distance to its surroundings as to consciously control orderings of these components as if they were new, not pre-existent, nor existing, irrespective of human presence or action. This human centralization is most evident in Vygotsky's assertion that 'learning awakens a variety of internal developmental processes that are able to operate only when the child is interacting with people in his [sic] environment and in cooperation with his peers' (p. 90). The child here is viewed as initiating its learning, and that this is required for an aspect of human progress or growth. In thinking about Vygotsky's theorizations it seems that once these processes are internalized, they become part of the child's independent developmental achievement.

Vygotskian theories on apprenticeship have been interpreted in education texts as growth-and-development-as-sequential-layering: 'the zone of proximal development notion is often used to focus on the importance of more competent assistance' (Chaiklin, 2003, p. 43). Children are seen as being guided by more experienced others, in a linear, developmental sequence (Bodrova & Leong, 2003; Chaiklin,

2003). Particularly, for Chaiklin (2003) this over-layering sequence should be highly ordered:

> ... childhood should be divided into periods, such that each period is characterized in a principled and unified way ... the concrete manifestation of the abstract relations must be discovered and characterized for the particular content of each age period. (p. 46)

Initially Chaiklin's interpretation of Vygotsky's apprenticeship theory seems to closely align with Deleuzian notions of apprenticeship: each offer commentary on the learner being exposed to abstract concepts, new signs, new information. Deleuzian notions trouble this easily determinable sequence, however, as they surface a child as an ever-shifting series of assemblages of the non-human, the uncontrolled, the unpredictable. The 'Deleuzian' child-as-series is not guided by age-defined, age-appropriate material offered to them by a more experienced other, nor is this material fully situated within curriculum, lesson content, educational principles. Deleuzian notions of apprenticeship prompt explorations of the fluidity of a child 'becoming' to some Other/Othered knowledges, a child as a continuously changing cluster of metaphysical, remembered, immersive forces and connections as they encounter education. Deleuzian notions also trouble the preoccupation sociocultural education has with culturally defining teacher and child identities (Burman, 2001). Culturally stabilized teacher and learner identities deny room for movements, shifts, or slippage. This is due to reliance upon a single, easily identifiable sequence of 'the' child being enriched, educated by 'the' more experienced other.

The popularity of applying sociocultural theories to education is, for Burman (2001), because they 'are records of a dominant culture, but one which has acquired such prevalence and predominance as to have become invisible, or presumed' (p. 7). Preoccupations with developmental theories (Dahlberg, Moss, & Pence, 1999; St Pierre, 2004) demonstrate a fear in shrugging off 'scientific' discourses around childhood in relation to curricular and classroom practice.

A steady increase in measurement testing perpetuates this preoccupation and puts pressure on teachers as they seek out 'lack of proper development; she/he is functioning as a detector of lack, an observer of error' (Borgnon, 2007, p. 267). The teacher here too is apprenticed; brought into this position by the stereotypical prompts around teacher identity. Not only are children drawn into conventionalized apprenticeship models, so too are teachers drawn into in conservative apprenticeship systems.

Becoming apprenticed

Pat Gavin (2008), an animator discusses how in kindergarten –

> Each morning our teacher would draw on the blackboard nursery rhyme illustrations just like the ones we saw in the school books... and [I] realized that the book pictures were made by somebody, they didn't just come in books, and I would watch fascinated as these squiggles and lines in bright chalky colours became a recognizable world like my own. (p. 46)

This account resonates with me too. I recall the moment when I realized the art pictures I looked at were made by someone, and that they did it by putting together separate marks, lines, shapes. I was about nine years old when this first happened, and it was as if I'd suddenly begun to see in a different way. I was very conscious of this shift because in that moment I realized that this image had been constructed, that it was created by a person, a person with enough skill to manipulate tools and materials to make this wonderful, life-like image. It was the moment when I became apprenticed to some of the signs of art, in this case an oil painting from the Renaissance. I made a conscious decision at that moment that I wanted to achieve these artistic skills, I desired to learn how to do that.

I became apprenticed to this particular swarm of signs through a poster on a wall in the classroom. In Gavin's (2008) account, the teacher, through drawing, exposed the class to a multitude of signs that were taken variously by different students:

> ... just before we went home I would always dread the moment when she would rub out this glorious thing that I had been enjoying all day... As far as I know Chris was less concerned than me. I suppose his interests lay elsewhere. (p. 47)

Something caught and resonated with Gavin but not in the same way for his friend.

These childhood accounts expose how we subverted dominant early childhood education sequences. We each became into art making, shifting into that space though not identically. I cannot speak for Gavin, but I began at this point to resist the pressure to immerse myself in other forms of learning because art became my productive force. I connected with swarms of signs not directed by my teacher, I daydreamed to direct my connections to swarms of signs. Much of this went unnoticed by my teachers as it didn't fit easily into a mainstream developmental growth model.

Thinking about drawing as communicating is useful because it challenges the deeply rooted dissemination norms that are embedded in contemporary Australian schooling; a system whereby particular developmental communication sequences are hierarchized, driven by pseudo-scientific beliefs around natural growth and brain development research (see particularly MCEETYA, 2008). I use drawing as an exemplar here because drawing makes highly visible how children can repeatedly make random connections to unpredictable signs, some of which they pour onto the surface of the drawing, some of which remain in a metaphysical state. Drawings offer visible evidence that educators need to rethink conventionalized notions around apprenticeship and knowledge acquisition.

In drawing, a child may draw objects of the world and pull on combinations of signs in the process. This can occur each time a drawing is produced, even if it is of the 'same' thing. This repetition of difference, this pulling on random signs is driven by a desire to make connection, to make apparent what hums below a surface, what is just out of view, just out of reach. A viewing of this drawing also makes connections, but it is a connection of difference. Here is the attraction with drawing, but also its downfall in the education system: it tries vainly to perform to the regulating practices but fails each time. But drawing must be included, must be advocated for because of this; it must because its incapacity simultaneously also puts up a resisting force against governing practices and situated interpretations entrenched in education discourses.

For Deleuze (1964/2008) 'we never learn by doing like someone but by doing with someone, who bears no resemblance to what we are learning' (p. 15). Curriculum is ineffectual if the expectation is regurgitation, a facsimile of a template or set of pre-determined achievement standards. This paper asserts that children require varied access to complex combinations of signs and should have opportunity to offer their responses in diversely literate ways. Drawing is a way for supporting that diverse response making.

Thought about through a Deleuzian apprenticeship lens perhaps, the act of drawing is seen as entering into a becoming. A drawer can be thought of as fully immersed in their learning. When children draw they often lose a sense of the boundaries of separation between themselves as a physical body, and the multitudes of impacting signs they encounter.

A majority view regards drawing as a pre-literate activity to assist in fine motor skill acquisition and character writing development. Mainstream use and regard for drawing can shape how children's drawings are valorized, determine the tools used, the context under which they are produced. Without vigilance, these ideas around drawing schema begin to surface as truths, immovable and without contestation.

In conventional settings, children are often left to draw by themselves, and youths are often dissuaded from drawing as their literacy skills improve, until, as adults, many do not draw at all. If educators can be persuaded to draw, however, this can bring forth an exposure, a realization that seeking out developmental schema in children's images ignores the multi-referential capturings of signs and instead reterritorializes them as pre-literate skill building exercises.

Developmental theories of education are problematic because they require educators to search amongst a multitude of signs 'from the macro-perspective of subjects and interpretations to the micro-production of signs' (Roy, 2003, p. 137) to extract predetermined meanings to justify the theory. To move away from main-stream theories and consider instead a child as an ever-shifting collection of signs, means educators must acknowledge the chaotic swarm of signs that a child might encounter in their learning. These unfettered influences/encounters/connections that come into a child's learning, such as 'gestures, language, semantics, speech, acts, color, support, lines, body movements, random thoughts, irritation, irregular breathing' (p. 137) can be attended to by educators, to help them build a profile that subverts more mainstream, predetermined learning sequences. Such attention enables educators to more closely examine the learning that is gained through a child's momentary lapses into unconvention, to discordance, to intercepted pathways, than the educator selectively seeking out signs that sustain developmentalist analyses.

This is a difficult request to make, however, because productive power forces (Dahlberg et al., 1999) act to motivate those who operate in the school system, including children, teachers, curriculum writers, politicians, parents, and others. For example, mainstream attraction to theories of childhood which regard the child as individualistic and self-knowing seem initially to celebrate young children. This positioning, however, oversimplifies details about children's learning, which in turn suppresses opportunities for educators to interrogate the difficult to explain, the messiness, the unexpected in a child's learning.

In a Deleuzian sense, this productive force underpins engagement in apprentice-ships and relates to a coming into, a becoming, a transforming into education, into the multitude of signs and power relationships encountered in educational sites and contexts. Because they influence virtually all areas of education, it is important that practitioners are aware of and consider the impact of these multiple forces. Of most interest in the context of this paper are the mainstream power forces that circle around childhood learner theories, and particularly, developmental theories of child knowledge and communication. These developmental power forces initiate a call to action 'to refuse to invest children with qualities of lost or true selfhood' (Burman, 2001, p. 17). These dominant views of the child as learner set up 'conveyer-belt' education sequences that seek to fill up an 'empty' child 'with knowledge, skills and dominant cultural values which are already determined, socially sanctioned and ready to administer' (Dahlberg et al., 1999, p. 44). Mainstream productive forces serve particularly to normalize childhood and learning as 'children [are] regulated and measured, surveyed and evaluated, in relation to fictitious norms elaborated by our models and associated practices' (Burman, 2001, p. 15). Not only do normalizing power forces extend beyond a view of the child as potential contributor to some future utopia; they reach into every crevice including the ideas, environments, food, clothing, interrelationships, leisure, and work that a child encounters.

Educators who consider Deleuzian notions of apprenticeship, or who, to think of it another way, resist conventionalized interpretations of childhood learning, face the challenges of resisting the mainstream. These educators 'have to learn to problematise what they are "seeing" and not fall into the trap of a naive realism; they have to experience themselves as joint producers of the sign regimes in which they participate' (Roy, 2003, p. 122). It is naïve and too optimistic to simply suggest that once we know, we can stop there. It is too optimistic to think that simply critiquing and removing oneself from the deeply institutionalized assumptions about childhood learning enables 'a fresh examination once we become apprenticed to the sign' (p. 122), and that this knowledge alone will affect change. Awareness, even in a Deleuzian sense of being apprenticed must additionally factor in action against the powerful, persuasive impact of affective governances on environment, space, stakeholders, curriculum. These are signs that are encountered which *become* independently to an individual, and they require constant vigilance and dispute to avoid commandeering our visions and analyses.

Thankfully the call to shift perceptions of early childhood education and care seem to be getting louder. There is a realization of the need 'to move away from the prototypical child as the developmental subject or the unit of development and talk instead of diverse children and childhoods' (Burman, 2001, p. 15). Awareness of the controlling mechanisms that thwart acceptance of diverse childhoods therefore must include thinking more broadly around how information is received, interacted with, retained, what that information is, and how a child rather than how a culture learns (Burman, 2001).

So, consideration of Deleuzian apprenticeships in educational settings must not only initiate in educators an awareness of the institutional effects on children, teachers, space, but must challenge and play out in analysis and judgment of the modes and visions by which children are seen to learn.

Swarms of signs

Some time ago a new job required me to move interstate to a new city. Despite my unfamiliarity I needed to find a place to live before I started my new job. I took a flat near to my place of work in the short-term because I didn't have a car and it meant I could walk to work. After about six weeks I decided to look for a longer-term option a little farther away. This search for a longer-term abode was interesting; I hadn't been in the town or actually in the state long enough to be fully apprenticed to it. Names of suburbs meant nothing to me; as I encountered different areas I was open to certain signs, but I was not yet apprenticed to many other signs including roofs, architecture, road widths, postboxes, vehicles, ornaments, histories, occupants. I could not interrogate the class distinctions of these suburban assemblages and I was not yet apprenticed to them. I relied upon the assemblages of signs I had available and made my decision.

This account does not pertain to a socioeconomic analysis because I do not believe that one assemblage is shared by all and I do not believe that the reputation of a place is conceived of or regarded as the same by everyone. I do not believe when the name of a suburb is mentioned everyone conjures up the same identical interpretation in their mind. Each is brought into their own combinations of signs depending upon individuating factors and each is brought in to their particular apprenticeship of that place.

For Deleuze, 'Signs are the objects of a temporal apprenticeship, not of an abstract knowledge' (1964/2008, p. 4); that is, signs of learning are encountered over time and are therefore not controllable or sequential because so many other intersecting experiences also occur for each individual over time. Furthermore, Deleuze's proposal that 'A man can be skillful at deciphering the signs of one realm and remain a fool in every other case' (p. 4) also supports a view that signs are not culturally organized or sequentially experienced, but are randomly encountered and understood by each individual.

Young children cannot be regarded as identical learners with identical sets of proficiencies, who learn in neat sequential blocks. Thinking about signs of learning as temporal, or randomly received, in Deleuzian terms, offers reason for persisting with education activism in resisting an Australian education system which strives to rationalize what is to be learnt, and conventionalize how children are to learn.

These preoccupations are grotesque gestures, simplistic and crass; perpetuating populist education conventions in relation to how a learner is expected to react and respond. Thinking differently about how children engage with signs of learning can assist in interrupting and resisting fixed beliefs around early childhood education and care. Theorizing about the multiple sign organizations at play helps to challenge linear/developmentalist childhood growth sequence discourses. As Deleuze suggests, a simple encounter with predetermined signs contained in instructional books cannot provide intelligence, a knowing. Deleuzian concepts of apprenticeship can help to think of children as skillful in deciphering, in chaotic and unpredictable ways, the multitude of signs they encounter in their education. Children can display great skill in becoming sensitive to some signs but not others, and each child can demonstrate ability to understand different combinations of signs. Furthermore, this acuity is not static but adjusts over time as new signs are encountered. Children need to encounter more than one type of sign to learn, to 'have' an education. There is a need to think diversely about how a child is apprenticed, and that this should not be unified or identical for all children.

School education is 'the result of an active clash of forces' (Roy, 2003, p. 124) as it simultaneously centralizes learning and institutionalizes learning. School education is constructed and fuelled by historical, scientific, political series of signs that seem on the surface to work together. Each instead works with such power and persuading force to canonize *and* detract from learning.

To consider conventionalized education aims, as being a liberator of the poor, the empty, the coarse; as introducing the world to a child; these conventions must take as their basis that 'education' is something already in existence, a canon of knowledge to be acquired and remembered. A conventionalized system cannot regard education as a new body of knowledge, whereby language, text, experiments, songs are continuously invented and discovered. Conventionalized education is already fixed and identified, and works its students towards a predetermined end point. It is rooted and monolithic and cannot be thought of as 'newly-invented' for each child.

Child learner immanence

Deleuze's (1964/2008) declaration that 'worldly signs are empty; they take the place of action and thought; they try to stand for their meaning' (p. 55) surfaces the demoralizing force of conventionalized education systems and puts out a call for 'subversive' apprenticeship alternatives. This is a significantly difficult call to make, however: in contrast to the grotesque gesture of the worldly sign (the instructional book, the report card) that contain and define childhood learning, sensuous signs (temporal, interconnecting, unrelated experiences) presents enormous challenges to conventionalized education constructions. Any education approach which is based on sensuous signs must reject the situated assessment strategies that pepper conventionalized education systems because they are almost impossible to measure, define, or rationalize – and they differ for each child, and for each child over time.

Why promote using Deleuzian notions of apprenticeship, then, if it requires such an enormous and fundamental intellectual and cultural shift? It must be promoted because it is already happening. Education *is* assemblage: adults, children, environments operate as individuated series-of-assemblages; of sights, memories, imaginings, desires – clusters of components that constantly shift. These series-as-assemblages are immanent, always in a fluid state, never fixed or situated, but transient. Fixed thinking about the child as learner helps perpetuate particular child-as-learner subjectivities and these operate at the mercy of stereotyped expectations. Particular stereotyped signs of achievement are looked for, to the ignorance or shielding of others that disrupt that. Children are persuaded to learn the same things in the same ways, striving for sameness in their apprenticeships, assemblages, desires and rhizomatic connections. However, using restrictive models or analyses invariably identify certain children as problematic. This questions the validity of the analysis and suggests that many children are positioned or constructed as problematic.

If education theorizations instead consider individuation and regard children as travelling along lines of flight, and that their unpredictable thought-strings encounter swarms of signs (the spatial, temporal, physical, metaphysical matter including furniture, uniforms, schoolbooks and resources, indoor and outdoor learning spaces, cultural concepts around education), such theorizations can help to dismantle the conventional analyses that construct children as certain types of learners. Thinking about concepts of individuation decentralizes the human and respects the mutability of this constant flux of components that are not the same for all and do not remain static.

EDUCATION AND THE POLITICS OF BECOMING

Although early childhood education has embraced hierarchical adult/child power relationships (Dahlberg et al., 1999) for some years, there is always hope that conceptual and theoretical shifts may occur. Sadly, new curricular and policy developments seem to establish new regimes of reality whilst bringing with them the residues of historic beliefs about young children and their learning. In relation to Australian early childhood, the Early Years Learning Framework (DEEWR, 2009) makes cognizant mention of this when it states: 'different theories about early childhood inform approaches to children's learning and development. Early childhood educators draw upon a range of perspectives in their work' (p. 11). These overt declarations help to make obvious the continued mesmerization of persuasive informing practices and conventionalized theories around early childhood learning and education.

New regimes also include the development of government initiative sites such as *My School* (DEEWR 2010), framed to support the new pedagogical preoccupations of the incumbent party into literacy and numeracy standards. While such sites proclaim to provide 'opportunity for everyone to learn more about Australian schools, and for Australian schools to learn more from each other' (McGraw, 2010) they primarily serve to initiate contemporary curriculum shifts, in this case a growing proliferation of testing and standards-driven delivery around two specific aspects of a curriculum. As Roy (2003) asserts 'it is crucial for the apprentice to become aware of these births and transformations, for they constantly lead us to view how new regimes emerge from old ones, and what residues they leave behind' (p. 128). Concreting childhood learner identities through embodied, dominant discourses (Dahlberg et al., 1999, p. 44) disregards learner *and* educator immanence and stifles opportunities for shifting perceived notions of good early childhood education and care practices.

To consider immanence (the potential) extends educators beyond fixating on trying make visible predetermined learner identities and expectations and encourages a practice of observing how –

> ... one thing/person is distinct from another because of some individuating essence – something that belongs to no kind, but which, though perfectly individuated, yet retains an indefiniteness ... has neither beginning nor end, origin nor destination. (St Pierre, 2004, p. 289)

Thinking about temporality/time in learning considers education as 'an individuation that was always starting up again in the middle of a different temporality, in new assemblages, never fully constituted, fluid, a flow meeting other flows' (St Pierre, 2004, p. 291). Temporality considers and acknowledges the impacting forces of systems of signs that intersect and intercept, that form a continually shifting set of experiences for each child. As an example, I see my daughter playing, sometimes with toys in the bath, sometimes with felt shapes, and I see that this play forms new assemblages, not just by her playing with those things, but by her encounters with her play space, the temperature of the room, the sounds around, the time of day, that day of her life. I see that she begins not at some starting point, but that she continues, folds, repeats, intercepts and that this never ceases; it is a continuous event, continuous learning. The bath, toys, felts are pre-existing, but the temporal significations of her play are unexpected and unpredictable because each time she plays she brings different combinations of signs to the experience.

The process of drawing exemplifies learner immanence. When drawing, the boundaries between papers and tables are lost, between papers and arms, between papers, fingers, crayons, breaths, muscles, thoughts are lost. Drawing subverts conventionalized concepts around learning sequences because, as it is undertaken, children connect to random clusters of things that are not singly theirs but that are connected to in a way that is particular to them. These random clusters are connected to in many ways and through differing experiences (taught, imagined, encountered) and each is a learning experience. The randomness of drawing also means that these learning experiences change and differ each time, even for each child. They are temporal, illuminating how random clusters can be encountered as a continuous series of cycles, not all running at the same speed or appearing in the same sequence.

I propose that drawing is education in Deleuzian terms. Drawing is a physical act, and also a metaphysical act. The bodily act comes from desire to produce, the body is without boundaries as drawing is carried out – an immersion takes place so that muscles, tendons, skin, hair are not consciously focused on but become into the surface plane and the drawing tools. Signs surround and may pour into an image, a drawer loses boundary surfaces as tools, paper, ideas, environment enact through the drawing. Metaphysical connections take place, the stops and starts, falterings, desires and other complexities can be encountered before a mark is made on a surface. Desiring may drive physical production, may manifest these stops and starts, these complexities, nevertheless as drawings are physically brought out much remains as metaphysical encountering, transient connection, momentary deterritorialising. Signs re-emerge but are repetitions of difference; the same is never the same, can never be reproduced but desire drives a perpetual attempt to try. Marks intercept and interrupt, signs connect rhizomatically and trouble the marks which surface, contingencies are made and subversions take place. Drawing dismantles individualization because it relies on production and receivership – it is momentarily suspended before being brought back into chaos as it is looked upon. This is not a linear process, against the persuasion of historical developmental canons, but a swirling, chaotic shifting, a continuous undertaking that has no beginning or end, but a rhizomatic, multiconnecting resonance with space, time, being.

Drawing is Deleuzian because it relies upon awareness and submersion into the 'flux that underlies the sign' (Roy, 2003, p. 139). This essay has focused on the need for a rethinking of conventionalized, dominant apprenticeship models in place in Australian early childhood contexts. Within an alternative approach to apprenticeship children's drawings are more than artistic activity, an aesthetic object, an attempt to create an artistic response. They are not neat, orderly or sequential, but host groups of signs that the drawer has pulled upon. If educators can acknowledge this and accept drawings in this way, they can begin to have exposure to the hugely diverse ways that children learn and process and disseminate information. If educators can think of drawings in this way, and if they make drawings too, they are exposed to multiple modes for working, of pressured frictions, convergences, interrogations on their own thinking, responding, theorizing. This exposure presents evidence to educators that children do not progress along neatly ordered sequential

EDUCATION AND THE POLITICS OF BECOMING

blocks, but that they respond to swarms of signs in unpredictable ways, and that this is affected by time and random interconnections.

References

Australian Curriculum and Assessment Reporting Authority (2010). *My School*. http://www.myschool.edu.au, accessed on 12 October 2010.

Australian Government Department of Education, Employment and Workplace Relations (DEEWR) (2009). *Belonging, being and becoming: The early years learning framework for Australia*. Barton, ACT: Commonwealth of Australia.

Bodrova, E., & Leong, D.J. (2003). Learning and development of preschool children from the Vygotskian perspective. In A. Kozulin, B. Gindis, V.S. Ageyev, & S.M. Miller (Eds.), *Vygotsky's educational theory in cultural context* (pp. 156–176). Cambridge: Cambridge University Press.

Borgnon, L. (2007). Conceptions of the self in early childhood: Territorializing identitities. *Educational Philosophy and Theory, 39*(3), 264–274.

Burman, E. (2001). Beyond the baby and the bathwater: Postdualistic developmental psychologies for diverse childhoods. *European Early Childhood Education Research Journal, 9*(1), 5–22.

Chaiklin, S. (2003). The zone of proximal development in Vygotsky's analysis of learning and instruction. In A. Kozulin, B. Gindis, V.S. Ageyev, & S.M. Miller (Eds.), *Vygotsky's educational theory in cultural context* (pp. 39–64). Cambridge: Cambridge University Press.

Dahlberg, G., Moss, P., & Pence, A. (1999). *Beyond quality in early childhood education*. London: Falmer Press.

Deleuze, G. (1964/2008). *Proust and signs*. (R. Howard, Trans.). London: Continuum. Originally published as *Proust et Signes,* Presses Universitaires de France, 1964.

Gavin, P. (2008). Reflection on time spent drawing: Towards animation. In L. Duff, & P. Sawdon (Eds.), *Drawing: The purpose* (pp. 45–56). Bristol: Intellect Books.

Kozulin, A., Gindis, B., Ageyev, V.S., & Miller, S.M. (Eds.) (2003). *Vygotsky's educational theory in cultural context*. Cambridge: Cambridge University Press.

McGraw, B. (2010). A note from ACARA. In *My School,* Australian Curriculum and Assessment Reporting Authority. http://www.myschool.edu.au, accessed on 12 October 2010.

Ministerial Council on Education, Employment, Training and Youth Affairs (MCEETYA) (2008). *Melbourne Declaration on Educational Goals for Twenty-First Century*. Accessed on 1 February 2010. http://www.curriculum.edu.au/verve/_resources/National_Declaration_on_the_ Educational_Goals_for_Young_Australians.pdf

Roy, K. (2003). *Teachers in nomadic spaces: Deleuze and curriculum* (Complicated conversations, Vol. 5). Bern: Peter Lang Publishing.

St Pierre, E. (2004). Deleuzian concepts for education: The subject undone. *Educational Philosophy and Theory, 36*(3), 283–296.

Vygotsky, L.S. (Author), M. Cole, V. John-Steiner, S. Scribner, E. Souberman (Eds.). (1978). *Mind in society: The development of higher psychological processes*. Cambridge, MA: Harvard University Press.

Multiple Literacies Theory: Discourse, sensation, resonance and becoming

Diana Masny

> This thematic issue on education and the politics of becoming focuses on how a Multiple Literacies Theory (MLT) plugs into practice in education. MLT does this by creating an assemblage between discourse, text, resonance and sensations. What does this produce? Becoming AND how one might live are the product of an assemblage (May, 2005; Semetsky, 2003). In this paper, MLT is the approach that explores the connection between educational theory and practice through the lens of an empirical study of multilingual children acquiring multiple writing systems simultaneously. The introduction explicates discourse, text, resonance, sensation and becoming. The second section introduces certain Deleuzian concepts that plug into MLT. The third section serves as an introduction to MLT. The fourth section is devoted to the study by way of a rhizoanalysis. Finally, drawing on the concept of the rhizome, this article exits with potential lines of flight opened by MLT. These are becomings which highlight the significance of this work in terms of transforming not only how literacies are conceptualized, especially in minority language contexts, but also how one might live.

Introduction

I want to take up the concept of discourse not so much as Deleuze might have (Deleuze & Guattari, 1987) but rather using a Deleuzian approach to the creation of a concept. As Colebrook (2002) stated, 'A concept is the creation of a way of thinking' (p. 20). It is a way to approach a problem. In this context the problem is twofold: the first centres on how discourse, resonance, sensation and becoming relate to each other and plug into Multiple Literacies Theory (MLT), and the second deals with what the links are to educational practice. Because MLT is both theoretical and practical, a theory-practice, this article presents concepts and also explores how these might work in practice. To this end, an empirical study of multilingual children acquiring multiple writing systems simultaneously is used as a lens to look at MLT as theory-practice. Significantly, neither the theoretical/conceptual nor the empirical data are privileged. The article is an assemblage in which these and other elements interact. What might this assemblage enable in terms of thinking about MLT as theory-practice for literacies education? To begin, I introduce the concept of discourse.

What is discourse? How does discourse function? I understand discourse as an event both virtual and actual. Discourse is a coming together of texts (at least two). Each text in the actual and virtual is a machinic assemblage. In the virtual, text is

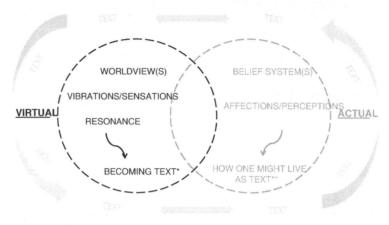

*Lines of Flight/ Deterritorialization
**Territorialization

Figure 1. The potentiality of discourse.

pre-personal, *asignifiying* machines. Text is actualized through an assemblage of heterogeneous forces that come together in a particular time and place (actualization of a sense-event). Text is a sense event, an outcome of virtual events connecting with actual experiences (Masny, 2009a).

Figure 1 is a visual conceptualization of discourse. The lighter colour relates to concepts in the virtual and the darker color to concepts in the actual. In the electronic version of the figure, these concepts are in constant motion as they intersect thus rendering the actual-virtual movement. Discourse and text in the virtual consist of sensations, resonance and worldview and in the actual, affections, perceptions and belief systems. The question becomes: How do they relate to each other and to discourse?

Worldview in the virtual is itself a machinic assemblage, and part of the assemblage that constitutes a text in the virtual. It is actualized as a set of beliefs in an open system. Worldview and belief systems plug into discourse and text for they are important to the deterritorialization (disruption) and becoming of texts and discourse. In the virtual, text and worldview, are considered blocs of sensation, that is, affects, and percepts. Sensations are vibrations. They seize each other and resonate. Deleuze provides an example: that of the sensations of the violin and sensations of the piano in a sonata, two bodies seizing each other and resonating.

> We know nothing about a body[1] until we know what it can do, in other words, what its affects are, how they can or cannot enter into composition with other affects, with the affects of another body, either to destroy that body or to be destroyed by it, either to exchange actions and passions with it or to join with it in composing a more powerful body. (Deleuze & Guattari, 1987, p. 257; see also Deleuze, 2004, pp. 39–41)

Resonance can produce a peaked amplitude, a flat amplitude or somewhere in between. A peaked amplitude can refer to bodies affecting each other with great intensity in unpredictable ways, whereas a flat amplitude is the product of bodies and affective intensities that reduce the power to act (e.g. sadness, in Deleuze & Parnet,

2007). This aspect of resonance, amplitude and the power to affect and be affected has important implications for discourse and educational practice.

The process, from sensation to resonance is a becoming *other* and a virtual text or texts (a discourse) emerge in the actual charged with affection and perception. Simultaneously, worldviews, pre-personal assemblages of asignifying machines, are actualized according to a particular context in space and time. They are actualized as an open system[2] of beliefs. It is within an open system that reading is disruptive and immanent. An open system allows for deterritorialization (of beliefs, affections, perceptions, texts and discourse) and becoming to happen.

What is produced? Through a coming together of texts, a discourse is produced and produces us. Discourse in the actual is a territory effected from reading, reading the world and self. For example, a sonata is a territory. It can be considered a discourse, a connection of different movements or texts. Composing, playing, visualizing, hearing and tasting a sonata happens with reading, reading the world and self *in situ*. The resonance conveys amplitude (peaked, flat, in-between) whose intensity impacts the power to affect and to be affected while the sonata interacts with one or more bodies (sadness, joy, pleasantness, and so on). The experience of affections and perceptions in relation with reading, reading the world and self disrupts and brings on the thought of (immanence). This event connects with how one might live.[3] The event of reading intensively brings on a deterritorialization (of experience), setting off rhizomatic lines of flight of becoming and transformation (immanence).

Returning to Figure 1, with each repetition from virtual to actual and virtual, from becoming to how one might live, the repetitions continue. However, it is different each time; assemblages differ each time. A discourse (and by implication, texts) as a territory in the actual deterritorializes in the virtual through reading intensively (disruptive) and immanently. This process opens up possibilities for lines of flight and becoming to happen and reterritorialize in the actual into another discourse and transformation of self. The discourses that produce us happen through the process of becoming and how one might live. Despite the graphic showing on one side becoming to be virtual and on the other side how one might live to be actual, 'the passage of the virtual into the actual does not exhaust the virtual; the virtual remains immanent within the actual ... and the virtual immanent within the actual is manifest as sensation' (Bogue, 2003, p. 183).

To summarize, in the virtual, discourse is pre-personal and consists of sensation (affects and percepts), resonance, worldviews, texts and becoming that transform how one might live, which is an assemblage in the current context of perception, affections, belief systems and discourse in the actual.

What is Multiple Literacies Theory (MLT)?

I explore MLT in terms of how it functions and what it produces. MLT, developed by Masny (2006) refers to literacies as a construct (machinic assemblages). Literacies consist of words, gestures, attitudes, and ways of listening, speaking, writing, the human and the non-human: ways of becoming with the world. They are texts, in a broad sense (for example, music, visual arts – both painting and sculpting – physics, mathematics, digital remixes). Texts are an assemblage of events from which sense emerges. Literacies can be are taken up as visual, oral, written, tactile, olfactory, and in multimodal digital. They fuse with religion, gender, race, culture, and power, and that produce speakers, writers, artists, digital avatars: communities. Literacies are actualized according to a particular context in time and in space in which they operate. Given the nomadic tendencies of literacies; they are not wed to a context, but are taken up in unpredictable ways across various contexts. Reading is both intensive (disruptive) and immanent (Masny, 2009a).

Literacies involve constant movement in the processes of becoming *other* (Masny, 2006). Transformations take on rhizomatic lines of flight involving creative processes that impact worldviews, becoming, belief systems and how one might live. Transformation, in this context, is about becoming *other* through continuous investment in reading, reading the world and self as texts in multiple environments (e.g. home, school, and community). It is from continuous investment in life experiences that connect that one is formed, transformed and becomes *other*. In short, literacies are about reading, reading the world, and self as texts and becoming *other*. MLT acknowledges the potential 'for transformation and becoming in all life' (Colebrook, 2002, p. 47) in order to understand how one might live (May, 2005).

Key concepts

Becoming

Becoming is about the untimely and implies indeterminacy. Becoming is a product continuously producing, while literacies are processes that form and shape becoming. Becoming is the power (*puissance*) to affect and be affected; life's power to form new affects and connections. Becoming is central to MLT. Becoming is the effect of experiences that connect and intersect. Transformations are continuous. What it once was could be no longer. It is different. It is through transformation that becoming happens.

Literacies as processes

By placing the emphasis on how, the focus is on the nature of literacies as processes. Current theories on literacies examine literacies as an endpoint, a product. While MLT acknowledges that books, Internet, equations, and buildings are objects, sense emerges when relating these objects as texts (assemblages, experiences of life) to reading, reading the world, and self as texts. Accordingly, an important aspect of MLT is focusing on how literacies intersect in *becoming*. This is what MLT produces: becoming, that is, from continuous investments in literacies literate individuals[4] are formed. A person is a text in continuous becoming. Reading and reading the world through text influences the text one continually becomes (Dufresne & Masny, 2001).

Reading the world and self as texts

Reading is intensive and immanent. To read intensively is to read critically. To read intensively signals that cognitive, social, cultural, and political forces are at work in reading critically. In so doing, reading critically is reading disruptively, and in interested and untimely ways. Moreover, because reading happens in untimely ways, there is no prediction about how reading is taken up. This leads us to reading as

EDUCATION AND THE POLITICS OF BECOMING

immanence. Take the example of watching a movie. How often do you see a scene that may transport you to think of what might happen next? Another possibility might be creating connections with your life and the thought of this happening to you or your dog. Not only is reading untimely, but is also is the thought of what can happen. In this way, reading as sense emerges and a power to become happens (Masny, 2009b).

Rhizoanalysis

In this section, the multiple literacies framework is the lens used to examine how competing writing systems in learning a second literacy transform children and become *other*. Methodology has been deterritorialized and reterritorialized as a rhizomatic process that does not engage in methodological considerations in a conventional way. It resists temptations to interpret and ascribe meaning; it avoids conclusions. St Pierre (2002) identifies two specific problems with received notions of qualitative data: (1) that they 'must be translated into words so that they can be accounted for and interpreted' (p. 403); and (2) that they are produced and collected, coded, categorized, analyzed, and interpreted in a specifically *linear* fashion. In this study, I find myself facing these same problems as I encounter what St Pierre has called 'transgressive data': data that escape language and become 'uncodable, excessive, out-of-control, out-of category ... [in short] the commonplace meaning of the category, data, no longer held' (p. 404). At the same time research processes become rhizomatic; the 'linear process is interrupted because the researcher enters this narrative in the middle' (p. 404). Instead rhizoanalysis views data as 'fluid and in flux', thus keeping the way open and working rhizomatic in-betweens to ask what connections may be happening between multiplicities.

Participant and activities

This study was conducted over a two-year period from 2005 to 2007 and involved five children, their parents, teachers, and day care educators. This article focuses on one of these children, Hello Kitty, a pseudonym selected by the child. Hello Kitty is 6–7 years old during the study. Her mother is Francophone and speaks English as well. Her father is a unilingual English speaker. The family lives in Ottawa and the children attend school where French is the sole language of instruction. Since the family resides in a majority English-speaking province and their mother attended a French-language school, minority language rights of the children to attend French language schools is guaranteed under the Canadian Charter of Human Rights and Freedoms (1982).

Data collection includes: (1) observations of literate events in class (two times in each year of the study) and at home (two times in each each year of the study); (2) interviews with the teachers, and Hello Kitty's parents about experiences with multiple literacies and the child's literate development; (3) observations of each child-participant teaching their mother tongue to peers to see what knowledge of writing systems were foregrounded (one session each year of the study); and (4) texts produced by the children. Hello Kitty was also given a photo camera and was asked to take photos of anything that was related to literacies. Before starting the activity, Hello Kitty was shown examples of photos the researcher had taken. There were

EDUCATION AND THE POLITICS OF BECOMING

photos of road signs, a sculpture, a musical score, a newspaper and math samples of additions and subtractions. Each one was discussed in terms of reading and reading each one differently. The specific vignettes below are drawn from interviews between the researcher and Hello Kitty after an observation of a Language Arts lesson in year 1 of the study, after a math lesson in year 1, and during the discussion around the photos Hello Kitty took in year 2. There is also a vignette from the researcher's interview with Hello Kitty's parents in year 2 of the study.

Analysis

Vignettes

Do not look to these vignettes as data and seeking to find concrete proof of transformation. Data in the more traditional way is about empirical data. Deleuze and Guattari (1994) have moved away from empiricism because it supposes a foundation grounded on human beings who seek to fix categories and themes. They call upon transcendental empiricism. It transcends experience (Immanence). It deals with perceptions and the thought of experience creating connections and becoming *other.*

The analyses presented at the end of each vignette are informed by the MLT framework. All interviews with HK took place in French.

Vignette 1

(HK = Hello Kitty, R = researcher, M = mother, F = father)

This vignette, from year 1 of the study when Hello Kitty was 6 years old, is taken from a conversation with the researcher after a language arts class. During the class the children had been writing stories about a recent field trip to the Cordon Bleu cooking school.

R: What do you put in a story?
HK: Period, capital letters, small letters, more letters.
R: What do you do with all these letters?
HK: Put them in a sentence.
R: What is a sentence?
HK: I don't know.
  (HK shows a sentence. She reads it.)
R: How do you know it is a sentence?
HK: The period.

The assemblage of sensations: sensations of the period, sensations of the sentence and Hello Kitty as a bloc of sensations seize each other and resonate. There is resonance. The questions then become: What amplitude is produced, and what intensities are there in the power to affect and to be affected?

A becoming of the worldview happens in the virtual and produces a belief system in the actual: bakers produce bread and biscuits (see Figure 2). Simultaneously, there are texts produced in the actual: the text itself, and other texts: the conversation with the researcher, the researcher and Hello Kitty. This assemblage of texts come

118

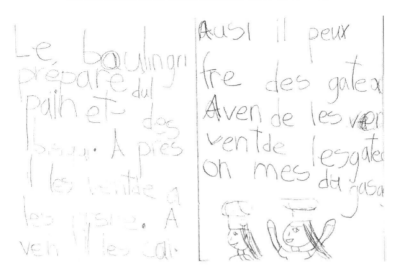

Figure 2. [Translation: The baker/bakery prepares bread and biscuits. After, he sells them to people. Before, he *** them. He also makes cakes. Before he sells them, we put icing.]

together to create a discourse. Could it be a story-discourse? Hello Kitty tells us what goes into a story; what a story should look like. The discourse focuses on its mechanics (rather than say its ideas, grammar elements of a sentence, or something different and unthought-of). How is it that one particular belief system (and not another) happens when the potential of the virtual is 'infinite'? MLT asks: What is produced? A worldview is actualized. It is a particular belief system produced out of assemblages connecting in the mind. There is a perception (and affection) of story in the actual. In the context of MLT, what reading, reading the world and self happen to disrupt and deterritorialize the current discourse about a story?

Vignette 2

This vignette is taken from a photo session in year 1 of the study when Hello Kitty was 6 years-old. This is a photo of Hello Kitty and her two sisters, one older and the other younger, doing a pencil and paper activity on the kitchen table. The following is an exchange between Hello Kitty and the researcher about the photograph.

    R: You like to draw?
    HK: Yes! A lot, a lot, a lot!
    R: Do you like to write sometimes?
    HK: Yes.
    R: When you write what is easiest?
    HK: Periods and capital letters.
    R: And what do you find difficult?
    HK: Exclamation marks and small letters.

In this vignette, an assemblage of texts (the photo, the conversation, Hello Kitty and the researcher…) produce a discourse. Reading Hello Kitty's responses, there are blocs of sensation: the period, capital letters, exclamation marks, small letters. These

Figure 3. Hello Kitty and her two sisters.

resonate in the virtual and become actualized as a belief system in the actual *in situ*, namely some are easier and some are harder.

A kind of discourse is being produced and is producing Hello Kitty. Could it be a territorialized school discourse? Within MLT (Masny, 2009b), literacies are actualized according to a particular context in time and in space in which they operate. School is a space where writing happens. Writing can be tied to a powerful (*pouvoir*) striated space (Deleuze & Guattari, 1987), an institutionalized space given to curriculum mandates that include the basics of writing. Deleuze and Guattari on Chomsky's work comment that –

> A grammar element is firstly a power (*pouvoir*) marker and secondly a syntactical marker ... You will construct grammatically correct sentences; you will divide each statement into a noun phrase and a verb phrase. (Deleuze & Guattari, 1987, p. 7)

Drawing on the potential of the virtual, it could be otherwise. MLT suggests that the 'otherwise' could happen as movements of smoothness create spaces that flow over striated movements, spaces in which the former deterritorialize the latter to open onto lines of flight, to transformation and becoming *other*. In sum, both striated and smooth spaces must be operational (Deleuze & Guattari, 1987). They can overlap. What is important to consider is that reading, reading the world

EDUCATION AND THE POLITICS OF BECOMING

and self constantly happen in smooth and striated spaces from disruption to restablization. In this event (the exchange between Hello Kitty and the researcher), might Hello Kitty's responses be related to the connections happening in the mind in relation to reading, reading the world and self, MLT?

Vignette 3

This vignette is taken from year 1 during a math class when children were experimenting with triangles.

> The teacher asks the children to do a triangle. Hello Kitty begins by making a triangle and other geometric shapes as asked. She first begins by drawing a circle. The teacher would like her to do a triangle. She converts her circle by putting 'triangles' around the circle.

Hello Kitty does a circle and says it is the sun. The teacher tells Hello Kitty that she has to use the adhesive points to do a geometric shape like a triangle. She proceeds to do several 'triangles' around the sun. In the end she counted 10 triangles around the sun. The teacher pointed out to the class that a triangle must have three sides. But Hello Kitty's drawing of triangles is different. What does this difference produce?

In this vignette, circles, triangles, worldview, teacher, Hello Kitty are blocs of sensations. They seize each other. There is resonance in a process of becoming. What is produced (actualized)? She complies by making triangles, but they are

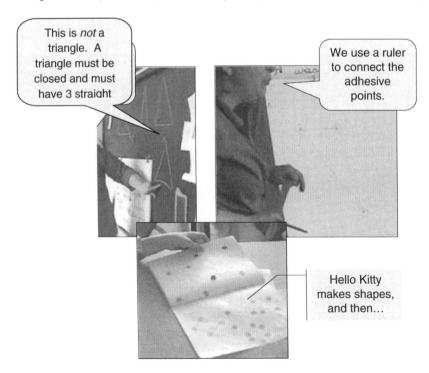

Figure 4. Hello Kitty's teacher gives a lesson on triangles.

EDUCATION AND THE POLITICS OF BECOMING

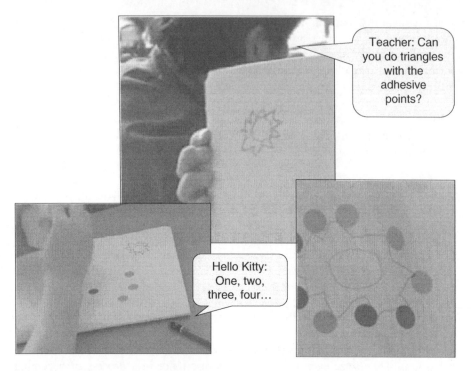

Figure 5. Hello Kitty completes an activity on triangles.

made on her terms (a belief system in the actual). In creating a sun (smooth space), combined with teacher instructions about doing a triangle (striated space), might there be affective resistance? Could resistance produce what MLT would consider an event? An event is an assemblage of worldview and block of sensations that seize each other and resonate emerging in the actual as affections and a belief system in smooth space (HK's triangles) over a belief system in striated space (curriculum triangles) producing ruptures, a potential becoming and transforming while reading, reading the world and self. Could creativity and desire effect (affect) a deterritorialization of math as geometry and reterritorialize it as something different: art, drawing? There is a further deterritorialization of triangles as having three straight sides and a reterritorialization of triangles as potentially having a curved side as in the case of the sun.

Might there be tension/rupture as art meets teacher? In this encounter affects are at work: powers to affect and be affected. In the affective exchange (i.e. resonance) between these bodies (human and nonhuman) becoming happens. Within MLT, could this be a sun-discourse? A math discourse? An art discourse? There is an assemblage of texts: the video clips, the teacher, Hello Kitty, the math class, etc.

According to MLT, literacies (reading, reading the world and self) as processes are about transforming and becoming. The assemblage (beliefs of teacher, beliefs of Hello Kitty ...) produced a rupture. Since literacies are processes, could reading, reading the world and self have brought a becoming assemblage in which the sun now has ten triangles?

EDUCATION AND THE POLITICS OF BECOMING

Vignette 4

In this vignette, year 2 of the study when Hello Kitty was 7 years old, she took a photo of a 'Miracle Bubbles' bottle. She then produced this drawing. Since the photo displayed a bottle with writing in English; I asked her if she could tell me a story about Miracle Bubbles in English. She refused and started to tell the story in French.

> R: Could you tell me a story about Miracle Bubbles in English?
> HK: I don't want to [in French]. Once upon a time, a boy played with bubbles.
> R: What is 'garçon' in English?
> HK: [In English] *Boy*. [Continuing in French] He had an animal. He had a mouth like a square.
> R: How do we say that in English?
> HK: I don't want to.
> R: It is because it is difficult?
> HK: Yes, because I forgot how to say it.
> R: So, the word '*bouche*.' What is that in English?
> HK: [in English] *Mouth*.

Once Hello Kitty starts the story in French, the researcher interrupted her to ask her what the word for *garçon* in English is. She responded in English and then continued her story in French. From time to time the researcher would ask for certain words in English, she would respond correctly and continue her story in French. Hello Kitty has the ability to go back and forth between English and French and maintain her storyline in French. In an interview, her mother insists on French being the language most often spoke at home. The school policy is that no English be spoken in school unless it is during the English class. The interviews with Hello Kitty and her mother took place at school.

Figure 6. Hello Kitty's drawing of 'Miracle Bubbles'.

EDUCATION AND THE POLITICS OF BECOMING

In the virtual, text, drawing, story, Hello Kitty, researcher, mother, father, home, school are asignifying machines and blocs of sensations. They seize each other and resonate. Amplitude, intensity and the power to affect and be affected happen. Worldview is actualized in a belief system. What kind of belief system? One that states that you cannot use English in school? Could this belief give rise to a resistance of telling the story in English? Is the connecting of bodies creating affective resistance? Virtual texts are actualized as an assemblage to create discourse. Might the power to affect and be affected actualize in affections and perceptions bringing on tensions, confrontation, struggle as part of the actual assemblage of the discourse? What is produced? According to MLT, while the assemblage produced the discourse, the discourse also produced us (Hello Kitty and researcher) in reading, reading the world and self.

Vignette 5

This vignette is from year 2 of the study and takes place during an interview with the researcher around a photo session. However, in this vignette, Hello Kitty is referring to a picture she drew of a man with bubbles. (See again Figure 6).

R: How do you know if it is French or an English drawing?
HK: I can just decide if the drawing is French or English.
R: If someone else does the drawing, how do you know which language it is?
HK: I will ask the person.
R: How do you tell in what language the drawing is in?
HK: I decide. It is what I want. I choose French all the time. Only sometimes English.
R: What do you do when your drawings are in English?
HK: I don't know.

Hello Kitty loves to draw a lot. In her mind, it is she who decides what language the drawings are in. She demonstrates considerable creativity. In a conventional world drawings do not have a language, but as desire connects up with creativity, a drawing is English OR French. It is interesting that it is not self-evident from looking at the drawing which language it is; for example, Hello Kitty has to ask someone if their drawing is French OR English. How does a drawing, in Hello Kitty's belief system at least, exceed conventional linguistic boundaries?

From a prepersonal, perspective, we would *not* say that Hello Kitty makes a decision, but rather a decision *happens* immanently. So, when a decision happens, it is based on affection (Cole, 2005). We are dealing with blocs of sensations: sensations of language, sensations of painting (art/drawing) seize each other. There is resonance. They become actualized in particular ways (as a French drawing, as an English drawing) depending on the context, on the event. This is an MLT moment when literacies are operationalized *in situ*.

A worldview, in the virtual, becomes actualized as a belief system. One can wonder if the Miracle Bubbles drawing, that Hello Kitty drew to accompany her story, is French OR an English drawing. What would she say? Could the English word 'bubble' be in a French drawing? Could the French word 'bulle' be in the drawing if the drawing were English? What of the relationship between intensity

124

EDUCATION AND THE POLITICS OF BECOMING

the resonance produces and the power to affect and to be affected? In MLT, the mutual seizing of affects and percepts – and actualized as affection in reading, reading the world and self as text – produce a French OR English art discourse. Discourse within MLT is a coming together of texts (Hello Kitty, the researcher, the Magic Bubble drawing, and other ...). For MLT, it is literacies as processes that transform and become *other*. Could it be different, something else outside this linguistic binary?

Vignette 6

(Interview with the parents, Year 2. Father = F, Mother = M)

F: When Hello Kitty writes a story she will say it is a story in French or a story in English. However, the script is the same regardless. [Comment: Dad reads English only] What she writes and what she tells you is two different things.
R: So she can distinguish between the two languages, but not in writing?
M & F: Yes.
F: Last year, she would say that this is an English story and bring a French book and vice-versa. She knows I do not know French yet I would ask her to bring me a story and she would still bring me a French book. Now she is able to make that distinction.

When comparing how Hello Kitty wrote and chose books in Year 1 and Year 2 of the project, each time, there is a different kind of assemblage going on. In Year 1, a book's language is not pre-established in conventional ways. The affects and percepts of the artwork in the book may have been involved as part of the assemblage in the virtual. Recalling the previous vignette, we can ask how the selection of books might be based on the language of the illustrations.

Deterritorializations happened in the process of blocs of sensations (percept and affect) seizing each other and resonating in the virtual, pre-personal language (drawings, letters, words). Text in the virtual gets actualized as texts (written stories written by Hello Kitty, story books presented to the parents in the different languages, linguistic conventions, parents as text, Hello Kitty as text ...). In addition, a worldview in the virtual is actualized as a belief system (choice of storybooks irrespective of the language of the audience to selection of storybooks according to language of the audience). Could a territorialization (of learning, of literacies, of language) be happening? Yet, as Hello Kitty encounters these texts (books, drawings, languages: French/English) how does reading immanently disrupt again to deterritorialize and reterritorialize otherwise? Each time, the assemblage is different. The assemblage is deterritorialized and reterritorialized in the process of reading, reading the world and self in becoming *other*.

The texts come together actualized as discourse. Such a discourse may be operating in striated space especially in year 2 as linguistic conventions establish the books to be in French OR English. What of smooth spaces related to becoming? What happens to texts that were once not fixed as French *OR* English? Texts are also becoming *other*. From an MLT perspective that works with the prepersonal, it is not so much Hello Kitty who chooses or decides if a book is French or English. Rather it is immanence: reading immanently as connections/assemblages happen-

125

ing in the mind-site, that bringing on the thought of ... a book in French (when in fact it might be in English), the thought of ... a book in English.

Lines of flight: Sensation, resonance, becoming, education, MLT

This article is at the crossroads of discourse, education and becoming. Within MLT, discourse is taken up as an assemblage of texts that come together as sensation (affects) and resonate in becoming. Within MLT, discourse is an event, a coming together of texts virtual and actual. In the virtual, discourse is an assemblage of virtual texts that are asignifying machines, blocs of sensations (becoming as affects and forces as percepts) (Deleuze, 2004) that seize each other and resonate. How does discourse function? When texts and worldviews come together in the becoming virtual, affects resonate. The result is amplitude, the extent to which forces as percepts are productive (Bogue, 2003). Amplitude communicates the intensity of the power to affect and be affected as bodies connect.

In the actual, discourse-as-event, is actualized as a coming together/assemblage of texts, based on a belief system charged with affection and perception. Central to MLT and discourse event is that literacies are processes, reading the world and self. It is about literacies-as-processes that transform and become *other*. It is about becoming with the world and that also begs the question: how one might live. Within MLT, how one might live is about immanence, reading immanently and intensively. Reading is connected to the power to affect and be affected, the power to deterritorialize that opens up to difference and to reterritorialize, the constant ebb and flow between the virtual and actual and difference. Within MLT, reading, reading the world and self disrupts, opens up to difference (becoming *other*), gives rise to multiple understandings of self and the world and creates multiple potentialities of the future.

Educational practice should lead us to render perceptible the imperceptible forces that populate the world and that affect us (Deleuze & Guattari, 1994, pp. 172–182). MLT can be the process whereby becoming is inherent to reading, reading the world and self as texts. Finally, what MLT can offer educational practice is for the latter to ensure that the goals of educational practice center on how one might live.

In the first three vignettes examined from Hello Kitty, language concepts – grammar elements, sentence structure, what constitutes a story, what constitutes a text (in language arts, in math and art) – can be thought of in terms of discourse as worldviews in the virtual actualized as belief systems about how language systems work. The becoming-literate of multilingual children like Hello Kitty is a process that involves a complex assemblage replete with affects and resonances. This research draws the attention of researchers and practitioners alike to the ways in which these discourses, as events, are produced by a myriad of sensations assembling, interacting, and resonating. Moreover, it brings forth important questions about the ways in which teaching practices are part of this assemblage, the ways in which practices can both territorialize *and* deterritorialize, that is disrupt, what literacies are about. The disruption of assemblages can work like resistance that produces different discourses about literacies. In turn, this might impact the becoming-literate of children like Hello Kitty and the text that she continually becomes through reading, reading the

EDUCATION AND THE POLITICS OF BECOMING

world and self. As such, the concept of discourse has important implications for the education of multilingual children.

In the last three vignettes forming the rhizoanalysis, an increased awareness of the way sensations resonate and produce becoming is particularly significant for educational practices in minority language contexts. It seems that the affective resonance, as French and English form part of the assemblage, is particularly intense, but what is the amplitude produced (peaked, flat, in-between)? How does this impact a body's power to affect and be affected? How might virtual worldviews actualize and what potential benefits could alternative belief systems have for seeing minority language education differently? This is a critical question to ask as it bears directly on becoming-literate in minority language contexts and on opening new lines of flight for how one might live.

MLT as a concept for educational futures disrupts the psychological perspective of reading and exceeds the boundaries of conventional literacies. Nomadic connections provide pathways to create reading as intensive and immanent. When connections happen they do so in relation to assemblages that disrupt/rupture while reading, reading the world and self. Learning is about the nomadic pathways travelled along uncharted unknowns (Semetsky, 2003). MLT as presented in the introduction of the article is educational and philosophical. MLT with its concern for creativity and concept creation is interested in becoming and how one might live. May (2005) states:

> ... the question of how one might live ... concerns the creation of concepts of difference that allow us to consider living at different levels. Among these levels we may find a variety of understandings of ourselves and this variety of understandings may open up a variety of futures to be lived. (p. 25)

> There is no creation without experiment. Whatever the difference between scientific and philosophical (and, my addition, artistic) language, functives are no more pre-given than concepts or sensations. (Deleuze & Guattari, 1994, p. 127)

MLT is experimenting and creating. It is a theory constantly becoming. It is a practice and as such has to be used; it has to work. It produces becoming. There is potentiality of MLT for the future of education.

Acknowledgements

I want to thank Monica Waterhouse for her careful reading of this article and her comments for which I am grateful. I also want to acknowledge the technical support I received from Monica Waterhouse and Brenna Quigley.

This research has been funded by the Social Sciences and Humanities Research Council of Canada and Heritage Canada's Official Languages Program.

Notes

1. A body can be anything: animal, sounds, mind, idea, linguistic corpus, social collectivity. (Deleuze, 1988, p. 127)
2. An open system is non-linear, not fixed and refutes essences. An open system allows for creativity and invention to take flight *in situ* (interacting with the environment). An example is the rhizome.

EDUCATION AND THE POLITICS OF BECOMING

3. How one might live (May, 2005) relates to a way of seeing the world that disturbs verities and 'opens up new ways of seeing and of conceiving this world ... are "remarkable, interesting or important" ' (p. 22). The word, one, does not refer to a privileged centered subject; rather it can be human, non-human, relationships, a mouth. One way Deleuze approached the question of how one might live relates to what might living consist of? Living consists in difference and actualization. Difference is a process alive with vitality. Within MLT, reading, reading the world and self disrupts, opens up to difference (becoming other), gives rise to multiple understandings of self and the world and creates multiple possibilities of the future. How might one live is both actual and virtual.
4. Individuals are not automatically human.

References

Bogue, R. (2003). *Deleuze on music, painting and art*. New York: Routledge.

Canadian Charter of Rights and Freedoms. (1982). *Part I of the Constitution Act*. Retrieved 31 January 2011 from http://laws.justice.gc.ca/en/charter/

Cole, D.R. (2005). Affective literacy. In J. Young (Ed.), Proceedings of the ALEA/AATE National Conference: *Pleasurable learning, passionate teaching, provocative debates* (pp. 154–165). Norwood, Australia: Australian Association for the Teaching of English.

Colebrook, C. (2002). *Deleuze*. New York: Routledge.

Deleuze, G (1988). *Spinoza and practical philosophy*. San Francisco: City of Lights Publication.

Deleuze, G. (2004). *Francis Bacon: The logic of sensation*. Minneapolis: University of Minnesota Press.

Deleuze, G., & Guattari, F. (1987). *A thousand plateaux*. Minneapolis: University of Minnesota Press.

Deleuze, G., & Guattari, F. (1994). *What is philosophy?* New York: University of Columbia Press.

Deleuze, G., & Parnet, C. 2007. *Dialogues II*. New York: University of Columbia Press. Revised Edition.

Dufresne, T., & Masny, D. (2001). *The makings of minority education: The Québec educational curriculum reforms*. Third Congress of the Humanities and Social Sciences, Québec City, Université de Laval; 16–19 May 2001.

Masny, D. (2006). Learning and creative processes: A poststructural perspective on language and multiple literacies. *International Journal of Learning, 12*(5), 149–156.

Masny, D. (2009a). Literacies as becoming. In D. Masny & D.R. Cole (Eds.), *Multiple Literacies Theory: A Deleuzean perspective* (pp. 13–30). Rotterdam: Sense Publishers.

Masny, D. (2009b). *Bridging access, equity and quality: The case for Multiple Literacies*. http://www.englishliteracyconference.com.au/files/documents/hobart/conferencePapers/refereed/MasnyDiana.pdf. Accessed on 12 January 2011.

May, T. (2005). *Deleuze: An introduction*. New York: Cambridge University Press.

Semetsky, I. (2003). The problematics of human subjectivity: Gilles Deleuze and the Deweyan legacy. *Studies in Philosophy and Education, 22*(3–4), 211–225.

St Pierre, E.A. (2002). Methodology in the fold and the irruption of transgressive data. In S.B. Merriam & Associates (Eds.), *Qualitative research in practice: Examples for discussion and analysis* (pp. 399–416). San Francisco: Jossey-Bass.

'We don't believe media anymore': Mapping critical literacies in an adult immigrant language classroom

Monica Waterhouse

> This article maps critical literacies conceptually and empirically in the context of adult immigrant language classrooms. It begins by describing Deleuze and Guattari's cartographic approach. Then it traces critical literacies situated conceptually within a Freirean paradigm before mapping them differently through the Deleuzian-informed Multiple Literacies Theory (MLT). MLT frames critical literacies as reading intensively, that is, disruptively. This alternative conceptualization is then mobilized empirically in relation to the problems and politics produced in the qualitative study of one language classroom. In this classroom, reading a newspaper article provoked a series of transformative events or *becomings*, a concept created by Deleuze and Guattari and which is central to MLT. A research cartography is presented as a series of vignettes weaving data and concepts. This empirical mapping of media literacies and reading intensively offers insights into the politics of becoming in adult immigrant language classrooms and opens conceptual lines of flight between critical literacies and reading intensively.

How might we think about different conceptualizations of critical literacies in relation to adult immigrant language education and how might this thinking be important in terms of producing more satisfying ways of 'how one might live' (May, 2005) pedagogically and with the world? In this article, I respond to these questions in two ways: conceptually and empirically. First, I conceptually map critical literacies as situated within two different paradigms in language education contexts, namely the Freirean-informed humanist tradition which I refer to as the received view, and the Deleuzian-informed Multiple Literacies Theory (MLT) (Masny, 2006, 2009b). Second, I mobilize MLT's alternative conceptualization of critical literacies empirically in relation to the problems and politics emerging in one adult immigrant language classroom where a newspaper article provoked a series of transformations, or in Deleuzian-Guattarian terms *becoming*. Through the lens of MLT, data from a qualitative study are creatively selected and presented as a series of vignettes. These vignettes offer a vector to see how a Deleuzian-Guattarian mapping of critical literacies might offer insights into the politics of becoming in adult immigrant language classrooms. In addition, I pay particular attention in the empirical portion of the article to how familiar qualitative research strategies are reformulated in terms of Deleuze and Guattari's cartography, a creative mode of inquiry that resists representation. Finally, I discuss some implications of these different mappings – between critical literacies and reading intensively – in adult immigrant language classrooms.

Conceptually mapping critical literacies

This section aims to conceptually map critical literacies within a Freirean-informed paradigm and within MLT. My use of the term 'mapping' is purposeful and refers specifically to Deleuze and Guattari's (1980/1987) notion of cartography. Therefore, it is important to devote the first part of this section to articulating cartography and its associated concepts: tracing, map, de/reterritorialization, line of flight, difference, and the power of life to disrupt. Cartography allows me to frame my discussion of different paradigm-specific conceptualizations of critical literacies in terms of mapping rather than comparison or critique. Notably, I return to the importance of cartographic concepts in the empirical section of the paper.

What is cartography?

For Deleuze and Guattari (1980/1987) cartography involves both the fixity of tracings and the creativity of maps. In cartography, the decentering of given structures and ways of thinking, the tracing, makes way for new structures and novel thought connections, the mapping. Notably maps can never supplant tracings because even the dynamic map may become fixed as a tracing. Tracings and maps are closely related and may become indistinguishable from one another. That is why Deleuze and Guattari (1980/1987) insist that 'the tracing should always be put back on the map' (p. 13), demanding that we attend to the relationship of tracings and maps and how they interact and transform each other.

How do Deleuze and Guattari articulate these interactive, cartographic processes between tracings and maps? Because Deleuze and Guattari are infamous for their concept creation and proliferation (Deleuze & Guattari, 1991/1994), we need to follow some conceptual links to the notion of territories. Deleuze and Guattari (1980/1987) refer to territories and processes of deterritorialization and reterritorialization which are, in turn, rooted in Deleuze's (1968/1994) ontology of difference. When a tracing or territory is decentered or disrupted, Deleuze and Guattari call this a deterritorialization or map making. A deterritorialization happens when given structures and ideas are interrupted by difference, shot through and ruptured by a line of flight, 'a path of mutation' (Lorraine, 2005, p. 145). A line of flight is created from the ontological realm of pure difference when relationships and experiences in life produce novel connections 'that release new powers' (p. 145). Ontologically, Deleuze (1968/1994) views these disruptions, deterritorializations, and lines of flight in terms of the power of difference and the connective power of life. Difference and life have limitless *potential* to open up new ways of acting and thinking, ways that are not predetermined by what has come before. By following a line of flight, a line of deterritorialization, cartography may produce maps of the new and different rather than simply tracings of the same.

And yet, returning to his ontology, Deleuze asserts that pure difference, the vastness of the potential of life, is never fully actualized. Only certain new structures, new ways of acting and thinking will become actualized. This brings about a particular actualization of difference and a specific reterritorialization on a new territory. However, the process does not stop there. These ongoing transformative processes, without beginning or end points, articulate Deleuze and Guattari's central concept, becoming. Becoming is driven by the ontological power of difference: the new territory once again becomes deterritorialized; the tracing is put back on the map.

The importance that Deleuze ascribes to the power of life as a productive and transformative process of becoming leads back to May's (2005) question that opened this article: 'How might one live?' The question refers not to the personal choices of an autonomous individual, but to life's power to produce new relations and different modes of becoming *with* the world. The following conceptual cartography of critical literacies is presented as an invitation to think along a line of flight and to invent new ways of becoming pedagogically in adult immigrant language classrooms. The cartography begins by tracing received conceptualizations of critical literacies bound to the humanist territories staked out by a Freirean legacy. Next, I deploy the Deleuzian-informed MLT to provoke a deterritorialization of critical literacies and a reterritorialization otherwise. Such a 'deterritorialization ... does not preclude reterritorialization but posits it as the creation of a future new earth' (Deleuze & Guattari, 1991/1994, p. 88) where we might think in the more uncertain and yet affirmative terms of a politics of becoming.

Critical literacy traced: Freire's legacy

The sociocultural turn in language education over the last decade has created in-roads for critical orientations to language education. These critical moves, often guided by Freirean critical pedagogies (Freire, 1968/1970), demand more deeply politicized ways of thinking about language teaching and learning, and recognize the interconnectedness of language and social processes. Critical literacies, forms of literacy that interrogate textual representations to reveal their underlying ideological assumptions and the cultural conditions of their production, have furnished one in-road to language pedagogies that take social justice as their guiding principle (cf. Schäffner & Wenden, 1995/2004 for a critical discourse analysis perspective). Luke, Luke, and Graham (2007), arguing in favour of 'a broad-based critical agenda for language education' (p. 10), position critical literacies on the front lines of the assault against neoliberalism. For them, working in the Australian context, these battles best waged in the classroom: 'Ironically, the anachronistic structures of state educational systems remain our best recourse' (Luke et al., 2007, p. 12).

The kind of critical language education called for by Luke et al. (2007) is also being actualized in classrooms in the US by the Literacy for Social Justice Teacher Research group. Rogers, Mosley, and Folkes (2009), members of this group, frame their Marxist version of critical literacy as 'literacies of labour' which are peda-gogically focused on exposing (economic) class conflict, challenging the workings of neoliberalism, and building alternatives to neoliberal policies. Rogers et al. present the example of one English language teacher's critical literacy approach in an adult immigrant classroom. The teacher talks to her students about workers' rights using a Powerpoint-based picture story. As the teacher's 'students are becoming more

EDUCATION AND THE POLITICS OF BECOMING

proficient with language and literacy, they are learning more about their rights as workers and how to be advocates for action' (p. 136).

At the same time critical literacies are being put into service to combat neoliberalism, the ever-increasing prominence of digital communication on a global scale is emphasizing the importance of critical literacies' close cousins: digital and media literacies. For example, in the UK, the government's digital inclusion initiative has put critical media literacy in the adult education spotlight (Clarke, Milner, Killer, & Dixon, 2008). Clarke et al. (2008) assert that without the necessary critical media literacy skills to evaluate web-based information 'individuals will be seriously disadvantaged, misled and probably confused by what they locate online' (p. 21). Varis (2010), writing in his capacity as the UNESCO Chair in Global e-Learning, supports this view and argues that critical media literacy should be incorporated into education efforts, including adult education contexts. He draws parallels between the 'complementary ... even synonymous' concepts of digital and media literacy stating:

> Digital literacy as media literacy aims to develop both critical understanding of and active participation in the media. Digital and media literacy is about developing people's critical and creative abilities. (Varis, 2010, p. 24)

In short, around the globe, critical literacies and critical media literacies are being recognized as key pieces in the adult education puzzle. However, I want to emphasize that even as critical literacies and critical media literacies are preoccupied with encouraging more politically-aware reading, they themselves are not apolitical constructs. The received conceptualizations of critical literacies outlined above are rooted in humanism and Freire's (1968/1970) pedagogy of the oppressed. Owing to this legacy, they presume, or at least aim at, emancipatory outcomes though dialogical processes involving both consciousness raising about social injustice (usually directly related to problems faced by students) and empowered action to effect social change. This is one paradigmatic territory for critical literacies and, despite critiques (Ellsworth, 1994), one that has gained a great deal of currency to become what Deleuze and Guattari (1980/1987) might call, returning to our cartographic concepts introduced earlier, a tracing. While this paradigm allows certain ways of thinking about literacies, it simultaneously disallows others. This is why Lather (2006) understands that investing exclusively in the tracing is a particularly dangerous thing and that 'paradigm proliferation is a good thing to think with' (p. 35). Following this advice, my objective in the next sub-section is to disrupt received conceptualizations of critical literacies, to break open territories and tracings, in order to map critical literacies differently with MLT.

Critical literacy de/reterritorialized: MLT and becoming

Although MLT is constantly on the move, it has, since its inception, been suspicious of the kinds of pre-given, emancipatory outcomes driving Freirean perspectives on literacy (Masny, 2005). Early on, the transformative powers of literacies were framed within MLT in the vocabularies of uncertainty, unpredictability, and uncontrollability (Masny, 2005). Then, in Masny's (2006) article *Learning and creative processes: A poststructural perspective on language and multiple literacies*, MLT explicitly drew on the Deleuzian-Guattarian concept of becoming to situate literacies as transformative

EDUCATION AND THE POLITICS OF BECOMING

processes. MLT 'is interested in the flow of experiences of life and events from which individuals are formed as literate' (2006, p. 151).

As a consequence of Deleuze (1968/1994) giving ontological primacy to difference driving transformative processes, becoming is opposed to the representational identity theories familiar in second language and literacies research (cf. McCarthey & Moje, 2002; Menard-Warwick, 2005; Nero, 2005). Identity theories often maintain an actively controlling subject at the center of the process, as in the case of Nero's (2005) description of 'acts of identity'. Identity theories also tend to express transformation in terms like $A \rightarrow B$ or $A + B = AB$ (i.e. hybridity). For example, McCarthey and Moje (2002) express the theoretical tensions between identities as 'coherent [A or B], yet hybrid [AB] and stabilizing [suggested by the equal sign, $=$], yet dynamic [suggested by the arrow, $\rightarrow$]' (p. 232). However, as Roy (2003) observes, becoming differs from these kinds of identity equations.

> In a Deleuzian conception, becoming is the transformation of life through the refusal of closed structures within which difference can be confined ... Becoming is not the becoming of A into B, but a state of openness to the movement of pure difference. (p. 77)

Beyond the constraints of representation and identity, Deleuze and Guattari's difference-driven transformation 'does not mean becoming the other, but *becoming-other*' (Semetsky, 2003, p. 214). Becoming-other signals the *untimely* aspect of becoming. We do not know a priori how becoming will unfold, what will be produced out of difference.

Engaging the concept of becoming, MLT frames literacies as untimely transformative processes that:

> ... take on multiple meanings conveyed through words, gestures, attitudes, ways of speaking, writing, and valuing. Accordingly, literacies constitute ways of *becoming*. Literacies are texts that take on multiple meanings and manifest as visual, oral, written, and tactile. They constitute texts, in a broad sense (for example, music: a music score, a symphony; art: sculpture, physics: an equation, architecture: a museum) that fuse with religion, gender, race, culture, and power, and that produce speakers, writers, artists, communities. In short, through reading, reading the world, and self as texts, literacies constitute ways of *becoming* with the world. (Masny, 2009a, p. 14)

Thus, MLT views the notion of text broadly such that even the individual is viewed as 'a text in continuous becoming' (Masny, 2005, p. 180). Consequently, MLT offers a powerful mode of thinking about the politics of becoming in relation to language and literacies education.

Just as literacies are reconceptualized as processes of becoming, so too critical literacies are reframed conceptually within MLT as reading immanently and intensively. Deleuze (1990/1995), viewing texts as 'non-signifying machines' (p. 8), describes reading as reading *intensively* 'in contact with what's outside the book, as a flow meeting other flows, one machine, among others, as a series of experiments for each reader in the midst of events that have nothing to do with books' (pp. 8–9). This intensive way of reading is taken up by MLT as critical literacies. Reading is always interested and involves reading intensively and *immanently* (Masny, 2006, 2009b). Reading intensively is a disruptive kind of reading that opens up to a multiplicity of

133

immanent lines of flight. Reading immanently connects with experience that brings on the thought of. 'The thought of ...' signals that sense emerges not as a priori meaning, but as an event in which experiences in life connect through reading, reading the world and self as texts. This ongoing process shapes and reshapes an individual's *worldview* – values, beliefs, politics, and principles about how the world works – and contributes to his/her continual transformation.

Another way to think about reading critically, that is disruptively, through MLT is to see reading, once again in Deleuze and Guattari's (1980/1987) cartographic terms, as a process involving deterritorialization and reterritorialization. Reading intensively produces a moment of deterritorialization, a disruption of a territory. The sense that emerges may destabilize the reader's understanding of how the world works, that is, his or her worldview (i.e. a territory). When worldviews connect and collide in this way, the reader seeks stability, a reterritorialization. This reterritorialization may entail a reorganization and transformation of the worldview. Thus, MLT allows for the consideration of the becoming that is produced when worldviews connect and collide in the course of learning a second language. Still, recalling the untimely (i.e. unpredictable) aspect of becoming, questions remain. *How* might worldviews shift? *How* will a reterritorialization happen?

Empirical entry points

Through the lens of MLT, this qualitative study considers multiple literacies as processes of becoming (i.e. transformation) in adult immigrant language classrooms, specifically within the *Language Instruction for Newcomers to Canada* (LINC) program. The LINC program is funded under the auspices of the Canadian government's department of Citizenship and Immigration and offers free English language classes for up to three years to any adult newcomer with permanent resident or convention refugee status. LINC's objective 'is to provide basic language instruction to adult newcomers in one of Canada's official languages .... The strategic outcome (objective) of LINC is ... to facilitate their social, cultural, economic and political integration into Canada' (Citizenship and Immigration, 2006). However, I contend that the straightforward relationship between learning language and successful integration implied in the LINC mandate elides the complexity of language learning and literacies as transformative processes in relation to the life experiences of learners and broader social contexts. In short, the mandate does not account for the politics of becoming which imbue the learning experience in LINC.

The data collection phase of this study took place during the first four months of 2008 and involved weekly videorecorded observations of classroom activities in two LINC classrooms in Ottawa, Ontario, Canada. The two teachers of these classes, as well as four of their students participated in a series of interviews in which we used the classroom video footage as a springboard into our discussions. During these interview sessions we often referred to relevant classroom artefacts (worksheets, student essays, newspaper articles read in class, etc.) and these were also collected. For the purposes of this article, I will draw on data from the Lakeside[1] LINC site to bring into focus the contentiousness of different conceptualizations of critical.

Qualitative research as cartography[2]

On the surface, our inquiry strategies might appear to be familiar ethnographic methods; however, as St Pierre comments on the experience of 'doing Deleuze' in research: 'Every single category of the structure of conventional, interpretive qualitative inquiry came loose from its moorings' (St Pierre, 2004, p. 293). Like St Pierre, I found that my engagement with Deleuze and Guattari's concepts have had the effect of deterritorializing methodology, transforming what it is to *do* educational research into a cartographic practice.

To reformulate qualitative inquiry as cartography, I will return once again to tracings and maps, but this time in relation to Deleuze and Guattari's (1980/1987) concept of the rhizome, as laid out in the opening chapter of *A Thousand Plateaus*. Rhizomes enable a reorientation to thinking about qualitative research as 'rhizomatous map making' (Alvermann, 2000, p. 118). In biology, rhizomes are horizontal plant structures such as those found in crabgrass. Unlike tree-structures, rhizomes are non-hierarchical and have no beginning or end points. They are always in-between. The rhizome is a connective structure that allows for propagation in all directions in response to immanent relationships with other elements (e.g. soil, water, minerals, sunlight, insects, etc.).

Taking up the rhizome as philosophical concept, its principles of *cartography* and *decalcomania*, maps and tracings, suggest how one might go about research. Decalcomania is a form of art that involves transferring an original image onto another surface such as glass or pottery. It reproduces a tracing of the Same. Rhizomes do not trace, they map. Guattari had a penchant for thinking in rhizomatic, cartographic diagrams: 'maps that are not content to merely illustrate, but which also create and produce' (Watson, 2009, p. 10). Research inquiry in post-positivist modes is epistemologically preoccupied with tracings which aim to reproduce and mimetically (i.e. accurately) represent a pre-existing reality.[3] In contrast, Deleuze and Guattari's (1980/1987) experimentation entails mapping and *creating* rather than tracing and representing.

> What distinguishes the map from the tracing is that it is entirely oriented toward an experimentation in contact with the real. The map does not reproduce ... it constructs ... It fosters connections ... The map is open and connectable in all of its dimensions; it is detachable, reversible, susceptible to constant modification ... A map has multiple entryways, as opposed to the tracing, which always comes back 'to the same'. (Deleuze & Guattari, 1980/1987, p. 12)

In practice, I produced a rhizomatous map that takes the shape of a series of interconnected vignettes drawn from the data. These vignettes 'seemed to be engaged or interjected in such a way as to make new relations possible' (Leander & Rowe, 2006, p. 440). Data in a cartographic research process are 'selected and assessed according to their power to act and intervene' rather than to be interpreted (Colebrook, 2002b, p. xliv). Interspersed with the cartographic display of vignettes are poetic encounters with the research participants: Tuzi and Maria,[4] students at the Lakeside LINC site. Assembled from participants' borrowed words, each poetic meeting is a simulacrum, a copy of a copy without an original model and thus having more to do with creativity than with representation[5] (Deleuze, 1969/1990). Within the cartography, discussion of the data involves posing questions in juxtaposition

EDUCATION AND THE POLITICS OF BECOMING

with the conceptual framework. The epistemological modus operandi of such cartographic research work is to produce *thinking* rather than knowledge. Mapping tends to pose questions rather than make interpretations. By affirming a multiplicity of elements and the connections happening between them, rhizomatous cartography endeavors to keep research ways open, to send thought off on a line of flight, and to spur thinking into ongoing movement because, as May (2005) argues, 'there is always more to think' (p. 21).

Cartography: Media and reading intensively in LINC

Throughout the LINC study, reading the newspaper during class time seemed to be associated with what Deleuze and Guattari (1980/1987) refer to as *affects* – capacities to affect and be affected – in other words, life's power to create connections and relationships that deterritorialize and effect a becoming. Thus, in the cartography, I explore the notion of reading media critically, that is intensively or disruptively in MLT terms. The cartography's entry point is an event at the Lakeside classroom that was initiated by the media reporting of protest rallies taking place in Ottawa during the lead up to the 2008 Summer Olympic Games in Beijing. Once again, *event* is a very particular philosophical concept which exceeds common usage as a bounded spatial-temporal phenomenon. Deleuze (1969/1990) derives the concept from the Stoics to describe how transformations, or becomings, produce the event. Put another way, the event is the expression of the transformative effects produced out of a dynamic interaction of forces. As Stagoll (2005) further explains:

> An event is neither a beginning nor an end point, but rather always 'in the middle'. Events themselves have no beginning – or end-point, and their relationship with Deleuze's notion of dynamic change – 'becoming' – is neither one of 'joining moments together' nor one in which an event is the 'end' of one productive process, to be supplanted or supplemented by the next. Rather, becoming 'moves through' an event, with the event representing just a momentary productive intensity. (p. 88)

Affective forces of deterritorialization move through the event that is described below in the LINC classroom and those forces flow out in ripples of transformation, potential resistance, and shifting worldviews.

> *Tuzi*
> I am forty-five years old.
> I come from China.
> Now we decided to settle down in Ottawa.
> I have been here for almost one year.
>
> The reason I come here just for my son.
> Because we want him to get Western education.
> Maybe when my son goes to university I will go back to China.
> You know, I'm a teacher in the university in China.
> Now, I work in an ice cream shop part-time.
> It's a job, but it's not the job I want.
>
> Now is the first time I studied in LINC class.
> Actually I think English is very important.

EDUCATION AND THE POLITICS OF BECOMING

So I come to school everyday to study English.
And to make friends.
This class makes me feel very happy.

Event: Pro-China rally

Approximately a month after Tuzi's final scheduled interview, she initiated *another* meeting with me. She had something she wanted to say about the local newspaper's front page coverage[6] of a rally she had attended on Parliament Hill in Ottawa in support of China hosting the 2008 Summer Olympics. This rally, involving approximately 10,000 local Chinese and Chinese-Canadians according to Tuzi, was held as a reaction to pro-Tibetan protests against the Chinese government that were simultaneously taking place in Ottawa and around the world.

Tuzi: In the [newspaper] article they report that rally, but they use the – they report the Chinese – the pro-Chinese and the pro-Tibet. The two groups. They use the most thin space to report. But you know that day just a dozen. I remember in that article it use a dozen Tibetans. Just a few Tibetans. And they interview some of them. So they use – they use the same space to describe them.

Researcher: So you feel that perhaps your event was a larger event, more people involved so it deserved more space in the newspaper?

T: Yeah. Deserved. And they should report all the – what people do or how the people feeling. What's – what were the people feelings. They should report this. Or – They don't – I don't think they need to report so many. They use so many space to report the Tibet feelings about that. So my classmate [Lily][7] was very angry. That day she was absent. But during the – at the break time she come to class ...

R: Ok.

T: On purpose because she was very angry. She said she can't stay at home. She wants to share her emotions to us. And LOOK! LOOK! This is the Western media. Because we know it's a big rally in Ottawa. And so many Chinese and organized very well.
...

R: So [Lily] just came for the break time on Monday to talk with her classmates about that?

T: Because she was SO ANGRY she can't stay at home! She said, 'Look, we all trust the media. Especially the Western media.' Because in China we always heard that the Western media: they are justice; they tell the truth; and they blame the Chinese media cover some truth. But here we feel that the fact is NOT that. We dis ... we don't believe the media anymore. And from this event, I think most of Chinese – most of the Chinese don't believe media anymore – the Western media anymore because they distort a lot. (April 23, 2008; Interview 4)

At first, Tuzi expresses a reading of the world that suggests a territorialization of media in Canada as trustworthy: 'We all trust the media. Especially the Western media.' Within this territory, that constitutes a worldview, Chinese media is read as

137

EDUCATION AND THE POLITICS OF BECOMING

corrupt: it 'cover some truth'. How could such a reading of the world interact with reading self as text; Tuzi as a Chinese woman living in Canada? How might this, in turn, affect becoming?

Life's power to disrupt and deterritorialize can 'cross a person's universe to appear seemingly out of nowhere' (Dufresne, 2006, p. 352). How might the affective relation of forces – a rally, a newspaper report, a protestor, a classmate – produce a deterritorializing event? How might media as 'justice and truth' be reterritorialized as 'distortion'? Reading disruptively, that is critically, in ways that may challenge worldviews creates this event.

In this vignette, what is the untimely response to investment in multiple literacies and reading the media itself as text? Anger? Dufresne (2006), who explores the role of affect and emotive forces in becoming biliterate, observes that 'once new knowing [i.e. learning] is introduced to this belief system [i.e. an individual's worldview], reactions and emotions can go from amazement and wonderment to disbelief, outrage, and outright hostility' (p. 347). The affective potential of difference *may* actualize a particular response to new learning: resistance. Another possibility is that worldviews are shifting. Through experiences of difference in reading, reading, reading the world and self, what transformations are produced in Tuzi and Lily as becoming follows untimely lines of flight?

Tuzi and I continued to discuss the newspaper's reporting about the rally and she drew my attention to the front page photograph accompanying the article. In the image, more than a dozen large Chinese flags wave over the crowd of protestors. A man in the foreground wears a red T-shirt that reads 'One China. One Family.'

> R: What was the conversation like in the class before [Lily] came. In the morning about that article?
>
> Tuzi: In the morning I just told them [interruption] that picture is very, very – it's a huge picture. And a lot of Chinese national flags, red flags so it's very noticeable. It's very noticeable. I told them I was there and I told them why I was there and what happened that day. You know just Chinese go – went there. And the other students they don't know. They didn't know what happened.
>
> R: Did you like the image that they chose to put on the front page?
>
> T: Yes. [Laughing shyly]. They just – very interesting. Oh, they [the classmates] were trying to look for me [in the picture] and ask me why I was there. And what happened. I told them.
>
> R: It was a good picture?
>
> T: Yeah. It's very, very good picture.
>
> R: The article though could have been better?
>
> T: Yes. I think. The picture is very good.
> . . .
>
> R: What did it make you think?

EDUCATION AND THE POLITICS OF BECOMING

> T: I think, uh – because I very angry about these things. The media they distort – distort the truth. I'm very angry. (April 23, 2008; Interview 4)

According to MLT, literacies are taken up in many different modes, including visual modes. In this vignette, Tuzi offers her take on the image that accompanied the front page newspaper report (described in the previous vignette). In contrast to her response to the written article, Tuzi responds very differently to the photograph: 'It's very, very good picture'. Through reading critically, that is intensively and disruptively, these texts take on sense and are becoming. MLT asks 'how a text works and what it does or produces, not what it means' (Masny, 2006, p. 152). So how is the media, as text, transformed through reading critically? The reader is a text as well; a text in continual becoming. Tuzi is a text. How is the media, through image and written word, constructing *her*? Remembering that ontologically Deleuze (1968/1994) sees difference driving becoming, an important question to ask is: How might reading of self in this vignette, in connection with this visual text and Tuzi's life experiences (Chinese woman, resident of Canada, protestor), *differ* from the reading of self in the previous vignette where Tuzi expresses a worldview in which Chinese media is seen as corrupt? How does this difference effect a deterritorialization? In a reterritorialization, how are Tuzi and a worldview transformed through experiences of English language literacies in LINC?

Reading intensively and immanently, sends thought off on lines of flight. How might this kind of critical reading of the image of the bright and noticeable 'Chinese national flags, red flags' form connections in the mind of Tuzi? It could bring on the thought of Tuzi's homeland, China ... the thought of family ... the thought of national pride ... something else. In short, how does critical investment in multiple literacies, by forming connections with life experiences, impact reading, reading world, reading self as texts?

Maria
I am forty.
We decide to came to Canada because Mexico City is – just a jungle.
That is the reason I am in Canada.
I think it's better for my children to live here. And for me also.

I need to learn English because it's the most important thing for do everything.
I decide to take the LINC program.
To make friends, to learn, to have SOMETHING to do is important.

I want three things:
I want to speak correctly.
I want to help my children with the homework.
I am going to feel very, very proud when I finally have a job and am working in English.
For me it would be a very, very BIG step.

Maria (Tuzi's classmate) also requested an additional, unscheduled fourth interview with me. She had thoughts to share about the newspaper reporting on the pro-China rally and Lily's reaction to it as well.

> Maria: There was a woman from China. She was reading the news about this Olympics problem ... She was very – REALLY, really angry about the article just last Thursday I think; no, last Monday maybe. She was really, really

139

EDUCATION AND THE POLITICS OF BECOMING

> upset. She can't stay at the school because she was upset about the
> newspaper.

R: Ahhh.

Maria: And I can't believe it. I say – I talked with her, 'Don't take it personally'. It's
      just, you know, this is very free country. So you can say anything. Just if you
      do something wrong to other people that people can go to the courts and –
      and you can get some penalty if you do something wrong. But this is a free
      country. You can write and say anything. Nah nah nah! [mimicking the
      negative response of her classmate Lily] She was really, really upset. She went
      to home. Just she – she doesn't – she couldn't stay at the school. And I can –
      I just was, 'My goodness!' . . . She was very upset. I thought it was too much,
      but ok. It touched something inside her. Ok. (April 21, 2008; Interview 4)

Maria seems surprised by her classmate's angry reaction, stating near the end of this
vignette that she 'thought it was too much'. She expresses a particular reading of the
world and self. Yet at the same time Maria says, 'It touched something inside her.
Ok.' Might the notion of being 'touched' express a becoming, the transformative
power of affects released through reading immanently and intensively (i.e. critically)?

The way reading is going on in Maria's case differs significantly from Tuzi. Sense
emerges as an event produced out of a complex flow of forces and experiences.
Maria's perspective, as a Mexican woman, is quite different from Tuzi's, as a Chinese
woman on this issue. The affects that come into play are, consequently, also different.
Reading Lily's reaction to the newspaper article, Tuzi responds with shared anger,
while Maria responds with incredulity: 'I can't believe it'. These different affects have
different transformative powers with respect to how becoming unfolds in the LINC
classroom. What lines of flight do these affective responses open?

Another aspect of difference actualizes in the reading of the Canadian media as a
text. In Tuzi and Lily's worldview the Canadian media should tell the 'truth', but now
they find, reading disruptively, that it 'distorts' the truth. Maria's worldview has a
different vision of Canadian media: 'this is very free country. So you can say
anything'. Is this a collision of worldviews? If so, what does this confrontation
produce? Anger? Surprise? Disbelief? Resistance? How does becoming unfold in
these affective flows producing the critical literacies event?

Deterritorializations and resistance

In the wake of these classroom events involving critical media literacies, issues
around Tibet-China relations were very much on Tuzi's mind. She worried about
what kinds of messages her classmates were getting from the 'Western media'. These
thoughts and concerns inspired her to deliver her in-class oral presentation on the
subject.

Tuzi: My topic is about Tibet issue. You know, it's a very, very controversial issue
      during these days . . . The media, especially the Western medias, reported a lot
      about Tibet issues. My topic is the – the REALLY Tibet. From my eyes, the
      really Tibet. Because I think, even if the media reported a lot about Tibet issue
      such as the Tibet riots.

R: Yes.

140

EDUCATION AND THE POLITICS OF BECOMING

T: The violent riots. And the independent – separate Tibet from China and the Tibetan asked for freedom and independent. And the Dalai Lama said the Chinese government have been genocide – the CULTURAL genocide for the Tibet, for the Tibet culture. But in my opinion, it's not true. In my topic I told my classmates about something – uh – told them something about Tibet because many students, they don't know, where is Tibet. They wonder: 'Is it true? Tibet don't belong to China – doesn't belong to China?'

        ...

R: Do you think you surprised your classmates with the information you delivered in your presentation?

T: I think maybe some students surprised because all the information they get – they have get – All the information they have get just from the newspapers, from radios, or the Internet. And, you know, this informations, I don't think they report Tibet issue in the justice or tell the truth. (April 23, 2008; Interview 4)

As an affective response to reading the media texts reporting on Tibet-China relations intensively and immanently (i.e. critically), Tuzi produces another text, an oral presentation, in which she explains to her classmates 'the REALLY Tibet from [her] eyes', the actualization of a particular worldview. Tuzi uses oral literacy practices in LINC to produce a counter-text. How might it produce lines of flight associated with 'life's power of deterritorialisation: a capacity to take any actual thing and translate it into a movement of flow' (Colebrook, 2002a, p. 65)? As such, Tuzi's text can be considered as an 'asignifying machine' (Masny, 2009b, p. 188), 'a flow meeting other flows' (Deleuze, 1990/1995, p. 8), including political, religious, social, and economic flows. So when a disruption happens through reading intensively, how will a reterritorialization take place as sense emerges expressing the relation of these flows? In other words, it remains to be seen how Tuzi's presentation, as a multiple literacies text, will get taken up. Here is how Maria talked about the experience of listening to Tuzi's presentation about Tibet.

Maria: I always have the idea that, uh – you know that – the people – these people – the Tibetan – the people in Tibet have problems. But [Tuzi] taught us something that is very important and maybe – maybe change my mind about that situation. Ok. You need to talk with her.

R: Oh? What [Tuzi] said might have changed your mind?

Maria: Yes a little bit because she told us that they are Chinese and they have a right – some rights different than that rest of the country. For example they can – they are able to have as many childs as they want. And you know Chinese doesn't have that right. And some kinds of – that kind of rights, different rights. And maybe – Ok, what kind of oppression are you feeling? No? Maybe – You know, maybe because I think I have read something from Dalai Lama and I like it.

R: Um huh.

Maria: And I – Now I am thinking, 'He's really true?' What happened with this guy, you know? Because he's the prophet. He's the person – more important person in this country. That now they are showing a face that nobody else knows about that.

R: Mm. So you even had a chance to rethink the Dalai Lama?

141

EDUCATION AND THE POLITICS OF BECOMING

Maria: Maybe not very – ... Maybe – Maybe he's not doing everything well. [laughing nervously] You know. Maybe – (April 21, 2008; Interview 4)

According to MLT's view of critical literacies, Tuzi's presentation involved reading critically which produced an event, a deterritorialization, disrupting what Maria thought she knew about the world. After listening to Tuzi's oral presentation, Maria tells us that what she learned, 'maybe change my mind about that situation'. How is reading immanently and intensively producing a becoming, transforming Maria? How does this untimely sense-event actualize? A rupture opens through reading intensively, bringing on the thought of ... difference. Maria wonders about the Dalai Lama: 'Now I am thinking, "He's really true?"' As Maria experiences these thoughts, how is a worldview deterritorialized in the process of becoming though critical literacies in LINC? Does Maria's uncertainty express the opening of a space of becoming where something different might flow as a reterritorialization takes place? What does the new territory look like as worldviews are shifting and producing an event expressing a becoming?

Between critical literacies and reading intensively

At the outset of this article, I took on the task of mapping critical literacies conceptually and empirically. Having done this, I now return to a key step in Deleuze and Guattari's (1980/1987) cartographic approach, putting the tracing 'back on the map' (p. 13). For my purposes, I am framing the received view of critical literacies within a Freirean paradigm as the tracing, and the alternative view of critical literacies involving reading intensively within MLT as the map. Once again the empirical example of the LINC study helps in examining the close interrelationship between the tracing and the map.

Although LINC does not have an explicit mandate to promote critical media literacies, by dint of including the newspaper as a daily in-class reading activity, the teacher at the Lakeside LINC site, Brooke, finds herself necessarily engaging certain forms of critical pedagogy. In one instance, Brooke described an annual presentation in which the local news producer for CBC[8] Radio came to the class as an invited guest speaker. Brooke summed up the pedagogical importance of his presentation as follows:

Brooke: The media has a duty to show both sides of a controversial issue and he tried to explain how both sides – we attempt to show both sides ... The students learn a lot from it [the presentation]. But we always try to make sure – (and I think he points it out too) we have to be careful consumers of information ... You don't sit and believe everything you that you read or everything that you hear. You take responsibility for information that comes in. (April 30, 2008; Interview 2)

According to MLT, literacies take on meaning within a specific context. In her comments, how do Brooke's experiences of reading and reading the world form connections between 'a duty to show both sides', 'responsibility for information that comes in', and what literacies are about in the Canadian society? The teacher's comments may be seen as part of, and contributing to, staking out a particular territory for critical literacies, one more closely aligned with a Freirean critical

EDUCATION AND THE POLITICS OF BECOMING

pedagogy than a Deleuzian-Guattarian view of reading intensively, disruptively. Critical literacies within a critical pedagogy paradigm interrogate the biases of media texts and aim towards a more balanced representation of both sides of the story, including the voice of critique (Banks, 2003; Luke, 2003). The critical reader, in this paradigm, is one who 'takes responsibility', as Brooke puts it, for critically assessing the information and messages they receive and who are subsequently empowered to effect positive social change. This is the familiar terrain of critical pedagogy with its corresponding tracing of the received notion of critical literacies.

Yet if this tracing is juxtaposed with the preceding research cartography mapping the movements of becoming involving Tuzi and Maria, a more complex picture unfolds, one in which critical literacies are experienced as disruptive events. However, my intent in this article is not to argue that we *should* shift our conceptualizations from a received view of critical literacies to reading intensively. On the contrary, as Brooke and her students at Lakeside have suggested, both tracings and maps are at work, overlapping and interacting in unexpected ways. Thus I am not advocating MLT as the 'best theory' for understanding literacies in adult immigrant language classrooms, but positing it as another mode of thinking, a theory that 'won't be totalized, it multiplies' (Deleuze, 2004, p. 208). The pivotal question then becomes: What can mapping critical literacies differently (through MLT and the work of Deleuze and Guattari) contribute conceptually to thinking about the politics of becoming in adult immigrant language learning contexts?

(1) *Power and the untimely*

By assuming that *all* readings are always already biased, in the sense that they are interested, value-laden, and political (the actualization of a worldview), MLT acknowledges that lines of power shoot through critical literacy practices. Freirean-inspired critical language and literacies educators view these lines as controllable to some extent, for example, they may pursue student empowerment by challenging the hegemonic power of neoliberal politics (Luke et al., 2007; Rogers et al., 2009). This is one way to think about power. However, MLT expands the conceptualization of power to also account for the disruptive powers of difference and relational, connective powers of life that produce lines of flight. Moreover, because the trajectories and intersections of these power lines cannot be predicted or controlled, reading critically as an intensive practice produces untimely transformations in the individual and the world. Thus, MLT allows us to think about the indeterminacy of critical (media) literacy outcomes in terms of the productive and affirmative power of difference.

(2) *Event*

Unlike conceptualizations of critical literacies that hinge on an individual humanist subject, reading intensively happens as the effect of complex and continually shifting connections and relations created by life's affective powers flowing through an event. Just as Deleuze and Guattari (1980/1987) demand that an event like 'the animal-stalks-at-five-o'clock' (p. 263) be read without pause, so too one can consider reading intensively as an event produced from the relation of forces. The dynamic interactions of these elements produce the event: a student, a teacher, a time of day, a newspaper, a radio, chalk dust, aroma of coffee brewing, sunlight, curriculum, immigration policies, an economic crisis, a protest rally, and so forth.

(3) *Affect*

The elements connected by life to produce the event have various affective capacities – powers to affect and be affected (Deleuze & Guattari, 1980/1987). Affective relationships create intensities moving through the event and come to bear upon critical literacies as processes of becoming. The concept of reading intensively, affirms a growing recognition of the need to account for affective forces in pedagogy broadly (Albrecht-Crane & Slack, 2007) and within literacy education specifically (Cole, 2005). (Re)introducing the role of affect in education is particularly salient in adult immigrant language and literacies instructional contexts which currently tend to be driven by policies based on human capital models prioritizing (sometimes myopically) the functional goal of job preparation (Warriner, 2007).

This article has approached the issue of critical orientations to language and literacy learning differently by leveraging Deleuzian-Guattarian concepts, bringing them into play through MLT. Pushing against the limits of how we think conceptually, critically, and pedagogically has the potential to (re)instate the adult immigrant language classroom as 'a site of cultural politics' (Warriner, 2007, p. 323) and to address the affective powers of becoming 'in ways that matter in the politics of everyday life' (Albrecht-Crane & Slack, 2007, p. 99). Thinking about education in Deleuze and Guattari's vocabularies of power, the untimely, events, and affect requires more complex and (perhaps) unwieldy pedagogical and research practices, yet as the same time invites more deeply political and ethical ways of becoming with the world.

Acknowledgment
This research was supported by the Social Sciences and Humanities Research Council through Doctoral Fellowship funding.

Notes
1. The name of the LINC site is a pseudonym which was established in consultation with the teacher.
2. For other instances of qualitative cartographic or rhizoanalytic work in literacies research see Alvermann, 2000; Dufresne, 2006; Eakle, 2007; Leander & Rowe, 2006; Masny, 2009a.
3. Notably, Deleuze's (1968/1994) work in *Difference and Repetition* shows that the onto-logical primacy of difference makes such a mimetic representation impossible. Nonetheless, he acknowledges that a tracing 'intends to reproduce' (Deleuze & Guattari, 1980/1987, p. 13) and 'always comes back "to the same" ' (Deleuze & Guattari, 1980/1987, p. 12).
4. All of the participants' names are self-selected pseudonyms.
5. Roffe (2005) elaborates Deleuze's reversal of Platonism with respect to the ontological status of simulacra. 'Simulacra do not refer to anything behind or beyond the world – they make up the world ... The simulacrum does not rely upon something beyond it for its force, but is itself force or power; able to do things and not merely represent' (2005, p. 250).

EDUCATION AND THE POLITICS OF BECOMING

6. This newspaper article ran on the front page of the *Ottawa Citizen*, April 14, 2008 (p. A1).
7. Lily is a pseudonym assigned to protect the anonymity of this student.
8. CBC stands for the Canadian Broadcasting Corporation. CBC is financially supported by the Canadian government and is responsible for providing both radio and television programming to the Canadian public. It also maintains a website with links to video clips, live audio streaming, and podcasts at www.cbc.ca.

References

Albrecht-Crane, C., & Slack, J.D. (2007). Toward a pedagogy of affect. In A. Hickey-Moody, & P. Malins (Eds.), *Deleuzian encounters: Studies in contemporary social issues* (pp. 99–110). Houndmills, Basingstoke, Hampshire and New York, NY: Palgrave Macmillan.

Alvermann, D. (2000). Research libraries, literacies, and lives: A rhizoanalysis. In E. St Pierre, & W.A. Pillow (Eds.), *Working the ruins: Feminist poststructural theory and methods in education* (pp. 114–129). London: Routledge.

Banks, J.A. (2003). Teaching literacy for social justice and global citizenship. *Language Arts, 81*(1), 18–19.

Citizenship and Immigration Canada. (2006, July 26). *Major Crown projects and horizontal initiatives.* Retrieved 23 April 2009 from http://www.cic.gc.ca/english/resources/publications/horizontal-2006.asp#linc

Clarke, A., Milner, H., Killer, T., & Dixon, G. (2008). Bridging the digital divide. *Adults Learning, 20*(3), 20–22.

Cole, D.R. (2005). *Affective literacy.* In the proceedings of the ALEA/AATE National Conference*: Pleasurable learning, passionate teaching, provocative debates.* Gold Coast Convention Centre, Queensland, Australia.

Colebrook, C. (2002a). *Gilles Deleuze.* New York: Routledge.

Colebrook, C. (2002b). *Understanding Deleuze.* Crows Nest, Australia: Allen & Unwin.

Deleuze, G. (1990). *The logic of sense* (M. Lester, & C. Stivale, Trans.), (C.V. Boundas, Ed.). New York: Columbia University Press. (Original work published 1969.)

Deleuze, G. (1994). *Difference and repetition* (P. Patton, Trans.). New York, NY: Columbia University Press. (Original work published 1968.)

Deleuze, G. (1995). *Negotiations, 1972–1990* (M. Joughin, Trans.). New York: Columbia University Press. (Original work published 1990.)

Deleuze, G. (2004). Intellectuals and power (Interview with Michel Foucault). In D. Lapoujade (Ed.), (M. Taormina, Trans.), *Desert islands and other texts: 1953–1974* (pp. 206–213). Los Angeles, CA & New York, NY: Semiotext(e).

Deleuze, G., & Guattari, F. (1987). *A thousand plateaus: Capitalism and schizophrenia* (B. Massumi, Trans.). Minneapolis, MN: University of Minnesota Press. (Original work published 1980.)

Deleuze, G., & Guattari, F. (1994). *What is philosophy?* (H. Tomlinson, & G. Burchell, Trans.). New York: Columbia University Press. (Original work published 1991.)

Dufresne, T. (2006). Exploring the processes in becoming biliterate: The roles of resistance to learning and affect. *International Journal of Learning, 12*(8), 347–354.

Eakle, A.J. (2007). Literacy spaces of a Christian faith-based school. *Reading Research Quarterly, 42*(4), 472–510.

Ellsworth, E. (1994). Why doesn't this feel empowering? Working through the repressive myths of critical pedagogy. In L. Stone, with G.M. Boldt (Eds.), *The education feminist reader* (pp. 300–327). New York, NY, & London, UK: Routledge.

Freire, P. (1970). *Pedagogy of the oppressed* (M. Bergman Ramos, Trans.). New York: A Continuum Book, The Seabury Press. (Original work published 1968.)

Lather, P. (2006). Paradigm proliferation as a good thing to think with: Teaching research in education as wild profusion. *International Journal of Qualitative Studies in Education, 19*(1), 35–57.

Leander, K.M., & Rowe, D.W. (2006). Mapping literacy spaces in motion: A rhizomatic analysis of a classroom literacy performance. *Reading Research Quarterly, 41*(4), 428–460.

Lorraine, T. (2005). Lines of flight. In A. Parr (Ed.), *The Deleuze dictionary* (pp. 144–146). New York, NY: Columbia University Press.

Luke, A. (2003). Literacy education for a new ethics of global community. *Language Arts, 81*(1), 20–22.

Luke, A., Luke, C., & Graham, P. (2007). Globalization, corporatism, and critical language education. *International Multilingual Research Journal, 1*(1), 1–13.

Masny, D. (2005). Multiple literacies: An alternative OR beyond Freire. In J. Anderson, T. Rogers, M. Kendrick, & S. Smythe (Eds.), *Portraits of literacy across families, communities, and schools: Intersections and tensions* (pp. 171–184). Mahwah, NJ: Lawrence Erlbaum.

Masny, D. (2006). Learning and creative processes: A poststructural perspective on language and multiple literacies. *International Journal of Learning, 12*(5), 147–155.

Masny, D. (2009a). Literacies as becoming: A child's conceptualizations of writing systems. In D. Masny, & D.R. Cole (Eds.), *Multiple Literacies theory: A Deleuzian perspective* (pp.13–30). Rotterdam, The Netherlands: Sense Publishers.

Masny, D. (2009b). What's in a name? Multiple literacies theory. In D. Masny, & D.R. Cole (Eds.), *Multiple literacies theory: A Deleuzian perspective* (pp. 181–192). Rotterdam, The Netherlands: Sense Publishers.

May, T. (2005). *Gilles Deleuze: An introduction*. New York: Cambridge University Press.

McCarthey, S.J., & Moje, E.B. (2002). Conversations: Identity matters. *Reading Research Quarterly, 37*(2), 228–238.

Menard-Warwick, J. (2005). Both a fiction and an existential fact: Theorizing identity in second language acquisition and literacy studies. *Linguistics and Education, 16*(3), 253–274.

Nero, S.J. (2005). Language, identities, and ESL pedagogy. *Language and Education, 19*(3), 194–211.

Roffe, J. (2005). Simulacrum. In A. Parr (Ed.), *The Deleuze dictionary* (pp. 250–251). New York, NY: Columbia University Press.

Rogers, R., Mosley, M., & Folkes, A. (2009). Focus on policy: Standing up to neoliberalism through critical literacy education. *Language Arts, 87*(2), 127–138.

Roy, K. (2003). *Teachers in nomadic spaces: Deleuze and curriculum*. New York, NY: Peter Lang Publishing.

Schäffner, C., & Wenden, A.L. (Eds.). (2004). *Language and peace*. London, Routledge. (Original work published 1995.)

Semetsky, I. (2003). The problematics of human subjectivity: Gilles Deleuze and the Deweyan legacy. *Studies in Philosophy and Education, 22*(3–4), 211–225.

Stagoll, C. (2005). Event. In A. Parr (Ed.), *The Deleuze dictionary* (pp. 87–89). New York, NY: Columbia University Press.

St Pierre, E.A. (2004). Deleuzian concepts for education: The subject undone. *Educational Philosophy and Theory, 36*(3), 283–296.

Varis, T. (2010). Communication and new literacies in the multicultural world. *Historia y Comunicacion Social, 15*, 13–26.

Warriner, D.S. (2007). 'It's just the nature of the beast': Re-imaging the literacies of schooling in adult ESL education. *Linguistics and Education, 18*(3–4), 305–324.

Watson, J. (2009). *Guattari's diagrammatic thought: Writing between Lacan and Deleuze*. London & New York: Continuum.

Bon mots for bad thoughts

Jason J. Wallin

> This article questions how the philosophy of Gilles Deleuze has been received and connected to the field of curriculum theory. In an effort to reconnect Deleuze-thought to its political force, this essay commences a series of arguments pertaining to the ways in which the revolutionary thought of Gilles Deleuze and Felix Guattari have been reterritorialized in all-too-conservative ways. Recommencing a connection to the political activism and radical psychoanalysis of Guattari, this essay aims to create a renewed image of Deleuze-thought for curriculum workers and arts-based theorists invested in rethinking the problems of representation to which much educational thought remains fundamentally committed.

Who is afraid of Gilles Deleuze? Gregg Lambert (2006) commences this very question in his book of the same name, arguing that academia has yet to take seriously the revolutionary potential of Deleuzian thought, birthing instead a host of exigetes and critical surgeons in whose hands 'Deleuze' has been poorly treated. It is Lambert's question that forms the crux of this essay. *Who is afraid of Gilles Deleuze in education?* As a reader of Deleuze and Guattari's *Anti-Oedipus* (1983) might speculate, the answer to such a question might very well implicate the educational bureaucrat, the priestly master-teacher, or that character of institutional resentment that organizes in advance those banal habits of thinking we might otherwise call *common sense* (*doxa*). Equally, it is in an encounter with the work of Deleuze and Guattari's *A Thousand Plateaus* (1987) that we might imagine the twitching of an anxious narcissist, the revulsion of a private fascist, or the spasms of an intelligentsia reliant on the perpetuation of certain automatic interpretation machines for confirming what is *always-already known*. Insofar as such institutional formations mark the varied legacy of transcendence in Western thought, the enslavement of desire under the will of the boss, and the formation of an apparatus for the production of governable identity formations, they become exemplary of the very institutional territorializations Deleuze and Deleuze/Guattari sought to deside-ment through the creation of a myriad anti-Oedipalizing, non-philosophical, and experimental deterritorializing machines (1983, 1987, 1994).

EDUCATION AND THE POLITICS OF BECOMING

While it seems that the organization of contemporary educational thought has much to fear in the thinking of Deleuze, it has become increasingly apparent that one might today answer the question *'who is afraid of Gilles Deleuze?'* with the riposte *'no one'*. While potentially impudent, such a response might alternatively be connected to two major symptoms pertaining to the reception of Deleuzian thought in educational philosophy and curriculum theorizing. The first of these symptoms pertains to the depoliticized reception of Deleuze in North American educational theory. Over the course of the past half decade, such depoliticization has become increasingly apparent through the systematic reduction of such inherently political formations as the *rhizome,* the *fold, smooth space,* and *nomadology* into vogue theoretical slogans. As Gregoriou (2008) critiques of the contemporary 'cut and paste' approach to Deleuzian thought in education, the painstaking argumentations and conceptual tools forged by Deleuze have been reduced to 'conceptual soundbites' (2008, p. 101; During, 2001, p. 165). This is to say that the development of Deleuzian concepts for education have not been rendered dangerous *enough*, falling back into the kinds of personal exploration, perpetual semiosis, and postmodern relativism eschewed by Deleuze. What might be called the second symptom of Deleuze's domestication into contemporary educational thought pertains to the dubious 'disappearance' of Deleuze's collaborator, Felix Guattari. Such an absence is telling, for it is in engagement with the revolutionary politics of Guattari that we might begin to cultivate a sense for what remains *most* dangerous in the collective Deleuzeguattari desiring-machine. As the work of Genosko (2002) cogently articulates, Guattari would come to compose the political 'outside' thought necessary to connect Deleuze's philosophy with the material practices of both institutions and counter-institutional forces. While we might contemporarily answer the question *'Who fears Gilles Deleuze?'* with the answer *'no one'*, this does not mean that Deleuzian thought falls short of revolutionizing the very notions of what it means to think, act, and live pedagogically. Rather, such an answer is symptomatic of the fact that Deleuze has been inadequately drawn into the political problematics of educational thought. This essay will attempt to relaunch an image of Deleuze that has not yet been made sufficiently *dangerous* for educational philosophy. In the course of this task, I aim to explicate the stakes Deleuze/Guattarian thought sets out for both curriculum theory and pedagogical practice. Finally, this essay will set out to mobilize the notion of *double-stealing* as a tactic for palpating a *line of flight* counterposed to those orthodox readings that threaten to mineralize the revolutionary political potential of Deleuze-thought for education. Put differently, this essay will seek to deterritorialize a particular image of Deleuze habitually traced in contemporary curriculum theory and educational philosophy. Insofar as there 'is no leaving the territory ... without a vector of reterritorialization' however, this essay will concomitantly relaunch Deleuzeguattarian thought along an alternative political trajectory (Deleuze & Parnet, 2008). Ultimately, this essay will attempt to rehabilitate the revolutionary impulse of Deleuze/Guattari for educational thought such that we might again *be forced to think*.

Importing Deleuze

The contextualization of *Deleuze-thought* in education owes much to the manner in which the name 'Deleuze' was enmeshed within contemporary curriculum discourse.

EDUCATION AND THE POLITICS OF BECOMING

In the curricular writings of the late twentieth century for example, Deleuzian thought would be imported under the general banner of 'French theory' and more specifically, as a prominent exemplar of post-structural thought (Aoki, 2005; Pinar et al., 2000; Reynolds & Webber, 2004). This is perhaps not a surprising maneuver insofar as the import of Deleuzian thinking under the signifier of poststructuralism would become an act of identificatory convenience for establishing relationality between such diverse 'French theorists' as Derrida, Foucault, Lyotard, and Deleuze himself. Yet, this is to address the particular image of poststructualism to which this heterogenic series of thinkers would be linked. In curriculum, the identification would be relatively straightforward, implicating a generalized intervention against the foundations, automatic-interpretation machines, and the closed-system paradigm promulgated via rationalist science. Poststructuralism would concomitantly mark a general repudiation of representational thought characterizing Western metaphysics since Plato as a means to forge a *philosophy of difference* in curriculum thinking. It is in such a manner that we might affirm the necessity of poststructualism for relaunching educational thinking from under the tyrannies of instrumentality and the freezing of life's *becomings* in the image of immutable psychological, social, and epistemological truths.

While the import of Deleuzian thought under the *arch-signifier* of poststructuralism enabled Deleuzian thought to enter into positive circulation as a tool for desedimenting methods of hierarchical categorization and judgment particular to the State inspired model of the modern school, it concomitantly enacted a form of violence that has contributed to the domestication of Deleuzian thought in education. Specifically, given the general acceptance of poststructural theory in curriculum discourse and the eventual turn away from its necessity as a tool for warring against the orthodoxies of educational thought, the question of how the thinking of Deleuze will live beyond the representational categories under which his work has been imported becomes imperative. On this point, two caveats should be advanced. First, the very notion of 'French theory' under which the name Deleuze has entered into curriculum discourse marks an errant essentialism. While Deleuze considered himself to be part of a 'strong' generation of such peers as Foucault, Althusser, Serres, and Châtelet, his life amongst these friends was something of an anomaly (During, 2001). While linked under the banner of 'French theory', Deleuze would reject the fatalism of Baudrillard and maintain distance to the deconstructive project of Derrida (Goodchild, 1996). The difference between Deleuze and his peers can be widened further insofar as his work bears little affinity for deconstruction, formal semio-analysis, psychoanalysis, or the general production of theory by which we might develop a taste for his particular style of thinking (Mackay, 2007). Deleuze and Guattari were keenly aware of the potentials for conformity and territorialization enabled by 'postmodernism' and 'poststructuralism', working carefully to avoid creating new fascisms of these theoretical *magic words*. Yet, while the import of Deleuzian thought into the field of curriculum was enacted under the *magical term* of 'poststructuralism', it is critical to note that this particular version of poststructural thought bore little affinity to scholars utilizing deconstructive strategies, psycho-analytic approaches, or genealogical approaches to curriculum. Given the vast singularity of Deleuzian thought, it remains to be asked how Deleuze has come to function and will function within contemporary curriculum thought.

149

Magic words

Concomitant with the increasingly popularity of Deleuzian thought in curriculum theory and arts-based research, Deleuze has come to be known as *the philosopher of the concept*. While this assertion deserves further articulation, is far from inaccurate. As Deleuze and Guattari develop in their final collaborative work *What is Philosophy?* (1994), a concept is more than simply a name attached to a subject or object. A concept is a way of approaching the world, or put differently, a way of creating *a* world through the *active* extension of thinking the possible. This image of the concept follows the affirmative task of philosophy set out by Nietzsche (1968), who asserted that '[we] must no longer accept concepts as a gift, not merely purify and polish them, but first *make* and *create* them' (p. 5). Even the most occasional reader of Deleuzian inspired curriculum theory and arts-based research will be familiar with such concepts as the *rhizome, the fold (le pli), smooth space*, and *nomadism*. Within the Deleuzeguattarian machine, such concepts function as devices for extending the field of experience, composing planes for the exploration of new artistic, political, and ethical actions that productively fail to correspond to an *a priori* image of thought. Put differently, the concept is neither a descriptor nor *signifier*, but rather, a machine for producing a style of thought capable of short-circuiting the image of the world *as it is*. Implicated here are those educational models of instrumentalism, standardization, and developmentalism which predetermine the becoming-subject and limit its desiring-production (*zoe*) into organized forms of moral, lawful, and representational *anti-production* (Agamben, 1998). Hence, insofar as the rhizome *might* operationalize a style of thinking capable of machining heterodox territories into temporary assemblage, it concomitantly functions as a probe-head or abstract machine for surveying how *a* life might go once the will-to-representation becomes inadequate for the instantiation of new and less oppressive styles of thinking (Roy, 2003).

While a Deleuzeguattarian inspired approach to concept creation is palpable in the works of Daignault (1989, 1990, 1992), more recent work in both curriculum and arts-based educational research is marked by a shift in the deployment of Deleuzian thought. Such deployments might increasingly be described via a method dubbed 'cut and paste Deleuzianism' through which concepts are reterritorialized as *brand names* procurable for virtually any kind of ideological operation (Gregoriou, 2008, p. 101). Such a reductionist trend in contemporary curriculum and arts-based theorizing has been similarly observed by Jagodzinski (2010), for whom the Deleuzeguattarian machine has been occasionally reterritorialized as an apolitical pseudo-philosophical pop discourse. This reterritorialization owes much to an overemphasis on the *discursive use-value* of Deleuzeguattarian concepts over an analysis of their operational potentials for instantiating new modes of thought and action (During, 2001). Simply, it has become sufficient to speak of Deleuzeguattarian concepts without pursuing what they can *do*, or otherwise, how they might be connected to preexisting social machines. Similar to the symptom of deconstruction's waning in North American academia, Deleuze and Guattari's conceptual toolbox now appears *ready-made*, betraying the Nietzschean (1968) provocation that *concepts must first be created*. To practise fidelity to Deleuzeguattarian thought means to extend, remachine and supplement rather than reify or popularize their philosophical concepts. The reterritorialization of Deleuzeguattarian thought into a vogue discursive capital marks a fundamental failure to engage the extra-textual modes of production operative throughout their work. Put differently, to approach Deleuze and Guattari's *conceptual toolbox* as a new lexicon for embellishing old habits or importing stealth fidelities is to botch the task of concept creation and further, to shirk the operationalization of concepts in relation with the material function of other social forces. The recent trend toward the reterritorialization of the *rhizome,* the *fold, smooth space*, and *nomadism* as heraldic devices marks more than intellectual gambit to conscript Deleuzeguattari for *any-use-whatsoever*. More drastically, it functions to depoliticize Deleuzeguattarian thought in an act that bears suspicious resemblance to the reductive and appropriative parasitism of designer capitalism.[1]

New models for old habits

Why would anyone have cause to fear Deleuze when his conceptual creations can be so easily by deployed in support of a myriad of ideological maneuvers? Today, curriculum and arts-based theorists laboring under the banner of *Deleuze-thought (le pensee Deleuze)* have repurposed the decentered multiplicity of *rhizomatics* for autobiographical and self-reflective inquiry, the concept of *smooth space* as an image for advocating deterritorialization without limits, and the lionization of *nomadism* with ideations of subjective liberation (see Irwin & de Cosson, 2004). Further, explorations conducted with Deleuze and Guattari's *conceptual toolbox* have been made to support connections to autobiographical, phenomenological, and hermeneutic thought despite the skepticism Deleuze and Guattari harboured toward such traditions[2] (see Springgay et al., 2008). Perhaps more interesting however is the recent trend toward the utilization of such Deleuzeguattarian concepts as the *rhizome* to recommence the postmodern project of perpetual semiosis in both the fields of curriculum and arts-based research (see Sameshima & Sinner, 2009). Further to this, by rendering the *rhizome* into a model for thinking, curricularists and arts-based researchers have been able to maintain a commitment to the hybridization of curriculum theory with other fields of research, hence constituting a weapon for warring against the canonization of the field. Intimate to the use of the *rhizome* as a beachhead against the termination of experimentation and essentialization of the curriculum field (see Reynolds & Webber, 2004), the *rhizo-model* constituted in curriculum research maintains its distinction from the root-tree or transcendent model Deleuze and Guattari refer to as *arboreal*.[3] Simply, the *rhizome* has been utilized to reinvigorate a binary image of structure/post-structure in which the *rhizome* constitutes the avant-garde alternative to the continual threat of essentialism in educational thought (see Cormier, 2008; Honan, 2004).

Primary amongst such prior fidelities is the function of representational thinking itself. The articulation of the *rhizome* in curriculum literature has commonly been organized abound such contemporary lexical buzzwords as *non-hierarchical, asignifying,* and *non-historical*. From rote, we know that the *rhizome* has no beginning or end, but grows in the middle (*intermezzo*). This familiar approach and modelization of Deleuzeguattarian thought marks a potentially unintended reterritorialization of the concept into an *order word*, or more asynchronously, the freezing of the concept into a representational fetish (During, 2001). More pointedly, the very conceptualization of the *rhizome* as a model that can be mimed marks a fundamental betrayal of the non-representational force Deleuze and Guattari ascribed to the concept. In other words, where such concepts as the *rhizome* have become reduced to encyclopedic exegesis or an image to be recaptured or retraced, they already bear the mark of becoming frozen images of thought. Clearly, this tendency is indicative of the move to mask a stealth affinity for representational thought. This is, of course, far from the intentions of Deleuze (and Guattari), who wrote in unequivocal terms that '[my concept is] not another "model"' (1987, p. 25). Indeed, for Deleuze, the quality of a philosopher can be judged not by their ability to represent a particular image of thought, but rather, to fabulate new concepts for thinking. Yet, where such concepts as the *rhizome* have become overdetermined, the task of fabulation risks being terminated. Reterritorializing the rhizome as an order-word functionally retards what a rhizome can do. What is to be feared in a scenario where the non-representational forces of Deleuzian thought are frozen as new orthodoxies or canonical images for emulation, encyclopedic repetition, and miming? Particular to our contemporary moment, there remains a paranoiac sediment amidst our schizophrenic desires.

A DeleUser's manual?

An approach to Deleuze is hence one that must remain vigilant against the desire to render his philosophy into an orthodoxy. As Boundas and Olkowski (1994) argue, it is with the gravest indifference to the work of Deleuze that his creations might be canonized or hemmed in by commentary and ceaseless annotation. Put differently, an inquiry into the deployment of Deleuzian thought in curriculum and arts-based theorizing might commence with a schizoanalysis of those stealth fidelities and representational desires upon which the Deleuzeguattarian toolbox has been reterritorialized. Such a task would begin with an analysis of the various *desiring-machines* at work in the curriculum field (Buchanan, 2008). Put differently, a schizoanalytic approach to the curriculum field might begin with the task of analysing how various curriculum machines have been assembled in the first place. This task posed, we have not yet broached the important question of how Deleuze *should* be used when so frequently deployed in service of double-dealing ideological purposes. However, the question of how Deleuze *should* be used cannot begin without addressing the ways in which Deleuzian thought has already been 'answered'. That is, I contend that there *already* exists in the field of curriculum studies something of a *DeleUser's manual* for approaching and working with Deleuzian thought. In other words, there exists in the curriculum field a *desiring-machine* connected to the noun *Deleuze*. This *desiring-machine* might in turn be characterized by a dual fidelity to *experimentation* and *deterritorialization* (see Ling, 2009).

Through an analysis of what *Deleuze-thought* has enabled for curriculum and arts-based theorists, we might begin to detect the particular functions of desiring production operative therein. Put differently, the question of how *Deleuze-thought* has been composed is less a question of surveying an 'authentic' Deleuze than an act of producing a particular *becoming* of Deleuzian thought. It is in this vein that the contemporary *becoming* of Deleuzian thought in curriculum and arts-based research has composed an image of *experimentation* and *deterritorialization* for educational

EDUCATION AND THE POLITICS OF BECOMING

thought. As Reynolds and Webber (2004) argue, such experimental approaches to curricular composition are crucial in an age marked by the overdetermination of desire by instrumentalizing, utilitarian, and punitive institutional forces. Following, it is only through practices of deterritorialization or rather, through the unfettering of desire from *a priori* patterns of thought and action that educational thought might be recommenced as a less harmful and potentially liberatory project. Simply put, it is in response to the stultifying organization of institutional life that Deleuze has become a herald of experimentalism and desire unleashed from those prior formations which unnecessarily limit what one could think or do.

The composition of *Deleuze-thought* as a herald of *experimentation* and *deterritorialization* is swiftly being rendered into a dangerous orthodoxy. Today, the word *experimentation* is being rehabilitated as a beachhead against overdetermination and the freezing of life under badly formed concepts. This is to say that curriculum theory is becoming habituated to the image of Deleuze as a philosopher of the disjunction and heterogenic synthesist of *x and y and z and ... and ....* Yet, even where the *and* perpetuates, it often remains relative to *something* that perseveres transcendently, be it the 'I' of autobiography, the latent anthropocentrism at the heart of the *artist-researcher's* creative act, or the dialectical ideal underpinning hybridic thinking.[4] In other words, what is dubbed difference within Deleuzian inflected curriculum writing has often yet to break from that notion of *difference in degree* by which difference remains relative to a *fundamental unit of reference* (Aoki, 2005). On an obverse trajectory, the experimentalism heralded by the composition of Deleuze in curriculum theory has reinvigorated the postmodern drive for unabated semiosis and *schizo-production* contemporarily synonymous with the Deleuzeguattarian notion of *lines of flight*. Such lines of flight are often wed to a benign image of *deterritorialization* through which a thing is productively released from material repetition (n-1) and reconstituted with difference. Today, *deterritorialization* has become a new password for *liberation* or, at the very least, a tactic for perpetuating curriculum's 'complicated conversation' through the intensification of semiotic production (Pinar, 2003). In some applications, deterritorialization has been lauded as a new image for the task of pedagogy while in others, as a critical tactic for routing codified thinking wherever it might be surveyed in Western thought.

Perhaps such a composition of *Deleuze-thought* in curriculum is not surprising provided the instructions that Deleuze provides for approaching his work. Perhaps most well known of these approaches appears via Massumi's (1987) introduction to the English translation of *A Thousand Plateaus*, where the approach of entering into and skipping through the text as one might listen to a record is most affirmatively advanced. Yet, the radicality of such an approach has led to an unintentional orthodoxy where readers of Deleuze have forgone more challenging 'tracks' in lieu of more 'listenable' or 'replayed' formulations (Holland, 2004). In curriculum theory, this has meant an overly concentrated focus on the introductory chapter of *A Thousand Plateaus* (in which the rhizome is introduced), or worse, the repetition of particular Deleuzo-slogans in educational theorizing. Yet, what does it matter? After all, does Deleuze not advocate an approach to philosophy that is at once both *collage* (as it is articulated in *Negotiations*) and *buggery* (as it is thought within *What is Philosophy?*)? If so, what pause would exist for not treating Deleuze as a host through which his monstrous progeny could be birthed for new purposes? Is this not how Deleuze asked his reader to approach the task of philosophical concept creation in a

153

time where students of philosophical thought had become 'bludgeoned to death with the history of philosophy?' (1997, p. 5).

It is in the work of Deleuze himself that the composition of a freely experimental and deterritorializing image *Deleuze-thought* is challenged. As Buchanan (1999) argues, Deleuze's style of philosophy is intimately linked to the consideration of a philosopher's work *as a whole*. As Deleuze (2006) comments on the works of Foucault, '[w]hen you admire someone you don't pick and choose; you may like this or that better than some other one, but you nevertheless take them as a *whole*' (p. 77). Above all other aspects of Deleuze's philosophical style, it is this approach to treating the work of a philosopher *as a whole* that Buchanan (1999) insists is necessary to our understanding of Deleuze's praxis. In unequivocal terms, Deleuze writes that unless one takes the work of a philosopher *as a whole,* 'you just won't understand it at all' (cited in Buchanan, p. 7). Specifically, it is by treating a philosopher, a filmmaker or musician *as a whole* that we begin to understand a syntax of style that emerges, that takes different directions, reaches impasses, and makes breakthroughs. Put differently, it is only by taking the work of a philosopher, an auteur, or musician as a whole that we begin to detect the machine that they create and the functions it operationalizes for thought and action (Buchanan, 1999). It is in contradiction to this aspect of praxis that Deleuze's own thinking has often been utilized. This is to say that Deleuze's own philosophical experimentalism practised a joyous affirmation for the style of a philosopher as opposed to a quotidian approach or reduction of a philosopher's style to a handful of conceptual tools or essentializing foils. As Michael Hardt's (1993) philosophical portrait detects, Deleuze emphasized the necessity of philosophical apprenticeship. Further, During (2001) writes, '[m]uch of what struck people as a revolutionary way of approaching philosophy was ... made possible only by Deleuze's precise knowledge of the traditional themes and problems that make up the history of philosophy' (p. 175). The deterritorializing maneuvers that would come to compose a contemporary image of *Deleuze-thought* would emerge through a protracted analysis of the social machines already operative with *a* specific milieu. It is in this way that Deleuze was precise about which master signifiers to release from material repetition (n-1) in order to operationalize a *line of flight*.

On the prospect of the next century *not being* Deleuzian

In a statement of uncertain intent, Foucault asserted that this century would become known as *Deleuzian*. While this assertion might very well have been posed as an incendiary in-joke,[5] the recent proliferation of *Deleuzian* thought in curriculum studies and arts-based research has come to constitute a revolutionary alternative to the lingering fascisms of transcendence, identity politics, and nihilism endemic to Western thought (Buchanan, 1999). For the fields of curriculum theory and arts-based research, the coming century might very well be *Deleuzian*. Across diverse fields of application and interest, theorist-practitioners are forming a *friendship* with Deleuze, locating in his work a new set of tools for not simply working on the problems of educational thought, but for instantiating an entirely new series of perplexions[6] for the future pedagogical thought-action[7] (Daignault, 1992; Roy, 2003; Semetsky, 2008). *Pedagogy is, after all, only as good as the problems it seeks to create.*

154

EDUCATION AND THE POLITICS OF BECOMING

The rapid increase of exegetical and exploratory curriculum works utilizing *Deleuzian* thought have overlooked a key caveat. 'Deleuze himself was not *Deleuzian*' (During, 2001, p. 184). Deleuze never aspired to the creation of a school,[8] nor did his work seek to fabulate applied models or rhetorical strategies. Unlike Derrida, Buchanan (1999) writes, 'Deleuze does not operate in a way that can be readily emulated once the principles are understood' (p. 9). If it *is* indeed possible to become Deleuzian, that is, to cultivate a style of thought that joyously fails to fall back upon a prior image of life, we may not yet have *become adequate to it* (Buchanan, 1999). In such an effort, however, it is crucial that contemporary curriculum theorists and arts-based researchers grapple with the task of ensuring that this century *not become Deleuzian*. Ultimately, this may necessitate abandoning Deleuze. Yet, such abandonment should not be equated with the abdication of an apprenticeship or commitment to understand Deleuze's philosophical style. Surely, that would be to lapse back into a postmodern stupidity. On the contrary, such abandonment might more adequately be thought as the *affirmative* attempt to avoid rendering Deleuze-thought into a hagiography. Put differently, to become an apprentice to the pedagogical thinking of Deleuze necessitates that we remain vigilant against the formation of orthodox schools, frozen concepts, and the canonization of *Deleuze-thought* into a representational circuit for educational theorists and philosophers. This move begins to evade the tyranny of representation that Deleuzeguattari continually attempted to return to thought. *The universal does not explain anything but must first be explained.*

To abandon Deleuze is concomitantly to follow the Deleuzeguattarian axiom that philosophy proceeds by succession. As Guattari (1995) writes of his collaborative work with Deleuze, '[w]ho knows what will be taken up by others, for other uses, or what bifurcations they will lead to!' (p. 126). Loath to the practice of criticism without creation, it is in apprenticeship to *Deleuze-thought* that the conceptualization of curriculum might be relaunched as something that must *first be made*. It is hence insufficient to conceptualize *Deleuze-thought* as a metaphor or model insofar Deleuzeguattari's practical philosophy is neither a prior condition of language or representational image. What is to be feared from a figure prophesized to become the singular philosophical event of the century? Put differently, what is to be feared in espousing one's affiliation with the philosopher by which the century will become known? Apropos Buchanan (1999), what is to feared in such an affiliation is the potential for Deleuzian influenced curriculum theory to lapse into hagiography or a mode of succession premised solely on the act of *criticism without creation*. This scenario leads to the *false answers* of rendering Deleuzian philosophy into either a monument or dismissing Deleuze without attending to the style of his thought. In this *Deleuzian century*, it is far more dangerous to begin an apprenticeship with *Deleuze-thought* in a way that begins by recreating the Deleuzeguattarian machine in relation to new subjective and social perplexions. This task might necessarily begin by asking how a pedagogy of affirmative betrayal that inheres the Deleuzeguattarian oeuvre. This might require that a particular conceptualization of *Deleuze-thought* be abandoned, or more adequately, taken up and launched toward a new problematic. Such a project is already underway in those areas of Deleuze studies attending to subjective and social phenomena unanticipated by Deleuze and Guattari themselves (see MacKay, 2007; Land, 2011). Such projects would be impossible to think if a monolith had been created of *Deleuze-thought*. Similarly, to recommence the danger of Deleuze for curriculum theorizing and arts-based research, we must ensure that this century *not become Deleuzian.*

Whither Guattari?

Perhaps the most striking omission operative within Deleuzian inflected curriculum theory and arts-based research is the general absence of Deleuze's collaborator, Felix Guattari. This omission is particularly worthy of our attention insofar as the collaborative works *Anti-Oedipus* (1983), *A Thousand Plateaus* (1987), *and What is Philosophy?* (1994) continue to be the most frequently cited of the Deleuzeguattarian oeuvre. What should be made of this ongoing omission, or rather, the reduction of the *Deleuzeguattarian* machine to Deleuze *alone*? Perhaps more adequately, we might begin by asking what the noun *Deleuze* operationalizes that the assemblage *Deleuzeguattari* makes unthinkable? Toward this, we might begin by following a Deleuzeguattarian pedagogy, that is, by addressing what the *Deleuzeguattarian* writing-machine *does.*

As Deleuzeguattari articulate in *A Thousand Plateaus,* the formation of their writing-machine had specific intentions, one of which was to not simply talk about multiplicity but rather, to *make the multiple.* 'Since each of us was several', Deleuzeguattari (1987) write, 'there was already quite a crowd' (p. 3). This practical approach to writing is irreducible to post-structuralism's skepticism of the subject. With *A Thousand Plateaus,* Deleuze and Guattari were attempting to write a different *kind* of book – one no longer recognizable according to the image of the *root-tree* that has come to characterize academic text. More radically however, it is through Deleuzeguattari's creation of a *pack* or *crowd* in the place of the author that the reader can no longer take either Deleuze or Guattari as an object of recognition. Hence, the composition of Deleuzeguattari's writing machine functions to ward against the will-to-representation by promulgating the author's *becoming-imperceptible*, or rather, the disidentification of the authorial *name* as the root (manifestor) of textual composition. Deleuze would detect this tactic of *becoming-imperceptible* in both the work of Nietzsche (Deleuze, 1983), who would escape the authorial *maxim* by creating an alternative style of *aphorism*, and Spinoza (1985), through the application of a geometrical method (Deleuze, 1988). In *Dialogues II* (2007), Claire Parnet would add to such tactics of *becoming-imperceptible* the 'writing *á deux*' instantiated by Deleuze/Guattari (p. 25). 'The dream' Parnet avers of Deleuze's collaborative style, 'would be that you are Felix's mask and Felix is yours' (p. 30). Such a tactic is crucial to Deleuzeguattari's process, since '[t]o attribute a book to a subject is to overlook [the] working of ... variously formed matters, and very different dates and speeds' (p. 3). Put differently, to attribute the act of writing to a subject is to fail to understand the ways in which a text already functions as an assemblage connected to other books, bodies, and *little machines.*

It is through Guattari that Deleuze's work is most fervently drawn into material conditions of subjective and social production. Put differently, it is largely through Guattari's influence that Deleuze's work becomes *politicized*. While such curriculum theorists and educational philosophers as Daignault (2005), Roy (2003) and Semetsky (2008) have drawn strong connections between *Deleuze-thought* and educational politics, the disappearance of Guattari's influence has allowed the continued utilization of *Deleuze-thought* as a depoliticized vehicle of *free-play.* After

EDUCATION AND THE POLITICS OF BECOMING

all, it would be in the wake of the May 1968 revolution that Deleuze would find in Guattari's revolutionary politics a way to make sense of the revolution (Genosko, 2008). This is to say that in much curriculum theorizing and arts-based research, Deleuze has become conceptualized solely in terms of his intellectual activity. It is alongside Guattari however, that such a conceptualization becomes difficult to maintain. As Genosko (2002) cogently demonstrates, Guattari is an *anomaly*. His work is neither traditionally psychoanalytic nor formally political, transpiring across literary criticism, ecology and architectural analysis. Where curricularists might celebrate Guattari as an interdisciplinarian, Guattari himself renounces the term, designating *interdisciplinarity* as an '*abracadabra*' word proffered by cynical pretenders well versed in none of their disciplinary reference points (Genosko, 2002, p. 2).

What is meant when one says Deleuze *and* Guattari, Genosko (2002) asks. Of the stakes Genosko attributes to this formation, it is the reduction of Deleuze *and* Guattari to an order word in which the accomplishments of the former continually overshadow those of the latter that seems most worrisome. Against this, Genosko posits a reversal of the order word as an act of resistance. What dangerous heterodoxy would be made of *Guattarideleuze* and what does such a disidentification war against? Such disidentification, Genosko develops, is aimed at

> ... all the little orthodoxies that mark the secondary and tertiary literature and support the order-word; the machine coupling of one 'Deleuze' after another 'Deleuze' ... the order-word: Deleuze and then Guattari. (2002, p. 42)

However, such an anti-dogmatic reversal of the order word should not be misconstrued. As Genosko asserts '[l]et's hope that this century will not be known as Guattarian' (p. 49). Of course, there are underlying consequences of disappearing Guattari from curricular and arts-based writing on *Deleuze-thought*. As Genosko demonstrates, Guattari was working on concepts often attributed to 'Deleuze' *post facto*. For example, Guattari's work in the field of astrophysics and ersatz totemic faces inform the abstract machine of *faciality* and the black hole/white wall system articulated in *A Thousand Plateaus,* while his theoretical work on the formation of an *integrated world capitalism (IWC)*[9] informs the concept of *control society* and critical relaunch of Foucault's thesis on the function of power. This posed, perhaps the most tragic aspect of Guattari's disappearance from curriculum writing on *Deleuze-thought* is the way in which such an absence discounts the contribution Guattari makes to relaunching pedagogy as a militant project and counter-signifying force. As Genosko (2002) develops, Guattari was notably influenced by the pedagogy of Jean and Fernand Oury, who updated the radical educational techniques of Celestin Freinet during the Institutional Pedagogy (IP) movement of 1960s France. The International Pedagogy (IP) movement and its particularized focus on psychoanalysis and case study writing would become an influence to Guattari, who would subsequently orient his theoretical activities toward a consideration of the ways in which subjects receive and incorporate institutional objects (Genosko, 2008). As Genosko writes, 'for educators working within the Freinet inspired IP, the focus on how the school itself created certain kinds of learning disabilities in its pupils formed a central concern (p. 62). Influenced by this concern, Guattari would begin to incorporate Freinetian tactics toward 'unfixing rigid roles, thawing frozen hierarchies, opening hitherto closed blinkers, and modifying the introjection of the local superego and objects' (2008, p. 63). Guattari would commence a life-long study on the 'therapeutic coefficient' of the institution, drawing upon the Oury's therapeutic approach to the *International Youth Hostelling* movement's 'roaming school', the Freinetian inspired potential of technology to mobilize forms of collective enunciation (groupuscles),[10] and practices of student/patient directed cooperative council (*counseil de cooperative*) employed by proponents of the Freinetian movement[11] (Genosko, 2008).

Contemporary curriculum thinking has much to learn from Guattari's practices *within* the institution. That is, while curriculum theorists have often conceptualized *Deleuze-thought* as *peripheral* to the institution, it is in the work of Guattari that the intensive reorganization of the institution's *unthought potentials* are palpated into being (Guattari and Rolnik, 2008). It is through such institutional practices as actualizing the therapeutic role of orderlies in a psychiatric hospital (*operationalizing transversal institutional subjectivities*), belief in the schizophrenics' right to self-enunciation, and the healing potentials inhering collective action that the work of *Guattarideleuze* might be better understood in relation to its neo-materialist import. With the notable exception of Roy's (2003) exceptional *Teachers in Nomadic Spaces: Deleuze and Education*, few proponents of *Deleuze-thought* in curriculum studies have taken up the *practical philosophy* of Deleuze/Guattari, or rather, the neo-material function of their conceptual deployments. Detractors of Deleuze/Guattari necessarily stop short in order that the familiar indictment of *otherworldliness* might once again be levied against their project.

In the field of curriculum study and educational thought, such indictments already mark a pedagogical failure. That is, the work commenced by *Guattarideleuze* was never intended to suit a reader's experience, to fold into epistemological debates concerned with the question of worthy knowledge, or to represent the world as it appears to us. Guattarideleuzian pedagogy is hence oriented not to what education *is*, but rather, *what it might do*. This is not an appeal to romanticism, although it does mark a weapon for combating the kinds of cynicism born out of postmodernity. Rather, such a reorientation points to the potential for transformation *already* inhering the material conditions of institutional life. What is to fear from a philosophy that is both otherworldly and unconcerned with the problems of the world from which it has departed? The waning popularity of postmodern philosophy and poststructuralism for curriculum theorizing are perhaps answer enough. However, the Guattarideleuze war-machine (1986a) is neither postmodern or poststructural. It is not interested in promulgating a skepticism toward systems or proselytizing the end of philosophy. The experimentation we are called to do through an encounter with *Guattarideleuze* is *practical*, for it is continually oriented to the liberation of enunciative potentials, the potential organization of collective movements, and the transformation of the institution and its neurotic presuppositions concerning the 'proper organization' of subjective desire. Into the twenty-first century, there will continue to be a great need for philosophical machines capable of palpating the *otherworldly* in *this* world, or rather, of creating a world for *a people yet to come*.

Bon mots for bad thoughts

In his editorial introduction to *Collapse Volume III* (2007), Mackay argues that those '*bon mots* that have entered into circulation as convenient slogans for "summing up"

EDUCATION AND THE POLITICS OF BECOMING

Deleuze have served his philosophy badly' (p. 35). Amidst the kind of 'tourist' approach to reading Deleuze/Guattari that might be encouraged in this ostensibly *post-Deleuzian* era, Mackay tasks us with first *understanding* how Deleuze and Guattari *work*. This is not simply to advocate that we make something *common* of Deleuze and Guattari. As exemplified earlier, most curricularists *already* know what a rhizome *is* (Mackay, 2007). What we have failed to do, Mackay argues, is to understand the ways in which concepts such as the rhizome *work* with the other conceptual tools composed in Deleuze and Guattari's philosophical machine. Further, we might pursue the ways in which such conceptual tools transform material conditions. In this vein, Mackay argues that we might recommence an engagement with the 'precision tools' created by Deleuze/Guattari, 'for any precision tool must be mastered before it is put to use' (p. 6). This challenge follows from the systematic style with which Deleuze and Guattari compose their own concepts and further, the care with which they are operationalized in the world. The threat of making a *bad body without organs*, or rather, of botching a creative gambit is immanent to any experiment. Of further danger is the fact that one might employ a precision tool however they like. That said, such an application would no longer practise fidelity to the careful pedagogical impulse with which Deleuze and Guattari *approach philosophy*. That is, the Deleuzeguattarian 'toolbox' is not composed of tools for *any-task-whatsoever*. Hence, what is necessitated today is a shift from *understanding* and *application* to *schizoanalysis*. Put differently, curricularists and arts-based researchers inspired by Deleuze/Guattari might recommence the question of *how* the Deleuzeguattarian toolbox works: With what problematics particular concepts be enjoined? With what subjective and social machines they might most 'productively' assemble? Not *'what is it?'* or *'how can it be applied?'* then, but *'what does it do?'* and *'how can it be made?'*. It is this practical problem that Deleuze and Guattari continually return to throughout their collaboration, modulating, transposing, and jettisoning various formulations as they were required or fell short of the problems with which they were brought into composition. Perhaps what is required today is a new host of concepts, images of thought, and tactics of disidentification capable of wresting Deleuze and Guattari from their internment under the very thing their work is mobilized against: *the unceasing desire for new orthodoxies*.

Notes

1. Conjoined to the mobilization of the rhizome as an image of complication and plurality persists a more insidious fidelity to the logic of neo-liberalism. That is, the potential of the rhizome to desediment and send territories into flight bears marked similarity to the deterritorializing powers of neo-liberalism, the machinery of which functions precisely by decoding and capturing social flows.
2. In Deleuzeguattarian terms, the rhizome becomes a way of thinking a decentered multiplicity without a centre of emanation or point of representational reference. In this way, the rhizome becomes a productive way of thinking about the composition of packs, swarms and fuzzy machined collectives. The *schizo-subjectivity* composed by Deleuze and Guattari renders the contemporary conflation of the rhizome with modes of autobiographical research dubious. Insofar as autobiography is preoccupied with the interpretation and representation of the subject, it counteracts the anti-hermeneutic, non-genealogical and asignifying impulses of rhizomatic thought.
3. As it is conceptualized in *A Thousand Plateaus* (1987), the rhizome is not simply an image of liberation. Rather, Deleuze and Guattari conceptualize the rhizome in a manner that is

EDUCATION AND THE POLITICS OF BECOMING

already populated by potentials for stratification. While heterodox elements might very well be connected 'rhizomatically', as in the case of minoritarian groups assembling in collective protest, this does not mean that they will not reconstitute their enunciation upon some microfascism or tyrannical image of life. In Deleuzeguattarian terms, the rhizome is populated by lines of flight (deterritorialization) *as well as* lines of 'territorialization' by which flows become halted, ordered, and attributed. As Deleuze and Guattari write, 'there exists tree or root structures in rhizomes; conversely, a tree branch or root division may begin to burgeon into a rhizome' (p. 15). Neither the rhizome (the potential for things to deterritorialize and enter into new assemblages) or the root-tree (the stratification of things into orders, taxonomies, or structures) is primary.

4. In some curriculum circles, hybridic thought conserves the idea of originary elements *prior* to mixing and further, the ostensibly uncontaminated status of these generative sources. It is in this vein that hybridic thought only minimally deviates from arborescent schemas and dialectical thinking, remaining wed to structural points of origin rather than facilitating a transversal exchange *between* such points.

5. In response to critic Michael Cressole (Deleuze, 1977), Deleuze comments specifically on Foucault's intent to raise the ire of the philosophical community.

6. Deleuze uses the term perplexion to signify the virtual state of ideas, hence bypassing the connotation of hesitation associated with the term 'problem'.

7. As Guattari articulates, 'Logical operations are phyiscal operations too' (cited in Buchanan, 1999, p. 6).

8. A Deleuze and Parnet (2007) detail, schools fall easily into arborescence through the production of manifestos, excommunications, official representatives, and bosses.

9. This important formulation was coined by Guattari in the late 1960s as a reformulation of the generic term 'globalization' and its obfuscation of emerging transnational economics specific to that period.

10. Overturning the institutionally alienated individual and the asymmetrical teacher student dyad, Oury would recuperate Freinet's use of a school journal (a collective correspondence within and between schools), a local printery (owned by students for the collective production and dissemination of texts), and an emphasis on cooperative council (the *refining-machine* of group organization led by the students themselves).

11. Freinet's first school, opened in 1935, was not organized around lessons, but rather, the mediating forces of the school printery and cooperative council.

References

Agamben, G. (1998). *Homo sacer: Power and bare life.* (D. Heller-Roazen, Trans.). Palo Alto, CA: Stanford University Press.

Aoki, T. (2005). Legitimating lived curriculum: Toward a curricular landscape of multiplicity. In W. Pinar & R. Irwin (Eds.), *Curriculum in a new key: The collected works of Ted T. Aoki* (pp. 199–218). Mahwah, NJ: Lawrence Erlbaum Associates. (Originally published in 1993.)

Boundas, C., & Olkowski, D. (1994). *Gilles Deleuze and the theater of philosophy.* New York: Routledge.

Buchanan, I. (1999). Introduction. In I. Buchanan (Ed.), *A Deleuzian century?* (pp. 1–11). Duram, NC: Duke University Press.

Buchanan, I. (2008). *Deleuze and Guattari's Anti-Oedipus.* New York, NY: Continuum.

Cormier, D. (2008). *Rhizomatic education: Community as curriculum.* Retrieved 16 January 2011 from http://www.innovateonline.info/pdf/vol4_issue5/Rhizomatic_Education-Community_as_Curriculum.pdf

Daignault, J. (1992). Traces at work from different places. In W.F. Pinar & W.M. Reynolds (Eds.), *Understanding curriculum as phenomenological and deconstructed text* (pp. 195–215). New York, NY: Teachers College Press.

Daignault, J. (2005). Hacking the future. Unpublished paper presented 22 November 2005 at the Complexity Science and Educational Research Conference, Loranger, Louisiana.

Deleuze, G. (1977). 'I have nothing to admit.' (J. Forman, Trans.). *Semiotexte, 2*(3), 111–116.

Deleuze, G. (1983). *Nietzsche and philosophy.* (H. Tomlinson, Trans.). New York, NY: Columbia University Press.

EDUCATION AND THE POLITICS OF BECOMING

Deleuze, G. (1988). *Spinoza: Practical philosophy.* (R. Hurley, Trans.). San Francisco, CA: City Light Books.

Deleuze, G. (1997). *Negotiations, 1972–1990.* (M. Joughin, Trans.). New York: Columbia University Press.

Deleuze, G. (2006). *The fold.* (T. Conley, Trans.). New York: Continuum.

Deleuze, G., & Guattari, F. (1983). *Anti-Oedipus: Capitalism and schizophrenia.* (R. Hurley, M. Seem, & H.R. Lane, Trans.). Minneapolis: University of Minnesota Press.

Deleuze, G., & Guattari, F. (1986). *Nomadology: The war machine.* (B. Massumi, Trans.). New York, NY: Semiotext(e).

Deleuze, G., & Guattari, F. (1987). *A thousand plateaus.* (R. Hurley, M. Seem, & H.R. Lane, Trans.). Minneapolis: University of Minnesota Press.

Deleuze, G., & Guattari, F. (1994). *What is philosophy?* (H. Tomlinson, & G. Burchell, Trans.). New York, NY: Columbia University Press.

Deleuze, G., & Parnet, C. (2007). *Dialogues II.* (H. Tomlinson, & B. Habberjam, Trans.). New York, NY: Columbia University Press.

Deleuze, G. & Parnet, C. (2008). Gilles Deleuze's ABC primer (P. Boutang, Director). Retrieved 13 December 2010 from http://www.langlab.wayne.edu/Cstivale/D-G/ABC1.html.

During, E. (2001). Blackboxing in theory: Deleuze versus Deleuze. In S. Lotringer & S. Cohen (Eds.), *French theory in America* (pp. 163–189). New York: Routledge.

Genosko, G. (2002). *Felix Guattari: An aberrant introduction.* New York: Continuum.

Genosko, G. (2008). Félix Guattari and popular pedagogy. In I. Semetsky (Ed.), *Nomadic education: Variations on a theme by Deleuze and Guattari* (pp. 61–76). Rotterdam, NE: Sense Publishers.

Goodchild, P. (1996). *Deleuze and the question of philosophy.* London: Fairleigh Dickinson University Press.

Gregoriou, Z. (2008). Commencing the rhizome: Towards a minor philosophy of education. In I. Semetsky (Ed.), *Nomadic education: Variations on a theme by Deleuze and Guattari* (pp. 91–110). Rotterdam, NE: Sense.

Guattari, F. (1995). *Chaosmosis: An ethico-aesthetic paradigm.* Bloomington, IN: Indiana University Press.

Guattari, F., & Rolnik, S. (2008). *Molecular revolution in Brazil.* Cambridge, Massachusetts: MIT Press.

Hardt, M. (1993). *Gilles Deleuze: An apprenticeship in philosophy.* Minneapolis, MN: University of Minnesota Press.

Holland, E.W. (2004). Studies in applied nomadology: Jazz improvisation and post-capitalist markets. In I. Buchanan & M. Swiboda (Eds.), *Deleuze and music* (pp. 20–35). Edinburgh, UK: Edinburgh University Press.

Honan, E. (2004). (Im)plausibilities: A rhizo-textual analysis of policy texts and teachers' work. *Educational Philosophy and Theory, 36*(3), 267–281.

Irwin, R., & de Cosson, A. (2004). *a/r/tography: Rendering self through arts-based living inquiry.* Vancouver, BC: Pacific Educational Press.

Jagodzinski, J. (2010). *Visual art and education in an era of designer capitalism: Deconstructing the oral eye.* New York: Palgrave.

Lambert, G. (2006). *Who's afraid of Deleuze and Guattari?* London: Continuum?

Land, N. (2011). *Fanged noumena: Collected writings, 1987–2007.* (R. MacKay, & R. Brassier, Eds.). New York: Sequence Press.

Ling, X. (2009). Thinking like grass, with Deleuze in education? *Journal of the Canadian Association for Curriculum Studies, 7*(2), 32–48.

Massumi, B. (1987). Translator's forward: Pleasures of philosophy. In G. Deleuze & F. Guattaris.), *A Thousand plateaus: Capitalism and schizophrenia* (pp. ix–xv). Minneapolis, MN: University of Minnesota Press.

Mackay, R. (Ed.). (2007). *Collapse: Philosophical research and development* (Vol. III). Falmouth, UK: Urbanomic.

Nietzsche, F. (1968). *The will to power.* (W. Kaufmann, Ed.; W. Kaufmann, & R.J. Hollingdale, Trans.). New York: Vintage Books.

Pinar, W.F. (2003). *What is curriculum theory?* Mahwah, NJ: Lawrence Erlbaum Associates, Publishers.

161

Pinar, W., Reynolds, W., Slattery, P., & Taubman, P. (2000). *Understanding curriculum*. New York: Peter Lang.

Reynolds, W.M. & Webber, J.A. (Eds.). (2004). *Expanding curriculum theory: Dis/positions and lines of flight*. Mahwah, NJ: Lawrence Erlbaum.

Roy, K. (2003). *Teachers in nomadic spaces: Deleuze and curriculum*. New York, NY: Peter Lang.

Samamshima, P., & Sinner, A. (2009). Awakening to soma heliakon: Encountering teacher-reaearcher-learning in the twenty-first century. *Canadian Journal of Education, 32*(2), 271–284.

Semetsky, I. (Ed.). (2008). *Nomadic education: Variations on a theme by Deleuze and Guattari*. Rotterdam, NE: Sense Publishers.

Springgay, S., Irwin, R., Leggo, C., & Gouzouasis, P. (2008). *Being with A/r/tography*. Rotterdam: Sense Publishers.

Spinoza, B. (1985). Ethics. (E. Curley, Trans.). In *The Collected Writings of Spinoza*, Vol. 1. Princeton: Princeton University Press. (Originally published in 1677.).

Index

Note:
Illustrations are in italics

absent space in policy prolepses *93,* 93–4
adaptive literacies 39, 40, *40,* 42
affect from interaction between bodies 9, 10,
  18n3, 49–50; affective events 11–13, 122,
  136
affection, concept of 70–1
affective sensing *91,* 91–2
apprenticeship in education 101–6, 107–8
arborescent thought 8, 81–2, 89, 151, 160n4
Arto 10, 11
assemblages, notion of 9–10, 11–16, 67–9,
  108, 114, 150; in discourse-as-event 124,
  126–7; of sensations 114–15, 118, 124, 125

Baudrillard, Jean 55
Bebo (social networking website) 10, 12
becoming, Deleuzian notion of 34, 36, 81, 89,
  116, 131, 133; becoming-musician 82, 83–4;
  becoming-other 51, 53, 54, 58, 115, 116;
  becoming-policy 90, 96; becoming-teacher
  21–2, 27–8, 29–30, 96; for Latino
  immigrants in Australia 42–4; politics of
  becoming 1–2, 42–4
Berliner, David 22–4, 28
bodies: affect of movement on 8, 9–10, 12,
  17, 114; and hesitation 62–3, 66, 71, 72
Boethius 81
Buber, Martin 54
bureaucratic literacies 38, 40, *40*

cartography 130–1, 142, 143; and qualitative
  research 135–6
cartoon doodling and multiple literacies *40,*
  40–2, *41*
child learner immanence 108–10
children as apprentices in education 101–11
choralism 75, 77
choral societies 77
concept, notion of the 113, 150
concepts and values in human life 52, 53, 54,
  55
confirmation and the ethics of care in
  education 54

control of terms and images, the 1–2
critical literacies 129, 131–4, 136–44
curriculum studies and *Deleuze-thought* 152–
  3, 154–5, 157, 158, 159
Curwen, James 77, 84n2
cyberbullying 6–7, 16–17, 17n1; sexual
  identifiers in 17, 18n5; and subjectification
  8–9, 10, 13, 17n2
cyberbullying in schools and online
  communities 5; research study on
  cyberbullying on social networking sites
  10–17

decalcomania 135
Dele User's manual, the 152
Deleuze, Gilles 24–8, 42, 44, 51–2, 92, 93,
  101; concepts for curriculum studies 147,
  148–51, 152–3; and critical literacies 133;
  ethico-political paradigms 47–9, 51, 53–4,
  57; and Guattari 156–7, 158, 159; notions
  of apprenticeship 103, 105–6, 107, 108;
  philosophical thought 147–8, 152–5–;
  theories of affect from bodily interaction 9,
  10, 18n3, 49–50 *see also* becoming,
  Deleuzian notion of
Deleuze-thought 152–3, 154–6, 157, 158
Deleuzian-Guattarian theories of affect 9, 15,
  38 *see also* affect from interaction between
  bodies
Deleuzian refrain, the 76, 79–80, 81, 82, 83
Derrida, Jacques 149
deterritorialization 122, 136–8, 141; in
  curriculum studies 152, 153; and *Deleuze-
  thought* 153, 154; of learning, literacies and
  language 125, 134; and lines of flight *114,*
  130, 159n3, 160n3; of music 80, 82–3, 115;
  shared deterritorialization 47, 53 *see also*
  reterritorialization
developmental model of teacher training 22–
  4, 26
developmental theories of education 108–9
  see also children as apprentices in
  education

INDEX

Dewey, John 51, 52
Difference & Repetition (book) 25, 27
digital communications 132
digital technology and education 1
discourses, significance of 7–8, 113–15, *114,*
  120, 125–7
'disinhibition' (anonymity) 6
double-stealing, notion of 148
drawing as educational apprenticeship 102,
  103–5, 110, 124–5

Early Years Learning Framework, the 109
education 2, 101–2; and Deleuzian thought
  147, 148–50, 152–3, 154; and the ethics of
  integration 48, 56, 57–8; and the learning
  process 51–2, 54
education policy 88–9, 91–4
emotional literacies 38, 39, 40, *40,* 42
ethico-political paradigm of Deleuze 47–9,
  51, 53–4
ethics of care in education 54–6
ethics of integration, the 48, 56, 57–8
event, as philosophical concept 136, 138
events and habitual patterns of cognition 61–
  3, 122 *see also* real-life events and a new
  pedagogy of concepts

fear and education policy implementation 95–
  6
Foucault, Michel 2, 71, 97n1, 154
Freinet, Celestin 157, 160n10–11
Freirean critical pedagogies 131, 132, 142–3
friendship and pedagogical assemblages 69–
  70, 71–3
fun and the politics of becoming 44

grievability and bullying questions 8
Guattari, Felix 48, 135, 148, 155, 156–9 *see*
  also Deleuze, Gilles

habitual patterns of cognition 61–3
hesitation and the body 62–3, 66, 71, 72
Hullah, John 77
human capital and organized schooling 52

Image of Thought 28–9
immanence and reading 116–17, 120–1, 125–
  6, 127, 133–4, 139–42
increased capacity of the body 62
intellectual hospitality and friendship 71, 72
intuition and the senses 91
IP (International Pedagogy) movement, the
  157

knowledge, meaning of 57

Latinos and literacy in Australia *see* research
  study into Latino literacy in Australia
learning and philosophical ideas 24–7, 34,
  48–51, 53
LINC (Language Instruction for Newcomers
  to Canada) 134, 142 *see* research study into
  multiple literacies as processes of becoming
lines of flight *114,* 115, 130, 159n3, 160n3 *see*
  also deterritorialization
literacies, types of 38–42, *40, 41,* 115–16, 122,
  126
Literacy for Social Justice Teacher Research
  group 131–2
literacy in Australia 33–4
living as a learning process 48–50
'logic of sense' 49, 91
logic of sense, the 89, 91

meanings of terms, change in the 15–16, 17
media literacy 132, 136–40, 142
MENC: The National Association for Music
  Education 77, 78, 82
Messiaen, Olivier 80
MLT (Multiple Literacies Theory) 39–41, 50,
  97n5 128n3; and critical literacies 129–30,
  132–4, 136, 138–9, 141–2, 143; as theory-
  practice for literacies education 113, 115–
  17, 119–20, 122, 125–6, 127
money and the politics of becoming 42
moral standards and the pedagogy of the
  concept 51–2
music 80–1, 83
music education 75–6, 83–4; pedagogies in
  75, 78, 80
music education in Canada and the US 75–8,
  82
Music Supervisors National Conference, the
  77

negative space 94–5
neoliberalism 131–2, 159n1
networks and the politics of becoming 42–3
nomadic families and literacy 39, 41
nomadic impacts of Mongols on European
  history 37
novice teachers 29, 30; replicating actions of
  mentors 26, 28

open system of beliefs 114, 127n2
Oury, Jean and Fernand 157, 158, 160n10

pedagogies in music education 75, 78, 80
pedagogy as assemblage 61, 63, 67, 68–9; and
  friendship 69–70, 71–2
pedagogy of the concept 48–51, 55, 56
perplexion 154, 155, 160n6
phantasm, notion of 92, *93*

INDEX

philosophical ideas and learning 24–7, 34, 51, 53, 55 *see also* pedagogy of the concept

policy apparitions 89–90, 95, 96

policy prolepses *91*, 91–4, *93*, 96–7; in education 87, 89, 90; through sense of fear 95–6

politics of becoming, the 1–2, 42–4

poststructuralism 149, 158

power and force relations and bodies 10

power lines and MLT 143

Pythagorus 81

qualitative research and cartography 135–6

reading 143–4; immanence of 116–17, 120–1, 125–6, 127, 133–4, 139–42

real-life events and a new pedagogy of concepts 47, 48–9, 52–3, 54, 55–6, 57–8, 143–4

refrain, the, and music education 76 *see also* Deleuzian refrain, the

relationships and teachers and learning 65–7, 68–70, 71, 72–3

Reproduction of the Same 26

research study into cyberbullying on social networking sites 10–17

research study into Latino literacy in Australia 34–44, *40*, *41*

research study into multilingual children acquiring multiple writing systems simultaneously 117–27, *119, 120, 121, 122, 123*

research study into multiple literacies as processes of becoming 134–42

resonance and amplititude 114–15, 118, 126–7

reterritorialization 134, 139, 141, 150; of the rhizome 151, 152, 159n1 *see also* deterritorialization

rhizomatic processes in music 82–3

rhizomatics and power relationships in qualitative research 35, 53, 135–6

rhizomatic thought 82, 89, 117, 127, 150, 159, 159n2–3; and reterritorialization 151–2, 159n1

RPiN (Redesigning Pedagogies in the North) project, the 63–7, 69–70, 72

semiotic sign-encounters and policy prolepses 90–1

sensations and the senses 114–15, 118, 124

September 11th terrorist attacks 55–6

sexual identifiers in cyberbullying 17, 18n5

sexualised affects 5, 8, 9, 10, 11–17

shared deterritorialization 47, 53

sign theories in education 101, 102, 105–6, 107–8, 110–11

simulacra 144n5

smooth space, concept of 151

SNSs (social networking sites) 10, 11, 12, 14–15

social control in music education 76–8, 84n3

sol-fa system of music pitches 77

spatialism and educational policy 94–5, 97n8, 120–1

Spinoza 49, 50, 70–1

status and the politics of becoming 43

striated (structured) environments 24

subjectification and cyberbullying 8–9, 10, 13, 17n2

teacher education 21–4, 26–30, 48, 55, 56–7

teachers and accountability policies 95–6

teachers and interpretation of policy 91

teachers and pedagogy in 'the north' 63–7, 69–70

temporality and child learning 109–10

terrorism 55–6

text 113–14, *114*, 115–16, 118–19

theoretical approach to analysis of school violence and cyberbullying 7–9

Thousand Plateaus, A (book) 24–5, 36–7, 81, 147, 153, 156

tracing, notion of 25–6, 81, 130–1, 132, 135, 142–3

transcendental empiricism 118

transformation through life experiences 116

unconscious, the 53

Varèse, Edgar 80

virtualization 62–3, 72

Vygotsky, Lev 102

Western art music tradition, the 80

Who is afraid of Gilles Deleuze? (article) 148

Why Pedagogy? (article) 67

writing, institutionalized spaces for 120